RULES
OF THE TRADE

RULES
OF THE TRADE
Indispensable Insights
for Online Profits

David S. Nassar

McGraw-Hill

New York   Chicago   San Francisco
Lisbon   London   Madrid   Mexico City   Milan
New Delhi   San Juan   Seoul   Singapore
Sydney   Toronto

Library of Congress Cataloging-in-Publication Data

Nassar, David S.
    Rules of the trade : indispensable insights for online profits / by David S. Nassar.
       p. cm.
    Includes bibliographical references.
    ISBN 0-07-135463-8
       1. Electronic trading of securities.   I. Title.

HG4515.95 .N375 2001
332.64'0285'4678—dc21

                                                                    00-061675

McGraw-Hill

A Division of The **McGraw·Hill** *Companies*

1 2 3 4 5 6 7 8 9 0   DOC/DOC   0 9 8 7 6 5 4 3 2 1 0

ISBN 0-07-135463-8

This book was set in Melior by North Market Street Graphics.

Printed and bound by R. R. Donnelley & Sons Company.

McGraw-Hill books are available at special quantity discounts to use as premiums and sales promotions, or for use in corporate training programs. For more information, please write to the Director of Special Sales, Professional Publishing, McGraw-Hill, Two Penn Plaza, New York, NY 10121-2298. Or contact your local bookstore.

This publication is designed to provide accurate and authoritative information in regard to the subject matter covered. It is sold with the understanding that neither the author nor the publisher is engaged in rendering legal, accounting, or other professional service. If legal advice or other expert assistance is required, the services of a competent professional person should be sought.
—*From a Declaration of Principles jointly adopted by a Committee of the American Bar Association and a Committee of Publishers.*

 This book is printed on recycled, acid-free paper containing a minimum of 50% recycled, de-inked fiber.

Dedicated to:

My sister, Rebecca:
You had a tough year,
but you handled it like the champion you are!

Contents

FOREWORD

Many books have been written on the subject of trading stocks and securities, and most focus on the mechanical side of the market such as chart reading, mathematical indicators, electronic trading systems, and other methods that would fall under the cognitive thought process of trading. Fortunately, there is an abundance of information available for understanding the mechanical nature of the market. But because the market is so dynamic, mechanical techniques and trading styles such as "scalping" are the most prone to change. With the explosion of electronic trading, recognizing this now is vitally important.

The most recent phenomenon to help make the point could be traced back just a few years ago to the "SOES bandits," as they have been called. Trading opportunities often were found by examining the depth of buyers and sellers at the inside market and determining how strong a market maker's propensity was to buy or sell a given stock by witnessing how long he stayed at the bid or offer and by how much he traded at a given price level. At that time, market makers would show size on average of 1000 shares, and the spreads were much wider between the bid and ask at the inside market shown horizontally on a Level II screen. *Note: Horizontal* simply means the difference between the prices at which market participants would buy and sell a security, theoretically the most favorable price at any given time. *Vertical* is the spread in price on the same side of the market (buyers or sellers). For example, if Morgan Stanley (MSCO) is the best buyer of

BRCM at the inside bid of $112 and the next buyer on the Level II is not indicating until $111, it would suggest a wide vertical spread among buyers of BRCM and therefore a thin or illiquid period of time for BRCM stock.

SOES traders traded these opportunities created by wide spreads, attempting to make money on market inefficiency, and many did! But much of that has changed due to changes in rules, much tighter spreads, lower size being shown to the market by market makers, and other events that have limited the opportunity for this mechanical trading style. Trading today for spreads alone is a mistake. While the opportunity still exists to a lesser degree, the spreads are so tight that success is not as attainable with this narrowly focused trading style. Therefore, traders must recognize changes in strategy and mechanical systems over time and adapt with the market.

Over the 30 plus years I have traded, including the time I spent on the floor of the Pacific Stock Exchange as a specialist, as a market maker, and currently as an EDAT trader, I have formed the opinion that enduring factors like personal and market psychology need much more attention. Cognitive, mechanical knowledge of the market is important, but what plays on a trader's emotions and how he or she reacts to events is of much greater importance and much less prone to change. That is what is so unique about this book and why I have agreed to contribute to and endorse it.

David concentrates on methods and insights that have been used by traders for many many years. Although there are few common denominators that are present in all markets, the few that do apply are the focus of this book. This book is a rulebook for trading, focusing more on the intangible assets that traders need over time than on the mechanical methods that will change and leave those that don't vulnerable.

The rules covered in this book are written from a trader's perspective. Few rules are new and original; most have been discovered over many years from many traders. These rules have grown and survived because they are not prone to change. Much is gained by "checking your ego at the door" and opening your mind to what could be taught only from many years of experience—experience that has been passed on through generations of great traders and multiplied exponentially over trading floors, hedge funds, institutions, and brokerage houses around the world and that cannot be duplicated by any one person in a single lifetime.

Those that understand this have already acquired the first and most important rule down: **The market has little room for arrogance and ego.** You must have the humility to admit when you don't know or understand something. To admit failure early when you are wrong and to cut your losses, and to learn from everyone, new or experienced, is the attitude the market rewards.

David makes the point that you need to be driven to build knowledge through your passion. I would add that if you think you already have the answers or possess the magic mechanical methods and techniques to trade, this book is not for you. Ego may have lead you to believe such "self-actualization" has been achieved in your trading, but time will correct that—just give it a chance. Many of us have gone through this stage of our trading, including me. Once you humble yourself and put your ego in check, your trading will improve directly with your wisdom. And wisdom is not as much mechanical cognitive knowledge as it is emotional intelligence. Both will be covered, with an emphasis on the latter.

Most books start with a wonderful promise of excitement and mystery and give you the feeling that if you only begin reading, you will find the destination you are looking for. This book's message is the opposite: You must learn the cold hard facts about the market and the rules that must be employed to engage it. I believe this lesson must be learned early, while keeping early excitement at bay. This book does an excellent job of introducing you to it. David approaches the subject of trading with the same honesty and humbleness you must approach it with. This approach centers on the fact that the market is not a destination; it is a journey. If you are expecting a book that will lead you to some destination at which you will find the financial rewards you hope to achieve, your expectations will not be met. Neither this book nor I support such illusions.

This book is a beginning of a journey. It relays the obvious as well as the more subtle nuances between successful traders and unsuccessful traders. Rules are an interesting institution. They are almost destined to fail on one hand because humanity has spent its existence testing them, stretching them, and certainly breaking them. On the other hand, where would we be without them? In the end, we all profit by following them to some degree and by breaking them to another.

Wall Street has had unwritten and written rules for too long. Thankfully day traders have had the courage to test them, stretch them, and even break them in order to create a brand new industry that now properly includes the average person. In this sense, we certainly have all profited from the breaking of the "old guard" and rules that have unfairly punished (financially) those who were not market insiders.

With the emergence of this new industry and pioneers of change, you will on the other hand find abuses of the rules that are put in place to protect us. Manipulations through chat rooms, margin requirements, lending practices, and hype certainly have found their way into this exciting new genre of electronic trading as well.

What David brings out in this book is a balance of rules that leads the electronic trader through the quandary of information that sends conflicting messages to what all market participants hope to achieve: clarity. I define *clarity* in the world of trading as a clear plan of action that leads to a statistical edge large enough to justify the implementation of an idea as to where stock prices are heading, called a *trade*. In the absence of such a plan, clarity will never be found consistently enough to yield sustainable results. Although the rules covered in this book focus on some of the mechanical practices required to find clarity, the psychological rules and attributes that have stood the test of time are rightfully covered in much more detail.

The question I ask others and myself is, Why do people trade?

I think the answer is in part that the market is a seductive institution. Experts from all walks of life have engaged it with all their expert skills, trying to find the perfect fit with the market based on what they know—mathematicians, psychologists, psychiatrists, floor traders, engineers, rocket scientists, software programmers, athletes, and on and on. Many have applied their deep understanding of their respective fields to trading, trying to pigeonhole their specialized skill and understanding into some literal solution to trading. Because many industries make up publicly traded markets, the market is a huge melting pot of services and industries. The irony is that, just as no one industry or discipline makes up the market, no one style or market mechanic will provide the trader with what he needs to trade. Hence, trading is more an art than it is a science.

Drawing from many fields of thought, many psychological, some mechanical, will be the melting pot of ideas that will give you the greatest chance for success. Diving too deeply into any one idea or any one mechanical system through software, technical studies, or mathematical formulas is too narrowly focused. Only by constantly reading and enriching yourself through exposure to the market can you gain the well-rounded base of knowledge you need.

I have read psychology books that make sense and have great application to trading, and I have read other books on mathematics and technical study that also do the same with explanations of how the math can quantify the psychology. But the lesson to take from this book, in my opinion, is to apply a combination of many views to ultimately form your own recipe for success. This recipe will be a living recipe that will continually change with your experience.

Among the tools and attributes most would choose to create the ideal recipe, magical software and technology seem to top the list. I have developed and contributed to some highly sophisticated trading systems. I was involved in the world's first electronic trading system on the Pacific Stock Exchange, and continued as the chairman and CEO of Instinet from 1983 through 1988. More recently as the cofounder and chairman of OptiMark Technologies, I can tell you that while technology has significantly enhanced the markets, it has yet to replace the essential characteristics that only the human mind possesses.

Unfortunately, in most cases, knowledge, research, and the psychological characteristics of traders often take a back seat to technology through excitement and greed. Technology and software unfortunately have been sold to the public as the solution or "holy grail" to finding the trading rewards that so many aspire to, but this ideology is no more effective than chasing leaves in the wind. Software has yet to replace the need for thinking, research, discipline, passion, commitment, and certainly the adherence to the critical rules of trading. These critical rules, as stated, have evolved over time through the mistakes, experience, and pain of many traders who have unknowingly written them by making the mistakes that you undoubtedly already have made or have yet to make.

David has done an excellent job assembling the key characteristics and attributes traders need that are often ignored. This book builds on the backs of many market pioneers who have, like the trail blazers of the old wild west, carved a pathway that, if trusted, will prove to make your journey toward your trading goals less painful and more profitable in much less time.

Software has certainly impacted electronic trading in a very dramatic and positive way, but software will come and go and change. The critical rules to trading are timeless, and they may change to some slight degree, but they will remain steady beacons of light for all to follow who engage the markets.

Because critical rules are never based on the opinion of just a few but rather on the experience of many, the rules stated are not all original. Some may even sound like clichés because they have been heard around trading pits for decades, but remember clichés become clichés because they are worth repeating and hold value. This book gives these time-tested rules a new coat of rhetorical paint and has added new rules based on the beliefs and attitudes of some of the best traders in the world. Regardless of their origins, if you put the axioms you find in this book into practice, it will make a real difference in whether you succeed or fail as a trader.

Because rules are more often broken than followed by new market participants, let me highlight an example that relates to the psychological demons that every trader has to deal with on a regular basis. When day trading, fighting demons becomes exaggerated because you have less time to rationally deal with them. You see a position run uncontrollably lower, knowing it must find support soon; but greed rears its ugly head and causes you to hold on, and before you know it, you are licking your wounds eating a major loss. Or perhaps you are in a trade going into the close and it moves against you, and you decide to hold the position overnight because you hope it will recover. "It's a good, solid stock" speaks the two-headed monster of greed and fear, who repays your misguided trust by taking a bite out of your net worth.

Greed and fear are just two of the many adversaries to the mind of a trader that will prevent many from reaching their potential. Fear of failing. Fear of succeeding. Fear of pulling the trigger. Fear steals confidence and paralyzes traders. Greed, on the other hand, creates exuberance at the expense of doing valuable research, which, in most cases, gives you exactly the opposite of what this useless emotion elicits, the desire for money. Unfortunately, in trading, the more you chase it, the harder it is to catch up to. Ultimately, you will recognize that doing the work born through your passion for the markets will build confidence through knowledge that replaces greed and fear.

Adopt the critical rules highlighted in this book and massage them to fit your own trading style and personality, and the enigma of the market will quickly dissipate.

Another example and component of this book David covers relates to technology. Technology has not just impacted trade execution. Imagine trying to conduct research today without the sea of information available through the Internet. In the last five years, the technology needed for the average person to trade fast and efficiently has come into its own, and if you are not taking advantage of it yet, the most likely reason is that you lack passion to trade or you are afraid of it. The first reason is a good reason not to trade; the second is not, and it is the result of ignorance. The point is, technology is here and will continue to impact many facets of our lives, and to remain ignorant and fearful of it will only spell regret in the long run. By reading now, I suspect that you have the passion to trade. As we say in the business, "Don't fight the tape!" Embrace your passion for the market; it is an advantage. For two centuries, the securities industry attempted to convince the typical investor that he or she was not capable of understanding the complexities of the stock market. The industry maintained that the market was so esoteric that only a highly trained, extremely experienced stockbroker could comprehend its intricacies. Today, you have the power to control your own investing destiny. Along with that power and control comes added responsibility in making your own stock selections. To push the envelope of responsibility, once in a trade, you must also decide when to exit—and that's often the most troublesome question for the amateur trader.

Remember that the word *amateur* is better defined as a state of mind than defined as a level of experience. I know many new traders who are true professionals because of their approach to the market, and I know even more amateurs who have been in the market for years. Their survival kit is made up of five parts luck, three parts hope, and two parts knowledge. This group has yet to face the music and in the meantime is being ground down by poor trading and blaming its dismal results on factors that it can't change, like interest rates, market volatility, bad brokers, commissions, and any other external factors it can think of. The truth is, these individuals will constantly blame others or events outside their control for what they don't have. They are usually very vocal, and they talk the most and accomplish the least, which earns them the title of "amateur." Professionals take responsibility, admit when they are wrong, learn from their mistakes, and move on down the road toward results. Results are the only true measure in the market, which is why the market is not political, but pure. Professionals believe that in most cases, like life, you get out of trading what you put into it. Professionals take responsibility for these results and often feel proud of where they are in their journey of learning, and they continually learn, while the amateurs are justifying and rationalizing to anyone who will listen and join their plight. The amateur stays in constant pursuit of the holy grail of market mechanics and technology that alleviates the responsibility to do the work. You decide which category you fall into, but if your past suggests some of these amateur characteristics, I strongly suggest avoiding electronic trading. It rarely works out for this type of individual.

While these words are tough and hard to hear, I told David when he asked me to write the foreword, "Don't expect me to 'run for mayor' and hold anything back." These are the facts I would tell a good friend or family member who aspired to be an electronic trader. This way, you can quietly and privately categorize yourself now, which may save you many thousands of dollars later. The fact is, trading is not easy and not for everyone, and only you can decide.

I share the same beliefs as David, and commend him on his candid and honest approach, which is the reason I have agreed to endorse this excellent book.

Warmest regards,
William (Bill) Lupien

ACKNOWLEDGMENTS

Thank you again to Stephen Isaacs and Jeffrey (Player) Krames for the opportunity.

Thank you to all our traders for your support.

A special thanks to Tom McCafferty for the contributions to this book and the hard work you provide each day.

A special thanks to my friend Bill Lupien. Your insights have helped me grow as a trader. I look forward to working with you on our new book!

To Stan Yan for the great illustrations. To Dr. Peter Berndt for your contributions. Paul Mann, CPA, for your appendix on taxation. To all members of Market Wise Securities, Inc., for the superb effort you give every single day.

To Jack Whitehouse for the insightful advice, daily support, and friendship. I couldn't ask for a better partner!

To my family:

Glenna A. Nassar and Gabriel E. Nassar, Sr., my parents who have always been there for me.

To my sister Rebecca who reminds me what strength really is.

To my wife, Tracy, and sons, Zachary and Weston, who remind me what is most important.

Disclaimer

Everyone who enters the stock market assumes the risk of losing money. This risk is amplified for those who make their own decisions and execute their own trades. It is further amplified if one day trades large positions on margin. In this case, the trader can lose even more money than is in his or her trading account. This book and the rules it contains will not protect you from losses. We have no way of predicting market action once you are in a trade or your reaction to an adverse market move. You must realize this before you actually trade and be prepared to assume responsibility for your actions. Always keep in mind, you are never under any obligation to trade—it is solely your decision.

This book is intended for educational purposes only. It is expressly understood that this material is not in any way intended to give investment advice or recommendations to buy stock or any other security or investment. The author and publisher assume no responsibility for the investment results obtained by the reader from relying on the information contained in this book. Investing and day trading is inherently risky and the results obtained by some investors may not be obtained or obtainable by other investors in similar or dissimilar conditions. The reader assumes the entire risk of investing, trading, or buying and selling securities. The author or publisher shall have no liability for any loss or expense whatsoever relating to investment decisions made by the reader.

The reader should understand that most people lose money day trading and that technology can substantially slow down during times of heavy market activity.

INTRODUCTION

Few disciplines are as pure as trading stocks. It is neither political nor does it discriminate, and the dichotomy is that there does not exist a more potentially rewarding or unforgiving financial endeavor. The only separation between amateurs and professionals are the critical rules that the market demands be followed. Obey them or become yet another victim of the dynamic enigma called the stock market.

Over the years that I have traded and trained people to trade stocks, I have come to the conclusion that some have had passion, but most do not. As cold and direct as that may sound, it is reality. I have been asked many times what the success rate is of students who come through our courses, as if to suggest the course is the sole solution to what traders need to know to trade successfully. I would love to tell you that our course and the education we provide is the "Shangri-La" of your trading needs, but I would be lying to both of us. The reality is, trading success can be found only within your own personal psychology and the passion you have for the market. Sure, education is critical. Sound understanding of the market and tools of the trade are imperative, but without the right attitude or willingness to form the right perspective and discipline, success will be elusive if not impossible.

At the risk of starting off on a negative note, we must begin by recognizing that many self-defeating mechanisms are present for the trader that constantly work against you. Chief among these self-defeating mechanisms are greed, hope, and fear. There are many others as well—not quite as vicious but just as expensive to harbor, such as laziness, revenge, and boredom. And the conclusion that I have come to is that successful trading is more a state of mind than a state of mechanical or cognitive understanding of the market.

The opportunity is simple. The growth of electronic trading has been and continues to be phenomenal. There were zero online accounts in 1994, and there are estimated to be 15 million online accounts by the year-end 2001.[1] This incredible acceptance of the concept of trading without the assistance of a broker is the result of several totally unrelated trends converging. One, of course, is technology. The Internet and the personal computer are not exactly recent inventions. Both have become very trader friendly. Other events, such as rule changes within the exchanges, and, more recently, increased market accessibility, including pre- and post-market trading, have also contributed to this growth. With the explosive growth ahead of us, I believe those that have the passion to embrace and learn to trade will have the advantage. After all, how many people would be trading today without a user-friendly user interface and a browser? Therefore, the number of traders and investors in the market today and the growth rate of more to come will provide tremendous opportunity and liquidity for a smaller crowd (smart money) at the expense of a much larger crowd (amateur money). The "smart money" crowd of traders are who I refer to as the "one percenters"—a small, esoteric group of active traders who continually write the rules of professional and semiprofessional trading.

The rules I outline throughout the book provide the rationale to avoid common pitfalls that traders before you and I have made. While trading nirvana is not realistic even after you master all the rules, you will become much more aware of common mistakes traders make, and if you learn from them and how to avoid them in the future, you will take years off your learning curve.

While creating this book, I interviewed many professional traders in order to assemble ideas and strategies that could be considered "rules of trading." What I have come away with in

---

[1]"Brokers and the Web," *The Forrester Report,* September 1999.

the process is that the truly enduring rules are small in number but enormous in value. Therefore, it is not my focus to highlight complicated technical formulas or chart formations that are prone to change. This information is already in vast supply, and I chose not to contribute to the "imbalance." Instead, I focus on a relatively small list of rules that, if followed, will provide far more value than the almost infinite amount of literal and tangible formulas now available to those who demand them. Unfortunately, it is this very information that defines trading as a science when, in fact, it is an art. Following the rules of trading that support the art is the primary focus of my work and of my personal trading methodology.

Whether it is day trading, swing trading, or longer-term trading you aspire to, there is no one right way to trade. Only the trading style that meets your personality, time horizons, risk tolerance, and personal goals married to the right mindset will bring the results you desire. Incorporating the right rules and discipline to that style will complement all trading styles.

Throughout the book, the rules are printed in a **bold typeface** and listed at the beginning of each chapter. As you develop your trading style and find your own way, alter the list, adding insights that only you can articulate based on your unique experience and trading style. Be patient on your journey, and allow yourself to continually develop as you define your natural propensity and style of trading.

I wish you success. Trade wise, and trade with passion!

1

PREPARING TO TRADE

Rules of the Trade

The rules are ever changing.

Get a mentor.

There are no silver bullets in this business.

Develop conviction.

Create a written plan.

Avoid holding positions over weekends.

Scared money never wins.

Get the knowledge.

With the emerging gateway to electronic trading opening wide due to revolutionary changes in the securities industry, a volatile stock market, and technological advancements, the first rule in preparing to trade is to understand that **The rules are ever changing.** With these changes and advancements has come an unprecedented explosion in demands to trade equities and securities. As a result, the markets have literally changed shape and form overnight when compared to the pace of change experienced in the markets since the New York Stock Exchange (NYSE) was first organized in 1792.

New methods of trading have created new paradigms and trading techniques that have fueled this growth. The "new economy" is rewriting the rules of trading in terms of price-earnings (P/E) ratios, technical analyses, and market opinions. Many professionals, analysts, and market participants have been predicting a great bear market at epidemic proportions, but they have yet to happen. Corrections (defined as 20 percent retracements in an established index) and even a crash have occurred during this bull market, but they have been shallow and short lived by comparison to its growth.

Another major change that is redefining trading strategies and paradigms is a shift of money flow, from institutional trading that historically dominated our markets to a more balanced trading pattern that includes individual traders and investors. These major changes, and others, have sparked an inferno that is sweeping across our country and enabling more individuals to take control of their own financial destiny. Many have rushed in and have been burned, while others are reaping great rewards. All contribute to changes that are continually rewriting the widely held rules of trading that relate to strategy and market mechanics.

Before we dive into what the more enduring critical rules of trading are, I raise the following question: What is the primary motivation that drives individuals to the trading arena?

1. Is it greed? *Merriam Webster's Collegiate Dictionary,* tenth edition, defines *greed* as "excessive or reprehensible acquisitiveness." In other words, as it applies to trading, *greed* is excessive emotional attachment to money.

2. Is it excitement? Gamblers often ride an emotional roller coaster that takes them from manic highs to depressive lows—they stay in the market for the thrill of the ride.

3. Or is it passion? Individuals who compete in the markets do so for emotional and financial growth.

My hope is that it is number 3: passion. The passionate are the ones for whom this book is written. Passion is really the only motivation that can lead to the desired results. The rules I will highlight throughout this book will build on what has been learned over many years by many professionals. That is why I will spend the majority of the time on rules that have stood the test of time as they have been adapted to fit today's marketplace. Few would argue that we are not in the midst of the most dramatic change our market has ever seen. Fair and equal access to the market through technology is creating increased market liquidity because of individual participation. The rules I cover still apply today, in spite of such dramatic change. Therefore, your interests will be best served to follow them because of these enduring qualities. I can make that statement with confidence not because I have written the rules but because I have used them, as have professionals who have traded over many years.

THE MENTOR

The second rule is **Get a mentor.** The Marines would tell you: "A well-executed plan today is far better than a perfectly executed plan tomorrow." In trading, a well-executed plan will always include a mentor. Professional traders tend to be loners, much like athletes who participate in individual sports, such as swimming, wrestling, golf, or tennis. These types of individuals have no one to rely on but themselves once the games have begun. But there is one person you will almost always see standing near a world-class winner at the end of an event. And there is almost always one person that is singled out for special praise when the champion accepts his or her trophy. That person is almost always the athlete's personal coach or mentor.

The success of almost every great trader reflects the influence of one or more people who took a personal interest in that person when he or she first entered the trading arena. Everyone needs a sounding board—someone to bounce ideas off, a trusted colleague to share plans with, someone to talk to when things are going well, and most importantly, someone to be there when you are not.

If you are fortunate enough to have a close personal relationship with a mentor and coach, then I think you have an advantage (assuming the mentor is worthy of that title). A coach does not take shots for a pro golfer. He or she does not do the swimming for the Olympic athlete, and he or she certainly can't be on the tennis court with the athlete for three hours at a crack. Mentors are off the field, on the sidelines. They watch. They think. They offer suggestions. They point out weaknesses and praise strengths. They cheer you up when you are down and bring you down when you are too high. They try to keep you from hurting yourself, and they push you to excel. They teach you what you do not know and tell you when you think you know too much. And they must do all these things well enough by game day so that you are ready to proceed without their physically talking you through it. What you want from this relationship is the lessons mentors teach in your head when you need them. When the opening bell rings, traders are on automatic pilot, making fast decisions without the time and luxury of overthinking. Instincts must kick in which are born from your efforts made prior to the opening bell. Mentors can help in these efforts. Remember, no one is an island; we all need coaching.

You cannot find good coaches easily because mentors and coaches have a difficult job. It is not exactly a job for which a person normally applies. Mentors and coaches are not always appreciated. They are not the ones that get the glory. Often, they are the ones that are blamed when things go wrong. Is it any wonder you rarely see ads for the position of mentor? Usually, these relationships already exist having been built up over many years, but have not been broadened to include the lessons of trading. Successful people you trust can contribute in many direct and indirect ways to your trading, even if they do not possess the direct skills of trading. While it is an advantage to have a mentor who is also a successful trader, utility can be found in professionals from different backgrounds. For example, the lessons taught in athletics have many applications to trading. Like sports, the results are black and white. You either win or lose at the end of the day. There are no shades of gray as there are in so many endeavors and careers that are evaluated by subjectivity. Because of this, facing reality is apparent in each trade, and this develops a tough skin on traders and athletes who are winners. Humility, discipline, and focus are additional attributes that are present in winners. Like almost all endeavors, winners are minorities, representing a very small percentage of the participants. In some endeavors, it is the 80/20 principle, where 20 percent of the players are getting 80 percent of the results. In trading, I believe the distribution is more extreme, where 5 percent of the traders are getting 95 percent of the results. And in the active trading environment of day trading, I seek to learn from the one percenters, where these individuals are at the very top of the food chain. The point is, in the absence of a mentor in the trading environment, an individual in the top 1 to 5 percent of his or her respective field most likely possesses many of the same attributes required to be a one to five percenter in the trading environment. These individuals and their experiences can teach you the personal psychology of winning and losing, and these lessons are transferable to trading.

Finding the mentor best suited to you and your trading style is not easy. Nevertheless, I would recommend you start by outlining the ideal solution—the combination of attributes that you feel is necessary to help you get the training and coaching you need, based on the style of trading you plan to implement. By writing down everything you need from a trading mentor, you engage yourself in a process that actually helps you define what kind of trading you will be doing and how much interaction with a coach you desire.

Many traders like limited involvement and would just want a person with whom they could share ideas, with little depth to the relationship. That might seem odd, but some trading schools and brokerage firms provide this very service: an objective, experienced professional that you can call from time to time to ask questions and who will point you in the right direction. Also, some services available through the Internet allow you to log into training sessions with seasoned traders where you can simply listen or participate more fully by engaging in a conversation with the professional. This type of arrangement provides a "Web mentor," which is attractive to people in remote locations. If you are fortunate enough to have a more intimate relationship in a *trading room,* in which a brokerage firm provides a trading floor equipped with all the tools and human support you need to trade, then take advantage of it. Regardless of which approach attracts you more, and even though trading is an individual endeavor, I suggest you find a market enthusiast or leader with more skill and experience than you have so that you can grow psychologically.

Many believe that there is an ideal mentor who can give you one winning trade after the other through a subscription service or chat room. But that assumption is unrealistic. Remember that **There are no silver bullets in this business.** There is no easy way to make money in trading. No one person, no one mentor, can provide perfect advice all the time. As a matter of fact, that is not even the providence of a mentor. Only a guru or an alchemist would claim to have the silver bullet. The problem with a self-proclaimed guru is that he or she is paid for his or her advice. In contrast, firms that will provide services free of charge regardless of the number of trades you make are firms I believe you can trust and that have your interest at heart. Think about it: A brokerage firm gets paid for your trading, regardless of how active, through commissions. It has a vested interest in your success. That creates a fair win-win relationship. The firm provides free support and continuing education; you provide your patronage. Paying for a subscription service that promises "winning trades" is denial for the amateur who refuses to do the work required and not the approach of a one percenter.

Mentors also help you develop conviction. I learned from my father to stand behind my convictions. Weak traders are easily influenced by news and others, but strong traders have conviction, and it shows in the way they make and maintain trades. The best traders form their opinions based on their solid research and hard work, and because of that, their opinions are theirs, adding credence to the cliché, "People support the things they help create." It is important to trust your instincts and convictions. Lessons like these are not always popular with new traders because they don't equate to tangible ideas that can be plotted on a chart or seen on a Web site. But having conviction in the course of action you have chosen based on your own research and instincts will give you a much greater chance for success than acting upon a whim or impulse.

Now that you have an idea of what a mentor is, what you expect from one is important to evaluate. Before evaluating what you need from a mentor, the first step is to ask yourself some important questions as outlined in the following section.

Personal Knowledge and Skill Survey for Traders

Check your level of confidence and competency in the following areas. In what areas do you need formal or self-education and which ones call for one-to-one mentoring?

	High	Medium	Low
1. General knowledge of how stocks are bought and sold	—	—	—
2. Specific rules governing the purchase and sale of stock:			
Over-the-counter versus listed issues	—	—	—
Electronic communication network (ECN) executions	—	—	—
Stock clearing rules	—	—	—
Crossed markets	—	—	—
Shorting	—	—	—
Stock selection	—	—	—
Technical analysis	—	—	—
Fundamental analysis	—	—	—
Opening positions	—	—	—
Closing positions	—	—	—
Margin requirements and rules	—	—	—
Account paperwork	—	—	—

3. Skill and trading experience
    Short-term (day trading and/or scalping)   ___ ___ ___
    Swing trading (one to three days)   ___ ___ ___
    Trend trading (three to ten days)   ___ ___ ___
    Medium term (less than one year)   ___ ___ ___
    Long term (over one year)   ___ ___ ___
    Trading strategies   ___ ___ ___
4. Years trading (over five = high;
    one to five = medium; less than one = low)   ___ ___ ___
5. Trading volume per month
    (200 or more = high; 199 to 51 = medium;
    less than 50 = low)   ___ ___ ___
6. Trading demeanor and passion
    for the market   ___ ___ ___
7. Computer and trading software   ___ ___ ___
8. Internet connectivity   ___ ___ ___
9. News and information gathering   ___ ___ ___
10. Financial backing   ___ ___ ___

Note that this is not an all-inclusive list. It is meant instead to provide insight into some of the key areas in which electronic traders must be competent. Because electronic traders are often replacing their brokers with themselves, they must self-impose a suitability profile in order to assess and improve their skill and knowledge. The trader must seek formal education, self-education, and a mentor for some of the more intuitive skills before accepting this responsibility. Many will maintain a combination of services by which they will continue to work with a broker as well as trade capital for themselves; either way, this information at a minimum must be known before electronic trading begins. In the absence or presence of a mentor, another cliché I use often is *"If it is to be, it is up to me,"* which properly states that the buck does stop with you. That is why, with or without a mentor and coach, you ultimately must be in control of your own universe. That control does not come with a quick motivational course; it comes with a plan.

THE PLAN

Before you begin trading and determining which stocks you will trade and on what time horizon, you must first set up a plan of action. The plan itself will actually help set the criteria for which stocks to trade and for how long. Many traders fail to plan their trading strategy and determine which stocks to trade, and consequently their mistakes are very real and very common. In fact, even ordinary. What is extraordinary is obtaining the knowledge, learning the rules, and developing the skills and attributes of successful traders before ever turning on a computer to trade. I often speak about the exuberant who are so anxious to launch their career at trading. They remind me of young sailors who cast off from the shore in their canoes instead of slowing down and remaining onshore long enough to build the proper ship. What good is a head start with a poor vessel? Smart traders build the right plan that can complete the journey. This leads to the rule **Create a written plan.**

This is one of the toughest rules to convince traders to follow. Time and again, they state they know exactly what and how they are going to trade. These same traders constantly find themselves confused and caught in losing trades. To avoid this trap, every 13 weeks I thoroughly review my own trading plan and adjust it accordingly. In Chapter 9, I include some aids to use in this process once you have begun trading, but before beginning to trade, the plan comes first.

A plan is composed of only two primary parts:

1. *The blueprint.* A blueprint is a preliminary action plan developed before trading begins. This step is accomplished before beginning to trade if the trader is new and inexperienced. If the trader is experienced, he or she should reevaluate the plan every 13 weeks. An inexperienced trader should review the plan more frequently. Either way, it is a "living written document" that evolves over time. For example, I always revise my plan for the summer trading season since summertime market conditions call for different strategies.

2. *The journal.* The journal is a day-to-day microadjustment of the blueprint. This is the document that requires you to adhere to your plan. Emotional aspects of trading on a daily basis are written in here. Questions such as

   - Did I follow my blueprint today?
   - Did I maintain discipline?

- Did I do the research required?
- Did I recognize support and resistance levels through volume?
- Was my methodology correct?

would all be good to ask yourself and answer in your journal. These represent intangible issues that technology cannot capture through a database. For example, traders will often lose money while doing the right things; nevertheless, they should remain on course regardless of the monetary outcome. A trade journal is ideal for reminding yourself of that. For example, in Chapter 9 I show the trading patterns of three traders. Each has a distinct style, but through a database, patterns in their respective styles can be seen, including where they are most profitable in terms of sectors, time horizons, and strategy, such as long versus short positions. But what the database cannot tell the traders are the emotional and instinctive qualities of the trade. The journal does, because often a trade is opened and closed for all the right reasons and indications, but the P&L does not reward the right behavior. The data is so objective that it does not reveal the fact that the trader did the right things in spite of a losing trade. If a trader acts on market action a certain way and is rewarded for the action 8 out of 10 times, then the 2 out of 10 times the trade does not yield a profit for the same action should not be questioned too critically. A journal is a good reminder to yourself that you would have done the same trade in spite of the loss. Conversely, if you abandoned your discipline, this too should be noted with your steps to avoid making the same mistake again. Questions like these should also be answered in the journal:

- What was my strategy (earnings play, split, momentum, etc.)?
- Did I exit on fear or logic?
- Did I do the right thing, and do I feel good about my decision? Why or why not?
- Would I make the same trade again in the same situation?

- Did I have confirming indicators when entering the trade?
- Was my discipline followed? Why or why not?

Before defining your trading style in your written plan, which we will do to close this chapter, examining why your plan should be written deserves comment. Writing stimulates thought. When you put your plan on paper, it somehow becomes more real than it is when it is just in your mind. You can more easily share it with a mentor or a fellow trader. Often a thought running through your head sounds great, but when it is in black and white in front of you, it seems unrealistic or improbable. And nothing is more expensive to a trader than trying to make something happen that is unrealistic.

Another very important reason for writing out a plan is that you cannot deny it. If your plan states you will not hold positions overnight but you do so anyway, you realize you have violated your own discipline. When the plan is only in your mind, you will find yourself rationalizing why holding that position overnight is wise, even prudent. Your discipline erodes like the sands of a beach; each ripple, wave, and tide of the market changes the land-scape of your discipline so that you evolve more into a jellyfish of the market rather than the relentless, unemotional shark you need to be.

Think of your written trading plan as one way of measuring your success in terms other than monetary. By comparing your plan to how you are performing, you can make minor adjustments as you need to, and then each quarter you can completely rebuild your plan, incorporating new rules, insights, and goals based on your most recent 13-week experience. Think of your plan as a way to keep score. Too often the profit and loss is the only barometer for traders to judge performance. Your profit and loss (P&L) is certainly important and cannot be underestimated since in the end, what we are all in search of is performance. But many more factors play into the process than just money. Emotions, accountability, responsibility, focus, and creative thought all get brought into the dynamics of trading versus a one-dimensional fixation on monetary gain. Writing down what these motivations and components are for you while tracking your adherence to them each day, through your journal, increases exponentially the likelihood that you will achieve your desired result. Let's take a closer look now at each component of the plan and the rules that apply.

Designing a plan is ultimately a very personal process. Only you know what you know. Therefore, the first place to start is to clearly state your goals and objectives by asking some additional important questions:

1. Do you want to be a full-time or part-time trader?
2. Is it your objective to make a living trading or to supplement your current income?
3. How much time and energy do you expect to put into electronic trading?
4. How many hours a day will you dedicate to research, and when will you do it?
5. Do you seek to become a day trader, swing trader (holding positions 1 to 3 days), trend trader (3 to 10 days), or an investor?

These are all critical questions you must ask yourself. Once answered on paper, the rules you follow for each style of trading will be much easier to incorporate. Each component of your plan should include a time horizon. Everything that follows in your plan keys off of this decision. Select a time horizon for each trade, rather than a single time horizon for all your trading. Like radar, when an opportunity presents itself, it will be recognized, especially as you gain experience. These opportunities will come, and if the criterion you recognize, such as the anticipation of earnings, is more associated with a swing trade, trade accordingly. Pigeon holing yourself strictly as a day trader, swing trader, or investor limits opportunity and also increases the likelihood that you will force trades out of boredom, trying to impose opportunity into a trade where none exists. In short, a multidimensional approach is always preferred to a narrow approach.

As a novice electronic direct-access trader (EDAT) or online trader, you should learn each trading strategy individually. In your written plan, you should state the order in which you plan to tackle each approach to the market. For example, you might state, "I'll day trade for the first two months of trading. This will take me into the earnings season, which is more conducive to swing trading, which I will focus on for that time." Also concentrate on one trading strategy at a time. Spend the first couple of months hitting nothing but very short term momentum trades. Then move on to adding swing trading for the next quarter. Mid- to long-term trading is probably what you have been doing, or have done in the past, if you come from an investing background. The research you do to buy a stock you are going to put in your individual retirement account (IRA) and hold for the long term is substantially different from the stock you would buy for a trade you think will last only minutes. For the former, you would do a lot of fundamental analysis to learn everything you can about the company and its markets, not to mention the company's past technical performance. This requires a considerable amount of time and effort. Precision execution is not dependent on research. Instead, market action momentum and pattern recognition are the focus. The evaluation process for a day trade is equally important but more intense, faster, and dependent on direct precision execution and timing. For a momentum trade, intraday volatility is critical, as is how the stock opens and closes. Unfortunately, too many "wannabe" day traders are not willing to work as hard as is necessary to become successful. You cannot park yourself behind a computer and start to day trade against the top market-making trading teams in the world and expect instant success. It does not work that way.

When you start working on your swing trading, technical chart patterns, breakout and breakdowns, moving averages in price and volume, and broader focus on Level II analysis become the tools and techniques of the trade. Since these trades last for several days, as opposed to several minutes or hours, you must decide—in advance of entering the trade—whether you will hold the position overnight.

While you may occasionally hold a position overnight, you should, as a rule, **Avoid holding positions over weekends.** The rationale is simple—time in the market is one of the three things you have absolute control over (stock selection and size are the other two). Since you have no idea what could occur over the weekend to influence the stock you are trading, why take the risk? Additionally, you can always reestablish your position on Monday if the trade still looks promising. Think of swing trades as trades you enter early in the week and exit by Friday. While not an inclusive list, these are examples of rules you would include in your plan.

From your decision on time horizons flows the rest of your trading plan, such as selecting stocks to trade as well as your entry and exit plan. For example, if you decide to begin with day trading, you should write down a criterion for the stocks you will trade. You would include characteristics like adequate daily volume, sufficient price volatility, correlation with leading indicators, major market maker participation, reliable technical indicators, liquid ECNs, tracking by analysts, and availability of news. Additionally, I find the more I trade a given issue, the more I become a specialist in that stock and recognize the patterns the stock exhibits. These are by no means the only criteria, but they are what I look for in the stock selection process. These characteristics will be discussed in greater detail in Chapter 4.

Table 1.1 will help you begin your plan, as it provides a set of criteria that should be followed for trades that last up to 10 days.

Day Trade Criteria (Intraday time horizon within an hour or less)

Day traders in the purest definition are rapid-fire momentum traders who take profits fast and cut losses even faster. They like anything that moves and shows a pattern or signs of follow-through. They are indifferent to going long or short, and they make the most trades in a day and have the tightest risk tolerance. There is no completely literal description of a day trader, but Table 1.1 is a good overview of considerations to follow.

Range Trade Criteria (Intraday time horizon up to several hours)

A range trader will carry a position throughout the day for periods of hours. These traders are trading the daily range of stocks based on pattern recognition and correlation to sector trends. Range traders don't like news on the stocks they trade. They prefer to move quietly through the market taking profits out of highly predictable ranges among the stocks they specialize in. They are a form of day trader, but they use a longer time horizon.

Swing Trade Criteria (One- to three-day time horizons)

The swing trade is more associated with minor trends in the market. Charles Dow compared (what later contributed to the Dow theory) the market patterns to the tides, waves, and ripples in the ocean. Primary trends are analogous to the tides, secondary trends to the waves, and minor short-term trends are associated with the ripples. Swing traders are looking for minor and secondary trends in stocks that reveal themselves over a few days. Day traders ignore these moves because they are intolerant of the risk associated with overnight positions. Many investors believe they are swing traders, but they lack the skill and experience to read the signals well enough to take consistent profit. Most will follow the "poke-and-hope method," waiting for the stock to move in their favor. Those trades that do are often liquidated and covered generally too soon, and those that don't become long-term investments until the traders can't meet margin calls any longer, forcing investors to cover at the worst possible time. Swing traders differ from investors because they employ a methodology that includes the discipline to cut losses when the data the market provides tells them to.

Trend Trade Criteria (Over 3 days, but generally less than 10 days)

Trend trading is very similar to swing trading but it works within a longer time horizon. This trader is often a systems trader relying on technical tools, such as *Omega Tradestation, TC 2000, Neovest,* and other alert systems. This trader tends to be the full blown technical trader, who will often employ options as well as equities to trade.

The criteria presented in Table 1.1 make up a guide to help you create a profile of which style or combination of styles suits your trading desires. While finding success in any style is hard work, all have the potential for substantial upside and downside. Because of this, mental preparation through a written plan will help set reasonable expectations prior to engaging the market to offset manic highs when success is found and depressive lows when inevitable losses occur. The key to surviving this potential emotional roller coaster ride is to look at trading like the trades

TABLE 1.1 Trade style criteria

	Capital Requirements	Time Requirements		Risk Tolerance
DT	Minimum $25,000 with 2:1 margin account or $50,000 cash.	Minimum 10 hours per day Example: 8:30–9:30 9:30–12:30 12:30–4:30 4:30–5:30 2 hours	Shaping up for the open/premarket. Trade the open and morning; sit out the first 15 minutes of open. Trade the afternoon and close. Account maintenance and journal. Evening work and research.	• Pure discipline. Tight risk stops (mental). • No overnight positions. • Trade heavy size. 1000 shares or more. • SIP. • Minimum 500,000 shares per day. • Volatility. Daily range of >$3.
RT	Minimum $25,000 with 2:1 margin account or $50,000 cash.	Minimum 10 hours per day Example: Same as DT.		• Risk tolerant/pure discipline. More risk than DT. • Slightly lighter size per trade. 500–1000 shares or more. • Limited overnights. • 500,000 shares per day. • Volatility. Daily range of >$1 or more.
ST	Minimum $10,000 with 2:1 margin account or $20,000 cash. No IRAs should be traded using this style of trading.	Minimum 6–8 hours per day Example: 8:30–9:30 9:30–11:00 2:30–4:30 4:30–5:30 2 hours	Shaping up for the open/premarket. Study market patterns. Watch/trade the close; clues on how a stock will open are often left at the close. Account maintenance and journal. Evening work and research.	• Risk tolerant. Timing less critical. • Trading ranges/trends. • Lighter size. • Larger point movements. • Overnight positions. • Smaller daily volume required. • Volatility. Daily range <$1 acceptable. • Stops important.
TT	Minimum $5000 with 2:1 margin account, or $10,000 cash. Self-directed IRAs often traded.	Minimum 3 hours per day Example: 9:30–11:00 4:30–5:30 Notes: • Marking to market should be done to evaluate margin requirements. • Evening hours vary according to research being done.	Positions are generally opened during morning hours or after the close. Account maintenance and journal.	• Same as swing trading.

Abbreviations: DT, day trader
IRA, individual retirement account
MA, moving average
RT, range trading

SIP, small incremental profits and losses
ST, swing trading
TA, technical analysis
T&S, time and sales
TT, trend trading

Analysis Tools	Analysis Techniques (Personal)	Psychology	Psychology (Market)
• Level II. • Time/sales. • Graphs/charts. • Index/future. • Charts/short term. • Precision execution.	• Specialist. Knows a handful of stocks very well. • Tape reading. • Levels and prints. • Support/resistance. • Relative strength. • Index correlation. • Futures market. • Fading and shorting.	• Spousal support. • Aggressive personality traits. • Hard worker. • Competitive. • Self-motivated. • Independent. • Risk tolerant. • Highly focused. • Humble.	• Microview of market. • Understands broad trends. of markets. • Fades over-reactions. • Avoids direct news.
• Same as DT, plus charts with short time using 10-, 20-, 50-, and 100-period MA.	• Same as DT, plus tape reading—larger range trading with a broader focus.	• Same as DT, plus average to aggressive personality traits.	• Same as DT, plus understands broad trends of markets as well. • Range trading. Looks for patterns. • Trades stocks correlated to market.
• TA/charts. • Online systems. • Conditional order entry. • Level II and T&S not critical but desirable. • Precision execution not critical but desirable.	• Filters through TA. • Sector strength. • Support/resistance. • Breakout/breakdown. • Shorting less active. • Gap trading is common. • Follows news more. • Research and fundamentals important.	• Same as DT and RT, plus average to moderately aggressive personality traits. • More analytical. • More time constrained. • Less active.	• Follows trends of markets. • Follows news more closely. • Range trading. • Technical market patterns.
• Same as swing trading.	• Same as swing trading except gap trading is avoided.	• Same as swing trading, except these traders tend to be very analytical.	• Follows the overall market trend. Shorting is rare.

themselves. Avoid the expectation of selling tops and buying bottoms, as you avoid exuberance and dismay. Find the "sweet spot" somewhere in the middle and run the long race by pacing yourself with limited losses. One of the greatest lessons any trader can learn regardless of trading style is to let profits run and crucify losses immediately.

CAPITAL CONSIDERATIONS AND MARGIN

Once you have profiled your trading style, the subject of capital is critical and must also be part of your written plan. How much do you need to day trade or swing trade? Should you open a cash or margin account? Does margin change if positions are held overnight?

Knowing what stocks you will trade and the size of the trade will help establish your account size. If you selected stocks of $100 per share and you plan to day trade heavily (large share-size), you would need at the very least $50,000 in a 2:1 margin account, and this would still substantially limit your opportunities because you would be confined to just that position while in a trade (assumes 1000 shares at $100 per share).

To determine how much capital you need, you should first decide whether to open a cash account or a margin account. In a cash account, you must pay for whatever stocks you purchase within three days. This is known as *T+3*, or the trading day plus three more days to settlement day. In a margin account, you pay for half the cost of what you purchase, and you borrow the rest from your broker. The amount of margin you can borrow is set by the Federal Reserve in what is known as *Regulation T*, or *Reg T*. The fed can adjust the figure up or down to slow down the economy or to heat it up, but at the time of this writing, Reg T is set at 50 percent, and it has been at 50 percent for a long time.

If you day trade, it makes sense to use a margin account for two reasons. One, it doubles your buying power, giving you more flexibility in higher-priced stocks and the number of shares you can trade. The other reason is that you generally will not have to pay any interest on the amount borrowed for intraday trades because the trades are offset each night at clearing.

However, if you hold a margined position overnight or for days, weeks, months, and so on, you must pay interest on the dollar amount borrowed. The interest is based on the *broker's call rate,* and it is usually a little above the prime rate.

Most brokerage firms have a minimum account size. Generally, it is lower for online trading accounts than for day trading. The reason is that the online accounts tend to be less active and therefore less risky for the brokerage firm. Some day trading firms seek only the most active traders, and their minimums are high, as much as $100,000. Other firms seek active traders who possess discipline and control—therefore, require less capital to begin, such as $25,000. All margin accounts, by federal regulation, must have at least $2000.

There is more than one type of margin and more than one type of margin call. A *margin call* is a request from your brokerage firm to add money to your account. A margin call can even occur in a cash account. For example, you have $5500 cash in your cash account. You place a market order to buy 100 shares of a stock priced a $50. What happens if your market order gets filled at $60? You owe $6000 plus commission. You get a margin call from your broker for the short fall. If you do not meet the call, the brokerage firm has the right, via the account papers you sign to open the account, to sell as much of your stock as necessary to satisfy your debit.

There are three kinds of margin calls. The first mainly applies to day traders, and it is called an *intraday margin call.* This means that at some time during the trading session you exceeded your buying power. This figure usually appears on your trading software, and it is calculated by doubling the excess equity in your account. The good news is that most trading software is designed to prevent you from exceeding your daily buying power.

The second type of call is the *overnight margin call,* also known as a *Reg T call.* This occurs when you exceed the amount of stock that you are allowed to hold overnight. You must have enough cash or securities in your account to pay for 50 percent of the stock you hold overnight. New money is required to meet this call. If you do not meet the call, your account is immediately put on *Restriction 2*—meaning nothing can be withdrawn and margin calls must be met the next day.

The third type of call is a *maintenance call.* This is the most common call of the new undercapitalized trader because once you have been holding a position in a margin account, if it loses value, you must maintain enough equity in the account to satisfy 25 percent of the current market value for long positions and 30 percent for short positions. If your equity drops below this minimum, you will receive a maintenance margin call. During the ".com crash of 2000" (as I believe it will be remembered—March 24, 2000, to May 25, 2000), many learned then that their tech stocks were not coming back (in time) to alleviate the maintenance calls, which forced sellouts and realized losses that ended many peoples' dreams of trading for a living or even as a supplement to their incomes.

This topic can be a bit boring, but these rules are expensive to break, so before opening a margin account it is best to understand the rules placed on your account. A final word on margin: These rules can be made stricter than the Federal Reserve requires, and often are. Each brokerage firm establishes its own *house rules.* House rules supersede all rules as long as they meet the minimum Fed criteria. I particularly like firms that have stronger requirements—it shows they are protective and careful, and I would much prefer to have my money in one of those firms as opposed to a loose cannon firm. Many firms have gone out of business and have put customers' capital at risk by having no coverage greater than the coverage provided by SIPC (Securities Investors Protection Corporation), which all firms must carry. I would suggest you diligently investigate the rules of the firms you are considering and not just pay attention to commission rates alone.

The next key area to consider is your financial situation. Much of what will shape your plan will stem from your capital available and the emotional attachment you have to that capital. The rule here is **Scared money never wins.** Before becoming an active trader, you should be on sound financial footing; without that, trading will be more associated with excessive fear than with reasonable confidence. This rule simply means you must be in a position to lose all your speculative or high-risk capital without the loss materially affecting your lifestyle. Before attempting any high-risk venture—and online or EDAT day trading should certainly be considered high-risk trading—you need to address some fundamental issues. For example, if you plan to trade full time, you must consider your cash flow and the money you will live on. Having a sufficient nest egg to handle unexpected emergencies and funds to cover major impending expenses (college for children, retirement, etc.) are all strong considerations, and is not money that should be put at risk. "Scared money" already puts the odds of succeeding against you through conscious or subconscious pressure. Additionally, you need to assess time commitment, support systems, and psychological aspects of trading to "brace yourself for losses," not winners.

Being financially stable takes a considerable amount of pressure off you as a trader. You can enter, exit, and manage trades more rationally. A trader, for example, who is in a losing trade and cannot afford to take a loss has the tendency to hold the trade too long—hoping it will turn in his or her favor. This can result in the violation of several of the rules that every trading plan should include whether new or experienced.

If this sounds like a lot to learn, you are absolutely right. But the knowledge you will acquire through studying will prepare you to decide which trading style will work best to help you meet your objectives. You will discover what type of research, markets, and securities attract you the most, and that insight will give you an advantage over the amateur who seeks every gap opening, split announcement, or other market event that screams "Trade me!" Headline events in the market are seductive to the aimless market participant, but the disciplined professional who stays focused on his or her plan and who executes trades that meet the criteria in the plan is positioned to run the long race. Successful trading is a marathon, not a 100-yard dash.

The rules covered this far lead up to one all-encompassing rule: **Get the knowledge.**

I believe a "fork in the road" has developed in terms of market education, instead of what should be more viewed as a scale, with a proper balance between mechanical understanding of the market and the psychological dynamics that determine how to use such knowledge. In one direction is the road to all cognitive, mechanical knowledge of the market. Because there is so much to learn and so much of it changes frequently, this road is very dynamic. In the other direction is the road to the emotional influences on the market that are often mysterious, esoteric, and even elusive. The fact that the two roads exist is not the problem. The problem is that most people choose one road to the exclusion of the other rather than spending time on both.

Cognitive learning, or the acquisition of "factual and tangible information," represents the road that most believe will bring the success they desire. Software programs are perhaps the largest and most sought after tool that traders focus on in order to look for the magic in trading that really doesn't exist. This one-sided focus occludes the psychological or emotional dynamics of trading that makes up the other road less traveled. The only true constant in the markets is the participation of humans who tend to react to similar situations in predictable ways. If we can understand our true motivations, chances are we can figure out a way to succeed. I believe now, after traveling a fairly long way down both roads, that successful trading does not result from equal devotion to both approaches. While both are extremely important, and one could not survive without the other, once a solid footing is secured in gaining factual information, it is understanding the psychological forces that will yield the greatest gains. Unfortunately, amateurs will continually choose the wrong road, wasting valuable time trying to strengthen their mechanical knowledge through software systems and decision-support tools, while the more important road (psychology) is traveled only lightly, if at all.

So there it is: The odds for success either fall significantly toward your favor with knowledge or significantly away without it. Ironically, that is the dichotomy of the market itself; brutally unforgiving of the weak and tremendously rewarding of the competent—a daily representation of Darwin's survival of the fittest, where success is measured most objectively, in dollars and cents. There isn't very much in between.

2

RULES FOR TRADING

Rules of the Trade

Know your strategy.

Use Level II as an indicator, not as an all-inclusive decision support tool.

Read the levels, not the ticks.

Know your order routes.

Never allow your order flow to be sold.

This chapter addresses the fork in the road I spoke of in Chapter 1, but it focuses first on the mechanical systems that we use to trade. While many people know a great deal about the stock market in terms of research and technical indications, which in today's marketplace are increasingly important, some of them have abandoned their methodology and trading techniques that have worked for them in the past, prior to the drastic improvements in technology. Many wise traders have formed strong opinions and strategies of what they should trade and for what time horizon but have lost their poise to stay with the opinion because of the rapidly changing action associated with "microtools" and real-time information now available with technology. The action plan for a given idea or trade can quickly erode under conditions of what I would call "market schizophrenia," which is often associated with real-time tick data. Real-time data have changed the course for many usually profitable traders to a new losing course because they have become intoxicated with studying stocks too closely under a microscope—a phenomenon that real-time information can provide. In this environment, many otherwise intelligent traders lose their conviction for staying with strategies that have served them well in the past. They lose the feel of reading the ebb and flow of the market or a given security when they view its behavior in an electronic direct-access trading (EDAT) context.

While these systems provide incredible power and the freedom to take control of your trading decisions and executions, to use them effectively requires something in addition to a deep understanding of their functionality. That addition is your own thinking. In other words, you must decide whether or not acting on the data will lead you to meet your trading objectives. Let me explain. I have met many professionals from various fields who have come to our school equipped with a pretty good trading experience. Some have told stories about how much money they were making and how they were going to abandon their successful careers—which have actually afforded them the time and money to trade full time. Unfortunately, when this irrational behavior is at its peak, words of caution we offer are no more heard than the words of a bartender to the drunk who has had one too many. The effect of the intoxication is the same even though the drug is different. The proverbial fork in the road is forged when this type of individual discovers the power now available through direct-access information and execution. Many fail to recognize that not only has their short-term success in the market been born of one of the greatest bull markets we have seen but also that the trading style they unknowingly adopted kept them further back from the gyroscopic, micromarket environment.

Until real-time information was available, the only market participants that had access to this trading environment were exchange traders on the floor, who were taught by seasoned professionals whose entire careers were shaped in that very environment. They were taught through the very delivery system and culture that had been built over many years and generations of traders associated with this environment. There existed, therefore, in this environment, many natural mentors to teach the next generation of traders.

This brings us back to our professional that I was speaking about. Perhaps he or she was a doctor, lawyer, small-business owner, entrepreneur, engineer, teacher, or any other professional you can think of. I think I have met most of them, and they have had a common experience. They have had some luck provided by the bull market, and their gain was protected by the natural safe barrier created by the delay in information availability through media such as brokers, the telephone, newspapers, and delayed Internet quotes. Thus many thousands, if not millions, of people have found some "perceived" success in the stock market. These people of course want more of that success, so they derail themselves completely or partially to travel on a new road with which they have absolutely zero experience. They have not been the recipients of training on an exchange floor. They have not had the benefit of mentoring from seasoned pros. Most have not been body slammed and stomped on by the market, and the few who have been have not stood back up and licked their wounds to return to fight another day, unlike the floor traders who are taught to do so by their mentors and who wear their battle scars like a badge of honor and beacon of hope for their young protégés. Instead, most online traders are ill prepared and intoxicated with a taste of success, and they have little or no knowledge but are still trying to day trade a living from the attraction of powerful real-time electronic systems. Therefore, the introduction of real-time market data unfortunately produced more money drunks than true professional market participants.

The statistics the industry reports are true: Only 10 percent or so of the people who engage in this sort of trading will be even moderately successful. This same 10 percent (if it is that high a percentage) are making fortunes, while the remaining are losing, falling to the sidelines like casualties of war. Is this because day trading successfully is not possible? Is this because the brokerage firms that offer day trading services are merely charlatans of the market, luring the unknowing into the "big top" just to take their money?

No. If day trading successfully were impossible, then no percentage of day traders would be successful, and if most brokerage firms were market charlatans, they would not be surviving either. The market is so pure that it has a powerful self-cleaning mechanism to rid itself of either party. Whether it is the ill-prepared amateur trader or the uncommitted sell-side brokerage firm, the market eventually punishes and purges both. Therefore, survival is possible, but to do so requires that the trader know and follow this important rule: **Know your strategy.**

The day traders' strategy, if defined as microtrading, is to take many small incremental profits (SIPs) from the market while strictly limiting losses. Novice online investors' strategy has been, and still is, to buy a stock based on some research, to take a good guess on what the stock is worth based on price association to where it may have been (ebb and flow), and to hold on to it until it returns a profit or the investor is taken out of the trade through a margin call and excessive losses. The bull market prior to March 24, 2000 (the beginning of the bear cycle of 2000 in my opinion), rewarded this behavior, causing novice online investors to believe they were "unconscious competents" or even "conscious competents" when in reality many were proven to be "unconscious incompetents" when the bear cycle arrived. A lucky few missed the carnage.

The term *conscious competent* comes from a psychological matrix that was created in the late 1960s and came into popular use without a real attribution to its originator. The competency matrix reveals a process whereby an individual progresses from one level of competence to another. The phases of the matrix as they apply to trading include the following:

- The *unconscious incompetence stage,* which describes a person who cannot trade successfully but doesn't know it. Too many online investors fit into this category.
- The *conscious incompetence stage,* which describes a person who cannot trade successfully and knows it. This person knows he or she should seek education and knowledge before proceeding.
- The *conscious competence stage,* which describes the person who can trade successfully by thinking about it and following a plan. Many have been confused into thinking they are in this phase when in reality they are experiencing luck in the bull market. While these traders seek knowledge, they learn the short side of the market.
- The *unconscious competence stage,* which describes the person who can trade successfully and consistently on pure instincts. While mechanical knowledge is dynamic, it is likely that these people can reach and remain in this stage because they know themselves well and they understand the psychological influences on their thinking. This stage is the goal of every professional trader!

Certainly other speculators exist that include money managers, individual traders with a longer-term outlook, and other market participants who could be defined as unconscious competents, but in all cases, before you set out in any direction, you should have a firm strategy in mind and on paper. Before studying the tendencies of successful market participants, we must first explore where most mistakes are made by novices.

Many have attempted to leave their respective careers to day trade full time under the illusion of a forgiving market prior to the crash of March 2000. Unfortunately most were humbled once the Internet "bubble" burst. Additionally, real-time systems contributed to the amateurs' failure while continuing to be the professionals' friend.

Many novices become victims of the market not because of the powerful tools they are using but because of the way they are applying those tools. If day trading is the strategy, micro imbalances in supply and demand is the approach for which the tools we are about to cover will be invaluable. Note that any strategy other than day trading will require an alternative application of these tools. However they are used, the new tools available provide tremendous application and utility, but proper use is imperative because improper use is unforgiving. What is to follow are the rules that should be followed while using the newest mechanical systems in the market. While I consider these rules to be critical, they are in no way a substitute for the even more critical rules, to be covered later, that relate to psychology. Knowing a great deal about technology, technical indications, mathematical formulas, and other tangible applications for the market will never replace or supplement the trader's self-knowledge. Those who do not gain and maintain emotional control once caught in the inevitable maelstrom of the stock market will find it impossible to find reason and clarity of thought.

That said, let's begin by defining what day trading was and redefine what it has evolved into today. A few short years ago, a day trader's primary mode of operation was scalping for spreads. Spreads were artificially wide due to market inefficiencies caused by events that are no longer important for the purpose of our discussion but are fully examined in other books such as the Secret of the SOES Bandits, written by Harvey Houtkin. Today, trading for spreads is a mistake, and the only profiteer in that equation will be the brokerage firm with whom the trader attempts this foolish endeavor. Supply and demand (S/D) imbalances have been and will always be the only enduring strategy for active trading. Ironically, the tools used by the day trading scalper of just two to three years ago are the same tools that today are utilized as confirming indicators for active traders, although they are not the sole literal decision support tools they once were.

Many "SOES bandits" of the past were able to make money off this temporary anomaly in the market, but the enduring strategies that have always yielded results are born from supply/demand imbalances.

The rules given in this chapter describe the "best-methods" use of these various tools available on an EDAT system. Since so many resources already exist explaining these various tools, I will not cover their functions in detail. Instead, I will prescribe the rules that should be followed to use them, making the assumption that you have already or will acquire an understanding of their functionality.

THE LEVEL II SCREEN

The Level II screen and the ticker, or tape, as it is called, are two tools that can highlight opportunity for the professional trader that recognizes trends created by order flow in the market. This is important since success leaves clues in most endeavors, and it does so in trading as well. These clues are left on real-time electronic systems in the form of S/D imbalances that suggest impending moves for stocks. The rule is **Use Level II as an indicator, not as an all-inclusive decision support tool.**

Level II price quotations are one of the most important tools for any short-term trader. I strongly recommend Level II to anyone actively day trading. Understanding Level II price quotations gives you a tremendous insight into micro imbalances in supply and demand of any stock, which in turn is your best signal for short-term direction of stock prices. While learning to accurately read the Level II window can take months of practice, without that skill, you put yourself at a distinct disadvantage. These benefits alone more than justify the use of Level II for any trading style, active or passive. However, the problem I see is that many traders still use it as they did a few years back when spread trading via the Small Order Execution System (SOES) was popular. The utility for this type of trading today is dead in my opinion and should be buried accordingly. Unfortunately, many firms and novice traders won't let it die and continue to lose money as a result.

Another risk of using Level II and the tape is that, if monitored too closely and too literally, it does become intoxicating, as

I stated earlier, and it creates a distorted view that does not reflect the true momentum or direction of a given stock. Therefore, Level II is best used in concert with other trend-following indicators that together shape overall momentum for a trade. Trend-following indicators, defined in many ways, including trading price levels, monitoring the futures market, indice strength, and technical indications, can be found in any good technical analysis book. Another strong attribute of the Level II screen is that it can help traders acquire precision execution skills. Level II creates transparency to a stock's liquidity, which identifies the market maker and ECN who is bidding and offering stock along with the size of their bid or offer. This is of great value because with this level of transparency married to direct execution tools, the need to ever place an order where you lose control, such as a market order, is eliminated. I will spend more time on precision execution methods, market versus limit orders, and trade entry and exit strategies in Chapters 5 and 6.

TIME AND SALES (TAS)

The rule regarding this tool is **Read the levels, not the ticks.** The TAS, or the tape, is one of the oldest tools there is for reading the market's direction and momentum. First invented in 1867, the ticker like the Level II screen can be intoxicating, and, in fact, even more so when it is viewed too closely and literally. I have seen traders work themselves into a state of hysteria one tick at a time trying to interpret what each and every print meant. Often those who think they know the most actually know the least as is obvious when they claim they can read the market strictly with this one tool. The better strategy when utilizing this tool is to read the price levels of support and resistance in real time while determining where prices are strong and well supported and where they grow weak and resistant. Think of this as "tape support" and "tape resistance," which simply explains where a stock is well supported from going lower and where it is resistant to going any higher.

Recognizing these levels is important, as is understanding the strength or weakness of these levels. For example, if CSCO trades to $60 on light volume from a support level of $50, the trader would see that as a strong indication that CSCO is strong within this range due to the light volume it traded as it moved 10 points. This would suggest that few sellers exist in CSCO within this range. If CSCO continued to follow through on heavy volume another $3 to $63, this would indicate that weakness may be setting in within this range due to the heavier selling volume. As profit takers come to market, the selling pressure builds. Although demand still exceeds the sellers, which is what allows for the additional $3 move to $63. The increasing, or "thicker," volume building is an indication that this move is nearing an end. A trader would trust anything within the $50 to $60 range much more than a move from $60 to $63 if the stock should pull back within this $3 range. For example, suppose CSCO comes in $9 from the high of this range ($63) to $54. I would consider the likelihood of CSCO trading from $54 ($63 minus $9), which represents a higher low, to $60 much greater than its trading from $60 to $63, everything else being equal. The strength or weakness of a stock's range can be measured through the Time & Sales screen and the volume of shares that trades through it. This is just one example of the power of this tool, but it is a good example of how to use it to read levels as opposed to every tick.

The utility of this tool is far greater than just the example cited, but the point to draw from it is that, if you attempt to interpret every print or tick with this tool, you force your mind into such a microview of the market that you will not see the forest for the trees. I find this is one of the most common mistakes amateur traders make when they enter the day trading environment. An example of how you can take the data from this tool and incorporate it into indicators that are more macrofocused within the day could be the *TRIN indicator*.

TRIN stands for "trader's index," and it measures advancing to declining issues against volume. For example, if the number of advancing stocks is growing at such a pace that it is disproportionate to advancing volume over declining volume, then the market may be approaching a top, and a reversal or downturn is getting closer. Without going off on too much of a tangent in explaining the value and the math of this indicator, the point I want to make is that many mathematical formulas such as TRIN exist to measure what an active trader is trying to measure through the information he or she receives from tools like the tape. The core difference is that, when you filter this information through your mind, instead of relying completely on filtering the information through a computer, your mind blends your feeling, intuition, and experience while reading these levels, something a computer cannot do at this time. As TRIN can highlight an improving or deteriorating market condition, the tape can be used in concert to identify stocks with relative strength or weakness that will lead the overall market. While TRIN represents overall market condition, it is important to remember that it is the alignment and confirmation of several tools that formulate trading decisions. TAS alone loses a great deal of its utility, but when combined with Level II, technical indicators like TRIN, and other indicators like sector strength, it is one of the strongest tools a trader can have. The following example also helps to explain.

PRESSURE POINTS

The following is an example of how the Level II and TAS work in concert with each other and act as a strong short-term indicator for trade entry, exit, and decision support. This example is easy to understand when broken down a piece at a time, and very effective when implemented by active traders who have the discipline to follow it. I call it pressure points. Pressure points describe areas of support and resistance for a given stock, which highlights reversals. Reversals are defined here as a breakdown after rallies at resistance and a bounce after sell-offs at support. These turning points often show signs of pressure before they release, and make what are often the biggest moves of the day for volatile issues.

Suppose you are reading a Level II screen with a Time & Sales screen, and the bid and offer for the stock in question is 85 to 85⅛. The prints on the TAS screen are showing that the volume of trading at that moment is trading at the bid, indicating sellers are in the market, hitting the bidding market makers and ECNs. As market makers and ECNs are being hit (buying), sellers are providing them with the stock they are buying. The indication to look for here is how aggressive are the sellers selling stock to the market participants who are bidding to buy, and how much appetite for the stock do the buyers have for the stock at any given price level.

Now most ECNs as a rule will not show you as much indication since they generally represent the retail market and the aggregation of many individual traders trading within any given ECN. Therefore, interest to buy or sell a stock at any given price level is difficult to read since no one person or personality reflects the sentiment in any given ECN. This is not true of a market maker who is only one or a few people making the market in a given stock at any given firm. For example, if CS First Boston (FBCO) has one market maker making the market (trading) in VRSN, you can read the intentions of FBCO as a whole much better than those of an ECN, which, as I stated, can represent thousands of traders. Therefore, as the market maker in this example is buying aggressively, evidenced by staying at the bid taking stock, he is showing you something about his sentiment for the stock (bullish). ECNs, due to the fragmentation within them, are not as strong a signal as an individual market maker. One exception would be Instinet, which is still more reflective of institutional order flow because there is less fragmentation in comparison to the public representation within other ECNs such as the Island ECN (ISLD), Archipelago (ARCA), or Speer Leeds Redi ECN (REDI).

Back to the example, as sellers aggressively hit these bids (evidenced by a fast-moving tape and high volume with bigger size prints such as 500 to 1000 shares), the indication to look for, in addition to the volume of trades on the tape, is how long and who is remaining as a buyer of VRSN on the Level II. Additionally, how fast are bidders getting out of the way (fading bids)? If bidders are fading fast, while sellers are aggressively hitting their bids, that spells weakness and indicates that the bid price in the market will be lowered. On the other hand, if the bidders are taking on a lot of stock while sellers are hitting their bids, market makers are revealing their hand by staying at the bid buying, showing their strong appetite for the stock. This will generally begin to show as the stock has already fallen or come in a bit and has begun to reflect buying strength to the upside as stock is getting to a support level. Also, this indication can be confirmed as ECNs begin to show up at the bid, evidencing that the other active traders in the market are also noticing what I just described and are beginning to buy at the bid price while the remaining sellers are fading.

Beside the ECNs' showing up while market makers are bidding strong, another confirmation that buying strength is building in this example is the absence of sellers. When sellers dissipate while buyers remain to own the stock, it indicates the turning point I spoke about where demand is building (bidders) and supply (sellers) are diminishing, which creates an imbalance of demand over supply, showing the impending price movement to the upside. Traders that make decisions with this mindset and recognize this type of indicator are indifferent to prices but very prejudiced to reaction.

I certainly will look for confirmation and subscription through well-correlated sectors and stocks, but as these indications confirm each other, they support a decision to act. In this example the action to open a long position would be taken, or in the case of a short position already on, a good time to exit and cover. The point is that these tools can be used for various strategies. The scenario I just explained would be more of a day trading strategy and definitely more microfocused, but not so narrowly focused that every print or trade alters my ability to read where stock prices are showing signs of support or resistance. Maintaining the discipline to react to changes in the market based on the strategy you are employing is at the core of the last two rules we covered. If the example above was confusing to you, this would be a good "leading indicator" that you need more time studying Level II, TAS, and the price action that can be viewed on these systems. Better to recognize this indication now and act responsibly than to rush into trading ill prepared, as do so many amateur traders who suddenly get introduced to Level II and TAS.

PRECISION EXECUTION

In addition to those decision support tools that act as confirming indicators, the new breed of electronic trader has direct access to professional tools like electronic communications networks

(ECNs), the Small Order Execution System (SOES), SelectNet, and SuperDot. All of which link to the exchanges and third-party markets to find what every trader wants: liquidity and market access. These systems will be covered briefly now, but extensive study will be required before implementing their use. The average new trader will need at a minimum one to two weeks' practice on systems that incorporate their functionality before live trading.

Essentially, through this technology, EDAT traders become their own order desks because there is nothing between their orders to buy or sell stock and the contramarket participant or entity that executes the order. The advantage of these systems means no more waiting for fills or being taken advantage of like the reactive investor who routes the order flow to professionals who often see the order before it is executed and trade against it (see "Know the flow" at the end of this chapter for more detail). With Level II, TAS, and direct order routes, precision execution puts you in control as the proactive trader. But with that control also comes responsibility, which is the basis of the first rule regarding this technology: **Know your order routes.**

Knowing how to find liquidity and the right tools with which to open or exit a trade are perhaps the steepest learning curves to scale when using an EDAT system. Understanding the market mechanics—such as knowing the difference between a limit order and a market order, when or where to place a buy or sell stop order, when to use leading limit orders in relation to momentum trades, which electronic communications networks (ECNs) work best in certain situations, etc.—is understanding the art and science of trade execution. The "rules of engagement" are what I am referring to.

Let's explore an example of how order routes through precision execution tools work in concert with Level II and the TAS screens. Suppose the market in Sun Micro Systems (SUNW) is 135 X 135⅛; 3000 shares X 1000 shares. What is the best order route to get the trade done? Would you go long with a market order? Would you use SOES to bid a price of 135⅛ for the entire 1000 shares? Would you use a leading limit order at 135³⁄₁₆ on the Island ECN? Or would you send a proactive order using the Archipelago ECN? How about a SelectNet preference to a market maker you suspect is a true seller at 135¹⁄₁₆? These are just some of the questions you must be able to answer when using EDAT technology for the best and fastest order route to liquidity. Many trades never get opened because amateur traders do not understand order routing while maintaining control of the trade in order to protect themselves. How much money is lost by traders chasing a fleeting bid when they want to sell? The answers are simple once traders gain this mechanical knowledge. While it is outside the scope of this book to explain every order route available, I will touch on a few examples to drive home the importance of order routing.

ECNs are essentially crossing networks that match buyers and sellers electronically without human intervention. When an ECN has an order that matches yours in its book of limit orders, you get an instant fill. If it doesn't have a match, it will either hold the order in its book of liquidity, send it to another ECN, or post it to the Level II market maker system, assuming that you are the best bid or offer (BBO). The actual routing depends on which ECN or system (SOES, SelectNet, SuperDot, etc.) you select.

Up until recently, there were separate ECNs for the over-the-counter market and listed securities, but this is changing. Systems are evolving every day in which listed and OTC stocks can be traded within the same ECN or a third-market execution system. Incidentally, *third market* means that there is now a new market to execute trades; it does not suggest by its "third-market" classification that it is in any way an inferior market. In fact, quite the opposite is true. When an issue is first offered to the public through an IPO, it is considered to be offered through a *primary market* made up of broker-dealer networks or underwriters who help private companies go public. The shares are primarily sold to investors who are already doing business with these firms through a distribution system normally made up of other broker-dealers in the selling syndicate. Once the IPO is offered to the public, it then trades in the *secondary market,* which we traditionally know as the exchanges. The New York Stock Exchange is the largest, and there are other regionals across the country, such as the Boston Stock Exchange (BSE), the American Stock Exchange (AMEX), the Cincinnati Stock Exchange (CIN), the Philadelphia Stock Exchange (PHS), the Chicago Stock Exchange (CSE), and the Pacific Stock Exchange

(PSE). The over-the-counter (OTC) market is also a component of the secondary market, now representing larger NASDAQ issues since 1970 when the NASDAQ was created.

Third-market electronic systems, while considered to be new to the market, really started with the formation of the first ECN, Instinet, in 1971. In fact, third-market systems existed even before 1971 with the telephone. New aggressive ECNs, like Island, Archipelago, and Redi, have been created just recently and have grown dramatically due to their capabilities: ease of access to market liquidity and ultrafast executions. These systems have gained the affection of active traders and the public because they allow for electronic crossing of orders and for trading with professional market makers, making the entire market more efficient and fair.

The point is that traders who understand these new emerging systems and how to use them during market hours, as well as during pre- and post-market hours, gain an advantage finding liquidity and therefore putting their orders ahead of the public's, who use inferior online systems. Example: A trader sends a limit order to buy 500 shares of VRSN at $180 per share or better (meaning less). If the ECN used for this trade has an order in its book of orders to sell 500 shares of VRSN at $180 or better (meaning more), it will match or cross the two orders at the $180 price immediately. The EDAT trader must know which ECNs do a large amount of volume in the stocks he or she trades. If, in this example, the trader is now selling the 500 shares it purchased and he or she places the order, which gets filled on only 300 of the 500 shares, what must the EDAT trader do? The trader is responsible for finding liquidity since he functions as his own order desk, and this is an example of where responsibility plays into taking control of your orders versus having a brokerage firm do it for you, which can cost you dearly.

Some of the possibilities are (1) leave the order in the market until it is completely filled (if the stock trades at or through the limit price); (2) send it to another ECN that has a strong book of liquidity in that stock; (3) cancel the unfilled portion of the order and send it at a price where there is a contra (the opposite side of the trade); (4) check the market maker window (Level II) and see if there is a market maker indicating and bidding the stock at a price at which you are willing to sell. If so, send in a SOES (Small Order Execution System) order, which is mandatory for the market maker to accept, or use SelectNet to send the order to all market makers as a broadcast, or select a specific market maker through what is called a *SelectNet preference*. Which is the best option depends on market circumstances. The point is the EDAT trader must be trained and prepared for just such an instance. This control creates the need for knowledge to trade with the most efficient means possible in the market today, but also creates a substantial advantage. This is what is meant by precision execution. In the next section, I explain the alternative. Once discovered, you will completely understand the advantage of using the decision support and execution tools of EDAT.

THE ORDER FLOW

Understanding how order flow works within the market and how it has worked for many years is important for reasons far beyond trivial pursuits. Precision execution systems provide the control if you accept the responsibility that comes with them. Assuming that is the case, a critical rule for active trading is **Never allow your order flow to be sold.**

When an online firm routes your orders to a wholesaling market maker instead of routing them directly to the market through systems such as the SOES, SelectNet, a variety of ECNs for NASDAQ issues, or through SuperDot for listed stocks, chances are very strong your order flow is either being sold or it is being worked by a proprietary trade desk owned by the online firm. This is common practice for online brokerage firms, selling the orders they receive from their customers to a securities wholesaler, or broker's broker who will pay online firms to send them their retail customer orders. The result is simple: These trade desks attempt to match the buy and sell orders of these customers while retaining the spread for the transaction. While not illegal, this is also not efficient. The activities of the trade desk cost you speed to market, which can lead to a market impact cost (MIC) through inefficiency of markets moving higher or lower, stock ahead where others with superior systems beat you to liquidity, and of course the inevitable loss of the spread retained by the market making community. The benefits to the wholesaler go beyond just the spread; they also enjoy the advantage of having insight to market direction through the aggregated orders. If a large bias toward the sell side were shown through thousands of orders in a given security at any particular time and you were the market maker, what would that tell you? If you would have a selling bias, your instincts are correct, and this is yet another advantage of buying order flow from online brokers and other trading operations.

From the perspective of the retail firms that sell order flow, they have the ability to create the illusion of cheap commissions while enjoying the opportunity to be paid on the back end from the wholesaling firm who is buying the order flow. "All that glitters isn't gold" comes to mind. Just because you are paying only $15 or even less to get an order done does not mean that you are getting the best price or fastest access to the market.

For the wholesaler who pays for the order, the opportunity created by spreads and order flow is enough reason to pay for an order. For example, if the spread in a given issue is only a ⅛th of a point, on a 1000-share lot order, that creates $125 in potential profits for the trading desks. If the wholesaler could buy the order from the retail firm for $0.02 per share, that would cost the wholesaler $20 on a 1000-share lot order. If a wholesaler can pay $20 for the opportunity to make $125, they are going to do it all day long, and many times the spreads are even greater!

Now to be fair to the wholesalers, I must tell you that they feel they have earned this opportunity for the spread because they have incurred market risk by providing the customer liquidity. This is true. However, the traders who wish to maintain control can retain the opportunity for the spread and the ability to find liquidity much faster while maintaining control of their order flow. Remember, seeing order flow is extremely powerful in and of itself. Think of a floor trader who is reading the crowd of buyers and sellers on a trading floor. The true value of a seat on an exchange is to recognize the imbalance of supply and demand in securities and then have the ability to execute in real time. Whether you are sending your order flow directly to a market-making desk or it is sold to a desk through paid-for order flow, the result is the same. You are contributing to the market makers' opportunity to recognize imbalances through the aggregation of order flow sent to them by you and many other online traders.

As you must realize, the electronic trading landscape is growing and is complex, and it is not easy to master at first glance. However, if active trading is your desire and passion, you can gain the knowledge and experience required. The roads you travel are within your control, and the decisions you make today will most dramatically effect the results you receive tomorrow. Professional market participants earn that title and are few in numbers because they make the right decisions and travel the difficult road. Yes, you will see carnage in the market, and it isn't fun all the time, but like the veteran exchange traders across the country, and the new breed of electronic traders of today, those that survive will also thrive wearing these lessons like a badge of honor as the mentors of tomorrow's generation of electronic trader.

RULES FOR THE ACTIVE TRADER

Rules of the Trade

Supply and demand determine prices.

Don't wait for certainty.

Let market indications lead you in and out of trades.

Be multidimensional.

Open positions early in the week and offset by the weekend.

Gaps tend to close.

Size the trade.

Amateurs control the open; professionals control the close.

Average winners, not losers.

Never let a winner turn into a loser.

Take profits often.

Never mix disciplines.

Never try to trade back a loser.

Don't fight the tape.

Few common denominators exist that are truly universal within all capitalistic markets, but this next critical rule is a law that controls all markets. Whether you trade derivatives such as options and futures, commodities, currencies, equities, or bonds, this rule is a law that must always be your beacon: **Supply and demand determine prices.**

As an investor holding a stock for an extended period of time, you are interested in many factors that are more fundamentally driven, such as any plans the company may have to issue more shares, open interest, management, and R&D developments. But as a trader, volatility and momentum swings as the result of an imbalance in supply and demand of the floated shares is what your focus must be. Supply and demand imbalances reflect all factors in the market at any given moment or within any given trend, regardless of how long it lasts, which reveals the true consensus of value of any given financial instrument.

As an active trader, you are simply looking for supply and demand imbalances on a short-term time horizon. In the end what every tool and software program ever written has set out to reveal to its user is where the buyers (demand) are exceeding sellers (supply) and where the sellers are exceeding buyers. Any imbalance that exists will result in an associated price change in the instrument being traded, and those that understand and remember this rule will remain at the top of the financial food chain in the market.

Countless systems and software programs are available today that promise the Holy Grail to uncovering profit in the market. Unfortunately, those that spend most of their valuable time and energy searching for the next trade secret or Holy Grail through software systems will chase their proverbial tail to the point of emotional and financial exhaustion, accomplishing nothing. In contrast, those who dedicate themselves to learning the mechanics of reading indicators that leave clues where these imbalances exist find success on average and move on to earn the enviable position of trader. I have come to believe through my own experience and many interviews and interactions with professional traders that finding an optimal combination of systems and tools is a very personal learning curve. Trading styles are as different as people, and few common denominators exist that are as truly universal as the laws of supply and demand.

When looking at supply, for example, from a marketwide perspective, some indications to follow that can speak directly to the issuance of new or additional shares of a given company would include IPOs, stock splits, secondary offerings, the release of treasury stock, or mergers and acquisitions, etc., all of which increase supply. As a general rule, this additional supply of stock decreases the price per share on an individual stock level. From a broader market perspective, an additional supply of stock through IPOs increases the total shares in the overall market, causing increased competition for money flow from institutional traders and individuals alike. Therefore, as dramatic IPO activity floods the market, weaker companies in terms of fundamentals stand the greatest propensity for decline, which can be measured through beta and other sensitivity formulas. The point is that as the supply of shares greatly increases in excess of demand, markets, as well as stocks, will fall. This law of supply and demand best describes the "bursting .com bubble" at the end of the first quarter of 2000, which was ignited by greed but ended in fear. This also explains the exodus of money from the value stocks during the rapid rise stage of the .com era in the preceding years. Well-capitalized, well-managed companies with strong earnings and revenues who traditionally trade at $80 to $100 per share suddenly retraced to unthinkable levels by comparison to their preretracement levels—all driven by the sentiment of traders in the market, causing an imbalance in supply and demand, pushing money into the .com sector of technology. Once this temporary weak demand dissipates, the market is left with excessive supply, causing the rapid downturn.

If a company decreases supply by buying its own stock—whether to meet obligations or to satisfy employee stock option redemptions or to do a reverse split for the sake of public perception—the price per share normally rises (see Figures 3.1 through 3.3). When supply and demand are in equilibrium, the

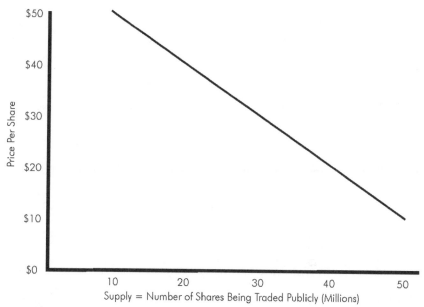

FIGURE 3.1   Supply curve

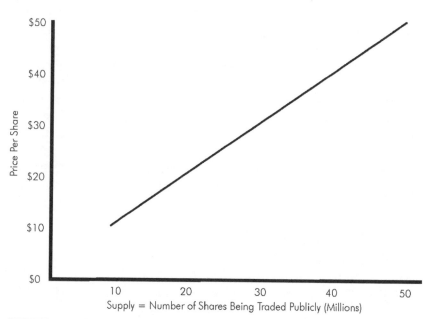

FIGURE 3.2   Demand curve

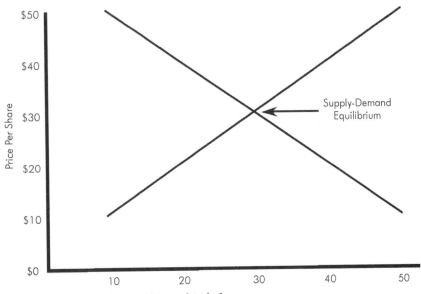

FIGURE 3.3 Supply and demand in balance

price of a stock is stable and will move sideways on a price chart. The understanding to be gained from this, whether looked at from a macromarket perspective or from a one-stock day trade perspective, is that this law is the king of all markets.

Day trading is perhaps the purest form of making this determination since day traders react to imbalances to either profit from followthrough where demand continues to exceed supply on microtrends or fade imbalances on reversals. The most common examples are trend reversals where traders seek to buy weakness at support levels and sell strength at resistance levels. Those that react to imbalances on a very micro minute-to-minute level are day traders. Others choose to evaluate these imbalances over a series of days, and this is where swing trading comes from. While others are longer term oriented and employ a myriad of techniques from quantitative analysis to fundamental analysis, day traders believe that anticipating and predicting movement too far in the future is difficult, risky, and much less profitable. Questions such as "How can Abbey Cohen with Goldman Sachs be a raging bull while at the same time five other analysts are predicting bear markets ahead?" are often asked. Very conflicting views of the market are saturating the media every day, so who is right? The day trader feels the future cannot be determined accurately with precision and chooses to ignore such views from these parties who seemingly have the best research money can buy but still conflict. If you want to see this phenomenon in action, just watch CNBC for a few hours, the current voice for the market it seems, and watch the guest analysts talk out of both sides of their mouth!

Swing traders and momentum traders are forms of day traders who have a longer time horizon and who believe technical analysis will reflect market reaction and trends from both bullish and bear perspectives. Technicians also believe that the psychology from both market crowds of professionals and amateurs is reflected in the charts and indicators. While amateurs are reacting to the news the market produces, professionals are generally fading their reactions. Many sell-side analysts and false market prophets erect the "big top" of the market where much of this news originates, such as analyst revisions and ratings, earnings estimates, and research reports. In the midst of all this is real news like earnings reports, lawsuits, product developments, management changes, mergers and acquisitions, etc., which is where professional traders and investors focus, depending on their time horizons. Fund managers learn early on through their training (such as apprenticeships with senior fund managers) to distinguish fact from hype or rumor. These are just some of the market participants on the playing field called the stock market. Some, like day traders, are rushing hard for 3 to 4 yards at a time, and others, like fund managers, are planning carefully through fundamentals in the huddle. But all are competing to find the imbalance in the supply and demand of the shares floated for trade in the market.

This proven theory plays itself out in the markets in many ways. Therefore, once you determined a bias, then you implement your strategy. The stock that will be the most sensitive to the impending imbalance to give you the best chance for profit based on what will move the most and fastest will reveal itself through relative strength or weakness. So reading imbalances must be viewed from a number of different perspectives. Whether on a one-stock level or an overall market level where competition for dollars occurs, the imbalance is best viewed as a cause-and-effect relationship. Price changes based on the money flow from competing markets form the *effect* that results from the reactions of professional and amateur market participants to news and events that are the *cause* of these price changes. An example is the activity of the arbitrageurs who trade futures contracts with equities: Money will flow from equities to futures, affecting a negative impact (selling equities) on stocks while money is flowing into (buying) futures, causing a higher valuation in futures. While this phenomenon is felt for only a short time in this scenario, the financial futures market is a vehicle for speculators to bet on anticipated price action of stocks in the very near future. The point is that supply and demand imbalances are the most accurate precursors to price action regardless of the vehicle being traded. The tools adopted and used to form a bias on a variety of time horizons will vary according to an individual's technique and style of trading, but in the end this common critical rule of trading does and always will operate in capitalistic markets. This first rule is the foundation of all rules for active trading, and all trading for that matter.

THE DAY TRADER MINDSET

Day traders must subscribe to this next rule: **Don't wait for certainty.** Before diving into this rule, think of stocks as either "thick" or "thin." Thicker (highly liquid) stocks generally show short-term trends over more time than thinner (less liquid) stocks since the reference to thick and thin relates to the price levels. A thick stock must trade heavy volume at each price before moving up to the next (or down) level. An example would be Intel (INTC) trading heavily on the offer price of $60 where sellers are offering INTC for sale, while buyers (bidders) are paying the $60 offer price. For INTC to trade higher, demand at $60 must exceed supply at $60 in order for the bidders to absorb all stock for sale at that price. This will force buyers to pay a higher price where sellers are incented to sell, such as 60⅛. The heavier the volume at $60 before exhausting the stock for sale at that price, the thicker the stock, and hence the more liquid but less volatile it is. Thinner stocks, with less average daily volume, tend to trade through price levels much quicker up or down since there is less subscription in the issue; therefore, as imbalances occur, thinner issues move more dramatically and faster on much less volume.

Day traders read these price changes on shorter time horizons than investors, but make no doubt about it, both disciplines are doing the same thing, reading supply and demand imbalances. The tools and techniques, as well as indicators, that help detect these imbalances are often different, but the desired outcome is the same: to recognize where the imbalance is to form a directional bias that will profit from the next pivot, breakout, breakdown, or reversal. Because active day traders will act quickly while trading stocks that have the propensity to move on thinner volume, this rule comes into play because professionals know that if they wait for the confirmation of news and rumors, they will miss many profitable opportunities. Amateurs feel compelled to wait for confirmations, which causes them to be late and gives the professionals another opportunity to fade their reaction. Amateurs tend to enter trades late and on the wrong side of the market as stocks become thicker and overtraded. Two very typical examples are splits and earnings reports, both major market events that tug hard on both ends of the rope of supply and demand.

Does this mean the professionals are reckless risk takers, trading ahead of news? The answer is no or they would not be professionals. It simply means they spend more time studying the market, have greater focus on their trades, have better analytic tools, and know what to look for when a trade is developing or breaking down. Once enough indicators confirm directional bias, professional speculators tend to act and trade ahead of the impending price move, hence putting them several waves ahead of amateurs who wait for news to break. Because of this, active traders must have conviction and confidence while reading and reacting to these indications. An aggressive trader acts on the volume and increased activity without waiting for news to be announced. It is often said that a chart and Level II tell the stock's story before the media do!

Conversely, the amateurs with less sophisticated technology and market acumen will wait for the news to be announced, putting them behind the professional trading community. As the public is also waiting for news announcements and certainty, professionals are often exiting on the news—"selling into strength" with good news and "buying weakness" on bad news—as the amateur rushes in or out providing liquidity. Although this is just an example, it illustrates the mindset of a professional who trades on market indications without waiting for the certainty of rumors and news. This takes us to our next set of rules.

TIME HORIZONS

The mindset of an active trader is directly correlated to the time horizon. Day traders begin by adjusting their discipline with stock selection and the time horizon of trades. They then continue to make adjustments once in trades in order to adhere to the discipline of day trading. Generally, the more actively you trade and the shorter your time horizon, the greater risk you assume since active traders tend to trade more volatile stocks. But having the control to enter and exit quickly is always an advantage that helps mitigate risk. The rule here is **Let market indications lead you in and out of trades.** How often and how actively to trade based on this rule is a very personal decision based on skill, risk tolerances, and desire, but a day trading style can reveal more opportunities for momentum, swing, and trend trading because of the high level of concentration required. Some argue that day traders can't see the forest for the trees, but I argue that the opposite is true. Day trades feed your macroview of the market as long as you don't define day trading as spread trading and try to read every tick the tape shows, as discussed in Chapter 2. The indications left to you by volume and price action will reveal the opportunities, but the patience to wait for low-risk–high-reward opportunities are the attributes that many amateurs who rush in on news lack, putting them in high-risk–low-opportunity trades. Day traders develop a keener sense of activity for stocks they trade by viewing price and volume activity together as seen on Level II and TAS that a chart cannot reveal.

The time horizon of a day trade is determined by the market action associated with a given stock. The indications that lead you into trades, and the time frame over which these indications are revealed, are important to correlate to the amount of time you remain in the trade. Deciding to remain in a trade for longer periods of time because the indications that led you in changed is not a good strategy. An exit strategy is not contingent on a profit and loss scenario, but instead based on the way the trade is acting defined by indications such as volume and price levels over a given time frame. Either way, adherence to the time horizon is the discipline. I am not going to turn what was a momentum trade into a swing trade if I am wrong. The rule here is to adhere to your time horizon based on the stock's behavior and remain a day trader if that was the intent of the trade. Remember, day traders' modus operandi is to trade heavily, which means trading a higher number of shares per trade while being more active. It would not be uncommon for an active day trader to execute a hundred or more trades in a day with each trade sized at least a thousand shares. Many trades are much larger in size, such as 10,000 shares or even larger, and these are referred to as *plungers*. The average trade might last no more than a few minutes. While I subscribe to both strategies noted above, I believe new traders should trade far less often, even as low as 10 trades per day, until their confidence and emotional stability are established. In the beginning, I strongly suggest that you focus your attention on reasonable liquid issues trading at least 1 million shares per day, in issues that are both optionable and marginable, meaning that they can be traded on margin and that there are options traded on the issue. These conditions automatically ensure good liquidity as a rule, but that does not preclude them from high volatility. Considerations such as these have an impact on the time horizon you set for trading, especially day traders.

MULTIDIMENSIONAL TRADING

A rule that is critical in the evolution and development of active trading is **Be multidimensional.** When having a multidimensional approach to the market, traders subscribe to a mixed style that includes day trades and swing trades. Sometimes a day trade is there and you must take the trade, while other strategies are designed to be of a longer duration. Never mixing the two is the key. Since we have discussed the day trading mindset, let's look closer at other forms of trading and review the rules associated with swing trading.

As a rule I recommend this: **Open positions early in the week and offset by the weekend** when swing trading (or sooner depending how the stock is acting). I am not a fan of holding positions over the weekend. There are times when it is appropriate, but these are few and far between. One reason for this rule is that imbalances occur in the largest form after the close and before the open because this is when most news is released in the market. The risk associated with this trade automatically increases exponentially because of this, and it becomes even more exacerbated over weekends. The imbalance in supply and demand during these periods create gap openings, which are essentially blank spaces in liquidity where little or no trading takes place. Let us say Juniper (JNPR) closed at $198 per share and opened at $190. This $8 gap creates exceptional risk. While substantial opportunity is also created once the stock opens, the high risk of a weekend position is simply not worth it. Because the entire world will see the gap once it starts trading, plenty of opportunity will still exist if you choose to engage the stock the next trading session.

This leads to my rule that **Gaps tend to close.** Without being too literal, and understanding that confirming indicators must be considered before making any costly assumptions, the basis of this rule is that prices often trade into the blank space or void. In this case you would expect JNPR to make up some of its losses and close some of the gap in the morning session. An important caution is to monitor the tape and other tools closely to confirm the bias, and not to blindly assume this to be the case in all situations. Certainly, follow-through can and will result in many situations, but a propensity for a stock to close some of its gap is reasonable to assume. The rationale for this is quite simple if you understand the mindset of a specialist or market maker. Because these market participants are charged with the responsibility to provide market liquidity, they don't want to trap themselves into a less-than-desirable position. Ask yourself this question, "If you were required to be a buyer of last resort in order to provide liquidity to sellers who would be expected to be strong on the morning following bad news the day before, wouldn't you bid the stock lower?" As a result, specialist and market makers will often do just that, hence opening a stock artificially low (gap down) so that they are not trapped in owning a stock at high prices. Therefore, they open the stock lower than reasonable, where they expect support. You could almost think of them as writing an overnight naked put, figuring if they get "put" the stock by panicking sellers on the open at these prices that are much lower than the closing price, they are in a better position to buy weakness.

For example, suppose you write the AMD April 35 puts at $2. If the underlying stock (AMD) is trading at $37 at the time, you sold out of the money puts since the put buyer is not going to exercise his or her put to you (selling) at $35 when the market is trading at $37. Remember, the put buyer wants to put stock at high prices relative to the strike price, not low prices. The point is, the seller of the put wrote the put because he or she does not mind being put the stock at $35 because the perception is that the stock is well supported at that level. If AMD trades to $33, the put buyer will exercise, forcing the put seller to buy the stock at $35 (the striking price). But because the put seller received $2 premium for selling the put option, his or her breakeven point is still $33 ($35 cost basis by buying the underlying less $2 received in premium). If the stock remains stable or trades higher, the option will expire unexercised, and the put seller will realize a $2 profit per share. This is the same rationale of the specialist or market maker who opens a stock lower, near a price level at which he or she perceives the stock to be well supported. In this sense, "gap" openings to the downside are like naked puts to market makers, since they are forced to buy stock as is a naked put seller, in order to provide liquidity to the market. Because of this, they once again will gap it as low as they can!

As other professional market participants recognize the perceived support price, the concept behind this rule is that buyers will come to market and force stock prices higher, while closing some or all of the price gap. Keep this general state of mind, and gap trading will work for you. When the trade moves away from you enough to meet your predetermined risk tolerance, exit, take your lumps, and move on! Don't expect to always be right. The profitable trades will take care of themselves; the losses require disciplined attention with this trade strategy, because if the stock does not find support at the open in this example, chances are very strong it falls much further as negative sentiment builds.

Gaps obviously occur on the upside as well. But again the important caution here is, do not be too literal. Gaps are simply good highlights to get your attention as well as the attention of others. Your skills as a trader need to take over from there. As a rule of thumb, down gaps are more reliable to trade higher at the open than up gaps. I think this is because traders are more inclined to be bullish and drive a good stock even higher when stocks gap higher, causing the gap to stay open and even expand with follow-through buying. My experience is that there is approximately an 80 percent reliability of a down gap filling to some degree, while gap ups are less reliable to close by trading higher at the open due to bullish follow through.

Additional rules that apply to swing trading require you to **Size the trade.** *Sizing a trade takes into account many considerations such as volatility, liquidity, daily range, trend patterns, and time horizons.* For an example of how this applies to swing traders, these positions should be light, which means smaller share sizes for longer periods of time and large point moves, since swing traders hold positions for longer periods of time. Where the heavy trader bought 1000 shares, for example, held the position for 10 minutes, and took a half-point profit, the swing trader might trade 200 to 500 shares for two days, expecting multiple point movement.

Let's say the swing trader executes 20 round-turn trades in a week. These well-researched trades are based on technical and/or fundamental analysis, whereas the day traders' moves are more instinctual and momentum oriented. Of the 20 trades, suppose half are profitable and half are not. Of the profitable, 2 generate the 2-point profit, which was the target, and the other 8 are just marginally profitable of ½ point each. With good discipline, the losers were held to an average loss of ¼ point. Commissions and fees cost the trader $1000, or $50 per round turn. This is higher than the day trader, but the day trader's volume of 50 trades a day is the reason he or she is paying lower commissions.

The math works out as follows. Two 500-share trades at a gain of $2 per share each is $2000. Another 8 winners at $0.50 per share times 500 shares is another $2000. The losers cost the trader $0.25 per share times 500 shares times 10 trades, which equals $1250. The commissions cost another $1000. The bottom line is a gain of $1750 for the week. Remember that the rationale is simple: The added risk acquired by taking overnight positions must be mitigated or at least reduced with lower share size!

I am often asked which approach—day trading or swing trading—works best for most traders. I cannot answer that unequivocally for every trader, but I believe in a multidimensional approach to trading when new. As a new trader, one discipline should be learned at a time. In your written plan, one plan is written for day trading and a second for swing trading. These plans are at the heart of the discipline needed to succeed. As the student develops into a professional or semiprofessional trader, one of the disciplines often emerges as the dominant approach. But we like to see well-rounded traders who can take advantage of quick-profit opportunities and still have the patience to work a trade over time.

NASDAQ TRADERS: WATCH THE OPEN— DON'T TRADE IT

My next rule for the active trader to know is this: **Amateurs control the open; professionals control the close.** Many people want to believe that there is some secret reason that things occur in the market and don't trust common sense because it is simply too simple. The fact is that amateurs do make most of their trades in the morning as well as early in the week. Some of the reasons for this are obvious, and some are less obvious. The obvious reasons are that most people get up early and go to work, take the kids to school, and so on. Therefore, if they have an idea about something, which in many cases is discussed with their spouse the night before or over breakfast, they act on the idea in the morning before, at, or near the open. The less obvious reasons are emotional. People are generally more positive in the morning with a fresh night's sleep. As I stated earlier, when opening a trade, most of the emotions associated with the trade are positive; otherwise, why open it? Who opens a trade they feel bad about?

With the positive feeling of a fresh new day, many new to trading and even long-standing investors feel compelled to act upon this burst of subconscious emotion through the act of trading. As a result, this is the most profitable time for professionals and the most costly for amateurs. Amateurs do things like place "market-on-open orders" to buy stocks that had good earning after the close the day before as they watch it on CNBC that morning. Don't get me started on this mistake. Giving a market maker a market order on the open after seemingly good news on a stock is like dropping fresh red meat in a shark tank—something is going to be eaten very fast!

This thought process helps explain what good technical traders think about and look for on the charts of stocks. You will hear terms like "overextended" to describe overbought situations, but it's important to pay more attention to the closing prices of stocks than the opening prices since amateurs influence the open while professionals influence the close. Which group do you want to follow?

This is an important rule, but it is also the most ignored. The open, particularly on NASDAQ, is known for erratic volatility. In the first 15 minutes of trading or so, market makers are often getting themselves in shape for the day (by closing any overnight positions they may have held) as well as processing all kinds of orders that have been placed overnight such as market-on-open orders. Additionally, news events reported between the close the prior day and before the open will tend to elicit overreaction from amateurs, while the professional market makers protect themselves with trade gaps. Opening stocks aggressively high or low based on the reaction to either stock-specific news or economic news is perhaps the most profitable opportunity for market makers of the NASDAQ and specialists of the listed exchanges. While the price swings are attractive, it is the single most dangerous time of day to open trades.

The moral of this story is "*Think like a pro—!*" and sit out the open for 15 minutes or so. Let the backlog of orders process, let market makers clean up their positions, and let news events in the market settle in a bit. Plenty of opportunity will exist after the immediate open. Be patient and pick your spots carefully. Fools rush in, and professionals take advantage of that. Another good reason for waiting 15 minutes or so to trade after the open is that sometimes market leaders, like AOL, Yahoo!, or Intel, will set the tone for the day in their given group and sector. A good or bad opening for one of these 900-pound gorillas can cast a shadow for an entire trading session, including the listed markets.

COMMON TRADING RULES TO FOLLOW

To close this important chapter, I have included a list of rules that I believe all new traders and most experienced traders should follow especially when employing an active trading style. While there are always exceptions to rules, these rules when followed will put the odds more in your favor:

- **Average winners, not losers.** Some brokers might tell you, "Don't frown, average down." I feel this is bad advice for most new traders. Adding to winning positions makes much better sense than putting good money after bad and averaging down. When you learn to average winners, you have learned discipline and you are managing greed—two very positive trading characteristics. For example, let's say you bought 1000 shares of a highly volatile, high-tech stock, PCMS. It makes one of its spectacular moves, advancing $10 a share in the first 45 minutes of trading. The stock comes in a bit on low volume (low-volume pullback). Therefore, based on this and other confirming indicators, you are convinced it is going higher. Here are two strategies you can deploy. One is conservative and the other very aggressive. Both are intelligent.

    A conservative approach would be to average your winner by sizing down your position—say, selling 500 shares for a $10 gain. You have lightened up your position. As we mentioned earlier, the size of your position is one of the two risk elements that are in your absolute control. You have $5000 in profits, less transaction costs. Now you are in a position to take some heat, meaning you will be able to withstand another small pullback if your analysis is incorrect and PMCS continues lower.

Many traders may well be taking some or all of their profits after the $10 run. So you should expect a retracement in price. If you expect a restart on the trend line after a small pullback, you still have a position while booking some profit. In this scenario, you have hedged your risk while leaving continued upside. This will help you grow a $5000 alligator suit to absorb additional heat if the pullback continues while reestablishing a higher mental protective stop.

The second strategy is much more aggressive. Instead of sizing down the position, you add to the position, hence "averaging your winners." This approach is based on your belief that PMCS has pulled back to a "higher low" and is reestablishing a support level during the low-volume pullback (indicating the sellers are not that aggressive). Sizing up the position during this pullback also makes sense and is a common strategy for the more aggressive trader. The mindset is that PMCS is in trend to the upside and is there for a reason, and it makes more sense to trade with the trend than against it. It is important to note in this scenario that the trader would be buying the pullbacks since stocks will generally come in at stages of a trend.

As experience grows, there are exceptions where it makes sense to average down. Averaging down has merit at times, and to categorically say that one should never do it is a bit bold. Most new to trading never drill any deeper into the issue and simply average down when things don't go their way. Many will evaluate the price of stock in relation to their cost basis in the stock. If they own BGEN at 60 and it falls to 50, the perception is often that the stock is low in price. Unfortunately, that kind of thinking is very injurious. When traders instead learn to evaluate stocks through filters such as technical indications, then subjective analysis begins to dissipate. Averaging down works best in conjunction with short-term trading strategies. On intraday trades, I often will begin to open a trade by scaling into it while buying weakness, for example, expecting not to buy the exact bottom. I will look for contracting volume through the tape to find signs of the sellers' dissipating. Additionally, I look for buyers to begin to emerge on Level II and monitor how long they hold their bids while sellers are hitting those bids. If the stock ticks lower, I continue to monitor the selling volume and buying sentiment. If a pivot is revealing itself through diminished selling and increasing buying, yet there is still a slight imbalance of sellers over buyers, I adjust my psychological risk fences and recognize that support is building. I often will scale in some more and buy some more weakness. This process may continue for several minutes, and as long as the indications support the idea, I have conviction to let the trade work for short-term strategies. Discipline, therefore, is defined by the ability to follow the market and stay with the trends it shows you rather than to panic and liquidate too soon.

- **Never let a winner turn into a loser.** Greed is perhaps the most likely reason for this completely inexcusable mistake. Let the market tell you when to exit trades. Your profit and loss in a trade has nothing to do with it! If your trade is acting well, as defined by key indicators, and the market activity is supporting your position, stay in. If not, it's go time! The last thing you want to do is let it become a loser. In the example of PMCS, if you let the 500 shares you still own drop $10 from your entry point, you would break even, not counting commissions and fees. This would be plainly irresponsible. Setting a mental stop-loss price as the stock trends higher protects profits that should never be given back to the market. Day traders, as a rule, use mental stops, rather than placing them in the market or with a broker as traditional traders do. This is because day traders are at their terminals while trading, and more importantly, are unwilling to reveal their exit price to a broker or other market participant such as a trading desk that buys order flow from online trading firms to know where your exit point is. Announcing your exit point is the equivalent of playing cards and letting your opponents know you need kings for gin! Never show your hand until you have found liquidity and are ready to exit the trade. This is another example of a proactive versus reactive order. A *protective stop* is the price at which you will exit the trade immediately. You also know that once a volatile tech stock starts to move one way or the other, it has a tendency to move very fast with thin liquidity at each price level; therefore, getting in front of the wave of liquidity will save you the market impact cost (MIC), which I will speak more about in Chapters 5 and 6.

Where should your stop-loss point be? There is no definitive answer. The stronger your conviction that PMCS is going higher in the next hour or so, the more heat you can take. In this case, without being too literal, we would consider a stop loss at halfway between where you entered the trade and where you took a profit. That way, you have at a minimum a total profit of $7500 (a gain of $10 on the first 500 shares sold and a profit of $5 on the remaining 500 shares). Another option available on EDAT systems is *conditional order entry* (COE). COE allows you to marry decision support tools with direct order execution to send an execution when the criteria that you set are met. What is powerful about this system is that the algorithm resides on your PC and does not indicate to other market participants where your buy and sell points are.

Back to our PMCS example: Remember that you can always reenter the trade. If after exiting your entire 1000 shares, PMCS begins to show strength again, you can always buy it again, and I promise you will be much more objective deciding to reenter the trade than you would be while in the trade. Never get in the mindset that the trade you happen to be in at the moment is your only chance to make money that day. Make it a habit to **Take profits often.**

- **Never mix disciplines.** If you open a day trade, close a day trade. This relates back to marrying losers; don't do it. Swing trades are meant to last for days; day trades are not. Never confuse the disciplines. An example would be to hold the remaining 500 shares of PMCS overnight. You have now taken a short-term momentum trade and made it into a swing trade—an obvious violation of our rule and a common practice of new day traders. You open yourself to the twin fears of market risk through time and heavy share volume through the day trade, and this is a bad combination. In the morning you will be either lucky or very sorry. While you would prefer to be lucky, as I said before, the market has no room for it, and you should not rely on it. Once a trader begins to depend on luck, he or she should take his or her business to the casinos.

- **Never try to trade back a loser.** Emotions get too involved when the last trade you made influences your next trade, especially when trying to press and get back a losing trade. This is generally a good time to walk away long enough to become objective again. Subjective traders lose; cold hard logicians remain objective and tend to succeed. If you have the good sense or instincts, developed through experience and knowledge, to dump PMCS if it started to retrace on heavy volume, for example, never look back. Do not be so convinced of your opinion of any stock that you continue to buy it once it begins a downtrend. Recognize that that is a shorting opportunity, and **Don't fight the tape.** This expression has been around Wall Street for many years, and it means that a trader should never fight the momentum of the market, which is reflected through the tape. If you think you should get back in the stock, wipe your mind of any opinion you have and evaluate the new situation for what it is—a completely new trade. Apply your trading criteria to the new situation as if you had never looked at the stock before.

RULES FOR STOCK SELECTION

Rules of the Trade

Trade liquid stocks.

Avoid chaotic stocks.

Match volume to time.

Specialize.

Trade stocks with good correlation.

Trade strong sectors.

Do the research.

Forget about chat rooms.

L et's assume you have followed the rules up to now, and you have a good idea of the type of trading you will begin with in terms of time horizons, research, sectors, and trading tools. Let's also assume that you are committed to gaining the mechanical and cognitive knowledge of the market through some sort of mechanism that helps you understand dimensions of trading that go beyond the scope of most introductory books. Some of these areas that require in-depth exploration and study are software usage, market terminology, the differences in exchanges (namely, NASDAQ and listed exchanges), order flow, and the way in which orders are routed to find market liquidity (touched on in Chapter 2).

Unfortunately, this introduction to the market is the exception, not the rule. Most new market participants introduce themselves to the market by trading the most volatile issues with the highest degree of risk. You may recall a program implemented for young juvenile delinquents called "Scared Straight." This program utilized the stories of convicted felons to instill fear of what the fate will be for those that break the rules of life. The program proved quite effective, but no such program exists for traders to scare themselves straight until it is often too late, when not only has the financial bank account been depleted but also the emotional bank account. I find that traders fail the fastest because of the stock selection process. This leaves the responsibility to obey the rules of trading on your shoulders. These rules will be discussed in this chapter, and they can be digested quickly and easily to help you avoid the biggest pitfalls in trading. This leaves the rest of your trading life to dedicate to developing and refining the intangible attributes necessary to trade successfully, such as strategy, technique, intuition, and confidence. Don't make the critical mistakes I will highlight throughout this chapter. Think of all the traders before you who are out of business as the convicts who, if they had the chance to do it all over again, would make much different choices the second time around.

We have done studies on over a thousand traders through database analysis, and I can tell you the correlation of failing traders to IPOs, sexy tech stocks that are in the news, and fast-paced chaotic dot com companies is amazing! More often than not, stocks that move big are stocks that have experienced their move before there was time to react. These moves are often over before they start! Chasing the seemingly exciting IPO that opens up 70 points over its initial public offering price will tame the senses quickly when the stock settles in the same opening day 40 points off its debut high. There is no reason to ever expose yourself to this chaos. You will hear all kinds of braggarts tell you what great success they had in these plays because their exuberance causes them to talk, but believe this: They are the most quiet people you will ever meet after their luck runs out and the market humbles them (Figure 4.1). Because of their false sense of wisdom created by any early luck they may find, they sooner or later fall, and they fall the hardest of all market participants! Don't be one of them.

FIGURE 4.1   Image created by Stan Yan, active trader and artist

LIQUIDITY

Liquidity is like oxygen to traders; without it, they are dead. Therefore, the first rule to follow for choosing tradable stocks is **Trade liquid stocks.**

The best way to explain liquidity in terms of the market is to consider it in the context of an auction. The Chicago Board of Trade (CBOT), the Chicago Board of Options (CBOE), the Chicago Mercantile Exchange (CME), the NYSE, and other regional listed exchanges across the country are all auction markets. To understand liquidity, ask yourself this question: Do you have liquidity in a thin auction market? Obviously, the answer is no. With no participants, you have no buyers to "lift offers" nor sellers to "hit bids." The term *lift offers* describes buyers' taking what sellers have for sale at any given price, while *hitting bids* refers to sellers' offering stock to buyers who bid to own stock.

Liquidity, therefore, is found with stocks that attract adequate buyer and seller activity. Like an auction, in the absence of buyers and sellers, markets become volatile and less efficient. Less efficient stocks increase risk exponentially, putting the trader in jeopardy. In fact, it is at this stage that risk management and discipline really begin to be important. Most believe that discipline is defined as cutting your losses, but I argue that discipline begins long before that. It begins when choosing stocks by evaluating their risk/reward characteristics, in which liquidity plays a big part. While it could be argued that illiquid volatility also creates opportunity through rapid price change, statistics prove that volatile issues move the most in the least amount of time. Therefore, most opportunity dissipates while downside risk looms.

Below are listed eight attributes of what I consider to be a tradable stock for a new trader. The first criterion is that it is being traded a minimum of 500,000 shares per day. Experienced traders often drop this figure as their skill grows, but before you do, you need experience in entering and exiting trades in thin markets. The mechanics you must learn, such as how to use limit and leading limit orders, will be a big contribution to your success.

Screen Criteria for Stock Selection

1. *Daily volume of at least 500,000 shares per day.* Stocks with daily volume at this level or greater provide you

with an exit means. No stock is worth trading without one.

2. *Sufficient intraday price volatility.* *Beta* is a measure of the sensitivity of a stock. Stocks with high betas such as 2.0 will move dramatically up or down on light news or *market wind* (economic forces). I trade stocks with a stronger beta but with tight risk tolerance. While there are no mathematical formulas to track this with a literal number, you can measure this by other criteria, such as relative strength. For example, if while trading Applied Materials (AMAT), the market is selling off in the Philadelphia semiconductor index (SOX) but AMAT is not participating, I look to go long as soon as the SOX regains footing.

3. *Correlation with major indices and sector leaders.* Stocks that track well against the groups they trade within are more readable. I rarely trade stocks that fade the index or group they trade within. Contrarian stocks usually have a reason they are bucking the trend, and those reasons are not well known or readable.

4. *Minimum of five active major market makers.* If there are not at least five active market makers of reasonable clout making the market in a given issue, I don't trade them. The best market makers trade the best stocks. While some would argue to stay away from these stocks for that very reason, I disagree. I want to watch the 900-pound gorillas trade and shadow them. They will leave clues while moving big money around, called *money flow.*

5. *Reliable technical indicators available.* I like "honest stocks." This simply describes stocks that trade true to the charts. When a stock establishes a good range or trend, the stock trades within these patterns predictably. When they break the patterns, I step aside and wait for the news that caused the pattern to change to dissipate from the market, or I day trade the extreme moves for a quick momentum trade.

6. *Strong book on at least two ECNs.* For the same reason I want good market maker activity, I want good subscription from ECNs. The www.nasdaqtrader.com Web site

can show you which ECNs and market makers are active in which stocks.

7. *Tracked by analysts.* Analysts do a lot of research, listen in on earnings reports, attend annual meetings, and have relationships with the Board of Directors (BODs). By reading research reports they produce, you gain a strong feeling for longer-term sentiment. While I avoid trading on their immediate news such as ratings changes, I do want to form a broader view of the stocks and sectors they report on through research reports.

8. *News easily available.* If I can't read about the companies I trade with current information, I don't trade them. Many stocks are reported on by only their own company officials, and there is little news about them from analysts and researchers. I avoid those companies. If the stock is not gaining the attention of analysts, it is not gaining mine. When stocks are reported on regularly, they set stock in motion since so many amateurs trade the news. I like to wait for the amateur money to rush in or out of stocks based on news and fade public reaction.

What fuels the rate and speed at which stocks trade is again supply and demand imbalance related. The appetite for stock (or lack of it) market participants have for a given security is what fuels price movement and liquidity. The speed at which these instruments trade is reflected through volume, which is the byproduct of liquidity and supply and demand. Therefore, volume is at best a coincident indicator of market participants' passion in any given issue. That passion will reflect itself as bullish where demand exceeds supply or as bearish where supply exceeds demand. As the aggressiveness of bulls and bears grows, volatility can actually fade through balances in supply and demand, even though volume is strong. As one side actually gains a strong advantage over the other, such as bulls over bears, it can become harder to enter to open a trade or to close or exit a trade because the stocks thin out at each price level as imbalances grow.

Liquidity, therefore, is found with issues that elicit enough response on both sides of the supply and demand equation to incent buyers (demand) and sellers (supply) to come to market at a rate fast enough to provide the trader ample opportunity to move in and out of trades. Without that "indication of interest" from market participants to trade a given instrument (stock), you are left in the same situation as the auctioneer trying to sell where there are no buyers. When absence of liquidity occurs, prices tend to become much more sensitive and volatile. This occurs because extreme measures are taken by one side or the other of the imbalance to create market reaction. One example of such measures would include ratings changes by analysts of sell-side firms (broker-dealers), that in almost all cases cause a market reaction. Liquidity and volume will measure market participation, but supply and demand imbalances will measure where the participation is dominant. For example, if there is an oversaturation of sellers in the absence of buyers at a given price level for a stock, sellers seeking liquidity from buyers tend to "dig deep" to find that liquidity and become aggressive sellers, hitting low bids. If PHCM (Phone.com) is trading 90 bid to 90³⁄₁₆ ask, for example, while buyers are evaporating quickly at 90, liquidity will be nonexistent for sellers at 90³⁄₁₆. As sellers become more aggressive when the 90 bids fade, prices at the bid will tend to spread out, creating more volatility. The next bid may be at 89¼, representing little or no liquidity at each price level between the 89¼ bid and the 90 bid that just disappeared. Even though PHCM may have been very liquid throughout the day, once a strong imbalance occurs (supply side greater than demand), liquidity can become elusive. As experience grows, thinner stocks may be traded, but risk increases dramatically.

Many who trade low-price *penny stocks* (stocks with a market value of less than $5 and low market capitalization) learn this critical rule when they are left holding the bag looking for buyers to take their stock when none are in sight for many price levels below their cost basis in the stock. We refer to this situation as *getting trapped* in a stock, and it is the last place you want to be.

As liquidity fades, stock activity become more chaotic, which leads to this related rule: **Avoid chaotic stocks.** This takes the other side of the spectrum when stocks have excessive market interest. These stocks often also lack liquidity and become chaotic.

Now you must be saying at this point, "Wait a minute!" The first section makes sense: After all, we have all seen scenarios in which a lack of demand has caused prices to adjust (fall) to incent buyers to come forward and create liquidity, but how can the direct opposite also be true?

The answer lies within another common scenario that we have undoubtedly encountered or experienced: a lack of supply due to excessive interest. The examples are endless, from the stampeding fools who trample each other to buy the last Beanie Baby on the department store shelf (a good reason to love Internet commerce!) to the multiple-hour wait for a table at the hot new restaurant in town. It is all once again about supply and demand. Whether there is a lack of dolls or tables, excessive interest can and will cause a lack of liquidity in supply and hence cause volatility.

When an IPO trades so rapidly due to excessive interest (*irrational demand*) and there is a limited supply of stock available (the *float*), stocks will trade with low liquidity at each price level or even each handle depending on the demand. That does not mean low daily volume or activity. In fact, excessive interest in a stock like an IPO or a stock that is the recipient of big news will cause the stock to trade big daily volume, but it will be thin at price levels within the trend line. As a given issue ascends or descends rapidly, buyers and sellers respectively are rushing in or out of trades while causing an imbalance in supply and demand. In the example with the rapidly ascending IPO, as buyers rush in to buy the stock with various types of orders, such as market orders, sellers are illiquid at current price levels on the way up, trading chaotically, moving the most on light volume while moving the least on heavy volume. This gives the illusion that there is good liquidity based on aggregate daily volume, when in fact the big moves throughout the day tend to occur on the lightest volume. This is certainly not always the case, but it is very common with high-volatility stocks like IPOs, or stocks that are the recipients of news.

For example, if an IPO is offered at 25 (prior to trading in the secondary market) but trades to or even opens at 70 (trade gap), a very low volume of stock would trade between 25 and 70. If the IPO opens at $70 and follows through to higher prices, more liquidity is found as prices rise. As prices rise, more and more sellers will be incented to offer their stock for sale to take profits, and therefore more liquidity is found as prices rise, with the most sellers available at the saturation point (resistance), the precise point at which buyers with market orders get filled! The saturation point will be the price level where sellers begin to exceed buyers, leading the way for a retracement. IPO retracements have a greater propensity for rapid price decline than most other market events once this saturation point is met, causing the wild volatility we know to be associated with IPOs and other big news stocks. Once the saturation point is reached, liquidity once again can be equally elusive when buyers disappear as the stock retraces or falls. This seesaw ride of misery seems to be the fate of many new electronic traders who fall victim to greed by selecting sexy stocks with poor liquidity. Liquidity for buyers on the way up is most prevalent at the saturation, which is where market orders will be filled, and the liquidity for the sorry buyers who now want to be sellers after being filled at the saturation point is also found near the lows of the day called *support*. These support levels are also the highest presence of market orders for amateur sellers. They become market orders of misery for the amateur as professionals buy their weakness, and market orders of greed as professionals sell them overpriced stock. Hence begins the seesaw ride of misery for those that trade chaos, putting them on the "victims' list" by not adhering to this critical rule.

In closing, think of a thin market as a shallow lake and thick market as an ocean. When a storm hits the lake, it becomes very rough, very quickly. The ocean, on the other hand, can absorb an enormous amount of energy from a storm before the waves begin to rise. Trading thin markets can be very tricky while balancing not just supply and demand but also risk and reward. Professional traders seek low-risk–high-reward opportunities in the market. Low-liquidity stocks generally do not fit this criteria and put the odds against you, and, therefore, they are simply not worth the risk.

If a less-than-liquid stock is to be traded based on sound research, follow the rule **Match volume to time.** By measuring average daily volume to the time horizon, you absorb the stock's price volatility to the trade time horizon you plan to trade. Therefore, if you want to buy an illiquid stock because you have reason to believe there is longer-term upside bias, price volatility becomes less critical assuming you are trading a lower-priced security that you expect to "put away" for a while.

Remember, volatility like market demand is a two-edged sword for active electronic traders. Without it, you have little opportunity. Active traders need a certain amount of volatility in order to take profits, but too much volatility due to poor liquidity, as defined, is dangerous. Conversely, if the price of a stock sits at one price or trades in an extremely narrow range, trading it for a profit is difficult or even impossible. Trading "balanced stocks" is what active traders are looking for. Balanced in that they have good volatility, but also good liquidity.

Highly volatile, low liquidity stocks are chaos and should be ignored for additional reasons. You have not had time to develop your skills reading Level II and the tape or the TAS screen. On very chaotic issues, prices can stream by so quickly that only the seasoned trader can make sense out of them, and even this trader is entering a high-risk scenario. The opportunity to spot the tape support and resistance levels and other patterns is a low-percentage trade and is best ignored. Instead, it should be traded from a swing trade (1 to 3 days) or trend trade (1 to 10 days) time horizon on much lower size, if at all.

SPECIALIZATION

My next rule is to encourage you to **Specialize.** As active traders, we want to "know the stock" characteristically. Knowing how your stock acts on a Level II screen and a TAS screen, how it ranges and trends on charts, how it acts within its sector or group, and who the dominant market makers are would begin to define the characteristics that are important to an active trader.

Too many new traders surf the market looking for anything that wiggles and jiggles, having no allegiance to any sector or basket of stocks. That is a mistake. Like a specialist on a listed exchange floor, learning how a stock acts through a variety of tools that make up an EDAT system tells the trader a great deal about the personality of a stock. Yes, stocks have personalities because the market segment that trades a given issue shapes that personality every day. NASDAQ market makers who are assigned to stocks can tell you a great deal about the stocks they trade. Specialists on listed exchanges can tell you even more since the listed market is not as fractured or fragmented as is the NASDAQ market. By becoming a specialist in a small basket of stocks within an active liquid sector, such as biotechs or semiconductors, you feed your ability to recognize patterns that will repeat themselves as the result of the trading tendencies from professional market participants. There is good reason why market makers and specialists are assigned stocks that they stay with for long periods of time. That same rationale should be adopted by electronic traders.

Certainly, news events will disrupt these patterns. This must always be kept in mind, but like a spinning top that is stable at high speeds, readable patterns can become known by studying and trading a few issues versus aimlessly surfing the market as many amateurs do. The news events can and will wobble the top (stock), and it is at these times that it pays to be more inelastic in terms of risk tolerance due to the excessive volatility often associated with news. But remember also that the most profitable and consistent trading patterns are usually associated with the stable top that provides adequate volatility with readable patterns. Stocks move quickly when unstable, and these moves are foolish to chase if you are not already in the trade ahead of the move. While they appear sexy in retrospect, they are the nemesis to traders' success. When news events occur, these patterns will change the range that you thought you knew, setting stocks in new trends and creating new ranges. It is at these times that it makes sense to slow down your active trading in these stocks and, instead, match a style of trading more conducive to trends such as swing trading. In time, new patterns that you will recognize will take shape and allow you to increase your activity once again in the issue.

Once you have specialized, I would tell you to follow the rule **Trade stocks with good correlation.** Correlation between stocks and major indices and sector leaders provides relative indications for traders. The correlation will indicate how a stock is moving in relation to the indices and sectors in which it is traded. For example, if the NASDAQ 100 is strong for the day, stocks that are also strong for the day within this group would be tradable issues if they are as strong as the sector if not stronger (relative strength). A few major indices and indicators I pay attention to are the U.S. Long Bond Futures Contract, the S&P

Futures Index, NASDAQ futures, and Dow futures and their respective price levels. The U.S. Long Bond Future Contract trades on the Chicago Board of Trade, while the other products all trade on the Chicago Mercantile Exchange (CME). Other strong measures of the market and sectors include:

- The biotech index (BTK)
- The technology index (TXX)
- The Morgan Stanley High Tech index (MSH)
- Philadelphia Semiconductor Index (SOX)

Good resources for these products and indices can be found at www.cbot.com, www.cme.com, www.amex.com, and www.phlx. com. Generally, futures contracts act as leading indicators to stock price movement. To illustrate this, let's do a basic overview of futures.

Buying a financial futures contract is essentially a bet or belief that stock (in this example) will increase in price in the future. By buying the futures contract, instead of the actual stock, money managers and arbitrageurs can leverage their investment substantially since the price of buying a futures contract is far less than the cost of buying the actual stock. A money manager for pension funds, for example, may not have received the capital yet to buy the actual stock he or she wants due to the lag time between payroll deductions. Money managers that perceive that stock prices will be higher in the coming days or weeks can pre-position themselves to own the equivalent of those stocks at today's prices without actually investing dollars or capital to buy the underlying asset (the stock). Simply stated, mutual fund managers might buy futures to take advantage of today's prices in baskets of stocks such as the S&P 500 until they receive their periodic influx of cash from 401k and retirement contributions. This is just one example of the activity that takes place in the futures market. To understand how the futures market can be used as a leading indicator, you must first understand how futures contracts trade and what the comparative impact is when viewed with the actual underlying assets of the index itself (the stocks).

Like stock, with futures contracts one party buys contracts and one sells, based on each's prediction of stock prices in the future. When the futures contracts expire (quarterly), you make or lose the difference between what the underlying basket of stock is worth and what you bought and or sold the futures contract for. Because futures contracts trade completely independent of stocks, an arbitrage opportunity is created. Futures trade on the Chicago Mercantile Exchange, while most stocks of the S&P 500 trade on the NYSE and other listed exchanges, with a smaller basket trading on NASDAQ. Because they trade independently of each other, inefficiency can exist whereby arbitrageurs, known as *arbs,* make money by selling one instrument (futures contracts) to free up capital to buy another (stocks), or vice versa.

As the two competing markets change their trend from up to down or down to up, you will see the associated basket of stocks follow suit, such as the S&P 500 Index (cash), NASDAQ 100, or the Dow Jones Industrial Average (DJIA). Therefore, if arbs are selling futures and buying stocks, the act of buying the stock leads prices higher, but the leading indication is revealed as futures are being sold with the expectation that stock will be purchased.

These patterns, led by the associated futures contracts, create a leading indication that should not be ignored. You also often find a similar pattern within a stock sector. For example, among chipmakers, if Intel moves higher or lower, it can pull the other chipmakers with it because of its size. We call this the *gravitational pull,* not unlike what occurs in the physical universe. When large issues like Intel move, they carry the weight of a leading indicator on many smaller stocks within their own sector. Sometimes the relationship is direct, while other times it is indirect. Understanding the correlation to major indices and futures contracts as well as major stocks is yet another critical rule to help spot market bias. The more bodies in alignment, the more strength that indicator has, giving you gravitational pull directly correlated to the indicator or inversely correlated. Either way, the indication is valuable.

SECTOR ROTATION

Another critical rule I personally follow is: **Trade strong sectors.** "Never push a bad position" simply means that where there is poor market participation, there is less opportunity. Sectors that are strong gain the attention of institutional money, traders, and—yes!—the amateur crowd. When the semiconductors are strong, I trade them. When money is flowing from one sector to another, I trade both. The fleeting sector is shorted while the recipient sector of money flow is traded long. This, by the way, is what true *hedge funds* do, whereas mutual funds generally only trade from the long side of the market. Hedge funds will trade both sides of the market while limiting overall portfolio risk by constantly being hedged. They make their money by taking sector risk, while eliminating market risk.

The stocks that lead the given sectors at hand are then closely monitored for relative strength or weakness in relation to the basket of stocks that make up the sector. These baskets can be researched at Web sites, such as www.spglobal.com and www.nasdaqtrader.com, that clearly indicate which stocks are strongest and weakest on a daily basis.

RESEARCH

Do the research. To help you get started, I took some information I included in my home study course, How to Get Started in Electronic Day Trading. At the risk of being redundant, I have added this content because I find that research is often the most neglected progression. My hope is that, as an active trader, you will discover how simple and enjoyable research can be.

As discussed previously in the rules for stock selection, it is imperative to trade strong stocks that are well suited to your trading style. Quality research is the key that opens the door to ensuring that you are always trading the stocks that yield the greatest chance for success.

To effectively achieve a high-quality list of tradable stocks, without burying yourself under a mountain of facts and figures that must be deciphered, using a sound research methodology is crucial. One approach I suggest is the top-down approach. (See Figure 4.2.)

This method is generally associated with technical analysis, and it begins with taking a macroview of the market and identi-

Top Down Approach

FIGURE 4.2   Begin by looking for strong sectors or indices within the economy. The indices that represent these sectors will allow you to identify which stocks or sectors are relatively strong within the index and uncover strong tradable activity.

fying those stocks within major industry groups that show signs of strength and activity. This approach is particularly useful for the novice or intermediate trader because it exposes him or her to a wide array of different companies, thus broadening his or her overall market awareness. At the same time, it narrows the often overwhelming list of all tradable securities down to a manageable selection.

The top-down approach essentially starts at a baseline of all available stocks and uses individually tailored criteria to filter out the vast majority of these securities from consideration.

First, identify a major index that fits your style of trading—the Dow, the S&P 100, the S&P 500, or the NASDAQ 100. Most traders tend to focus on either the S&P 500 or the NASDAQ 100 as a beginning place for searching for tradable stocks. The S&P 500 is often selected because (a) it includes both listed and over-the-counter stocks and (b) the vast number of securities within the index virtually guarantees that all industry sectors that make up our greater economy will be well represented. Despite the continued dominance of the S&P as a starting ground for selecting stocks, the NASDAQ 100 has seen significant growth in terms of its importance to traders. Primarily composed of technology issues and the recent focus of the day trader industry, the NASDAQ 100 is now a great place to start finding technology-related stocks that can quickly gather the momentum appealing to shorter-term traders. As for the Dow, it is unlikely it will provide a significant list of stocks for you to trade; nevertheless, due to its continued importance as the bellwether index and its inclusion of the strongest of the large cap companies, it should still be watched closely as an indicator of overall market health.

Once you have chosen a major index as a starting ground, analyze which sectors within that index also appeal to your interests (e.g., financials, technology, biotechs, or semiconductors). The Standard & Poor's Web site not only lists each of the stocks within the S&P 500 but also gives a description of each company and the sector and subsector classifications of each (http://www.spglobal.com/ssindexmain500text.html). Many of you might ask why you need to find sectors that are of particular interest to you, rather than just picking the sector du jour. The reason is *passion*. If you don't have passion for the industry sector in which the stocks you are about to research reside, then you won't have the desire to actually do the research to the best of your abilities even when you are tired from a full day's work. If you don't do the research thoroughly, you won't have the facts you need to gain the requisite knowledge; if you don't have the knowledge, then you won't have the confidence you need to replace your fears; and then you might as well be throwing darts at the *Wall Street Journal* along with the monkeys who often outperform both the professional and the dumb money in their quarterly contest.

Once you have selected the sectors that appeal to you, reexamine the lists of stocks within that sector. Are there enough stocks within that sector to continue refining your research, or should you use the sector description to expand the list of stocks within that sector, even if the additional stocks are not within your major index? It is likely that you will have to conduct additional sector research to find a full list of stocks within that sector, which you can then continue to narrow down. Several good Web sites provide excellent research about particular groups of stocks that can be used to create a robust list of stocks within each sector, including the following:

- **www.amex.com** The American Stock Exchange Web site provides lists of stocks within each of the Select Sector S&P Depository Receipts (Select Sector SPDRs) as well as information about the stocks within the various Merrill Lynch & Company Holding Company Depository Receipts (HOLDRS). These are great sector groupings in which to find stocks within a particular sector. See http://www.amex.com/structuredeq/holdrs_tth.stm for an example of a listing of securities within an HOLDRS sector.

- **www.phlx.com/index.stm** The Philadelphia Stock Exchange Web site lists the stocks within several sectors, including the closely watched semiconductor sector, thestreet.com Internet sector, and the wireless telecom sector. The S&P Global Web site provides a listing of the stocks in the S&P 500 index and their sectors. If you have chosen a large sector such as technology, you may need to further narrow your choices to telecom, chipmakers, box makers, or some other subsector of technology.

Once you have created a significant listing of stocks within the sector or two that are of interest to you, you need to narrow those lists down to those stocks that are the most tradable. Refer again to Figure 4.2.

After perusing the data available for each of the stocks within the sector you have chosen, next choose five or six stocks from the sector to specialize in and add them to your interest list on your trading system before preparing for the next phase of research.

When you have a selection of stocks on which you will focus your trading, the real research is about to begin. While too much general market information can often hinder a trader's ability to focus on the behavior of one stock, when you are acting as a shepherd over a few stocks within one or two sectors, it is to your benefit to garner all the knowledge you can about those stocks. What follows is a list of various tools and methods you can use to gather information about these stocks.

First, visit the company's Web site and spglobal.com to understand how the company desires to be portrayed within its sector as well as to obtain an accurate picture of the product or service in which the company specializes. For example, doing this research on a few of the above-listed semis, you would learn that AMD "designs, develops, makes and sells a variety of industry-standard integrated circuits which are used in product applications such as telecommunications equipment, data and network communications equipment, consumer electronics, personal computers and workstations." In contrast, AMAT, although also a member of the semiconductor sector, "develops, makes, sells and services semiconductor wafer fabrication equipment and related spare parts for the worldwide semiconductor industry (*source:* www.spglobal.com/500mainframe.html). These descriptions describe two very different companies whose customers and company-specific risks are also quite different.

Second, you can search the company's Web site for press releases and all of their recent Securities and Exchange Commission (SEC) filings, which can be found at www.edgar-online.com. This is an excellent site for reviewing all recent SEC filings. These filings can relay a lot of information regarding insider trading, major company acquisitions or product releases, issuances of additional shares, or other events that can foretell the future turn of stock prices.

Third, familiarize yourself with key upcoming announcements for the company, particularly earnings announcements, since many trading opportunities exist, both short and long, in the weeks surrounding these quarterly announcements. See http://biz.yahoo.com/z/a/a/amd.html for a sample screen of pertinent earnings information.

In addition to using research to make informed decisions about trading a stock prior to its earnings announcement, you can now use the Internet to make better decisions about the future direction and strength of the stock as a result of the earnings announcements. The quarterly conference calls—at which a company announces its earnings, releases a statement, and then typically holds an informal question-and-answer session, all formerly available only to those with connections to major trading firms or members of the press—are now available on the Internet. Sites such as Yahoo! (www.broadcast.com/Business_and_Finance) and ON24 (www.on24.com) provide direct links to the quarterly conference calls where you can listen in. Much information can be gathered not only from what the company has to say but also from the inflection in the voice of the CEO as he or she answers what can often be very pointed questions.

Fourth, conduct routine technical analysis of your stocks to stay informed of any significant changes in the longer-term outlook. Where are the stock's key levels of support and resistance? What do analyses such as the stochastic charts have to say about the stock's being overbought or oversold? Has volume been showing any significant changes: What indications does the MACD show? While technical analysis alone is not the best basis for trading, it is an excellent way to graphically illustrate the changes in supply and demand that have occurred and often highlights clues as to what can next be expected.

Fifth, gather trading information on your selected stocks. For over-the-counter issues, NASDAQ Trader (www.nasdaqtrader .com) has excellent historical data on each issue. Information such as monthly share volume, monthly short interest, share volume by market maker, and other data compilations are available. In addition, visit www.cboe.com to gather information about your stock and its derivatives, including the open interest in the stock's options, the put-call ratio, and implied volatility. While each of these bits of data alone is not overly significant, taken as a whole they provide an accurate picture to the reason behind price movements. In addition, significant changes in the data may also foretell pending price movement; for example, if the short interest is declining, one would surmise that the formerly pessimistic shorts are buying to close out their short positions, thus creating an imbalance of demand over supply, causing the stock price to temporarily move up due to a potential short squeeze.

Sixth, visit www.nasdaqtrader.com to determine who is the key market maker in your stock. Who is the ax? The trading data listed by market maker will give you a strong indication of which trading firms are aggressive participants in that stock's market. Thereafter, when you see this market maker staying on the bid and refreshing his quote, you know that an increase in price may soon follow given that market maker's historically stronger-than-average appetite for this stock.

It simply translates into work and dedication. Stocks that meet the criteria set in this chapter are all that are needed to get started. Once a handful of stocks are selected and added to your interest list, specialize in them and get to know them intimately. Understand their patterns. Know when they release earnings and when their competition releases earnings. Study their reaction during strong market days and weak ones. Know which market makers are most active in the stocks. Trade them often. This is how trading expertise is found.

There are no magic mathematical formulas or filters that will replace good old-fashioned familiarity that is found through trading. Research is important and rewarding, as highlighted above, but too much research and not enough trading equates to too much expectation and emotion associated with the overresearched stocks. Traders often marry stocks they invest too much time in before making any trades, and this is not considered specialization. Active participation mitigates emotion and makes you more logical and familiar.

I close this chapter with this rule: **Forget about chat rooms** and stock picking services that claim to do the thinking for you. If it were that easy, the market wouldn't have any value. Remember, the benefits in these situations belong either to the manipulator who front runs the stocks that are highlighted in the chat rooms or to the recipient of the subscription fees that charge for such so-called services. Instead, invest in yourself by doing your own work and gaining confidence, and save your capital for more useful applications like trading in the market. The market is the best teacher, and although you can count on tough lessons, these lessons offer the most utility.

RULES FOR ENTERING TRADES

Rules of the Trade

No clarity, no trade.

Size the open.

Watch fair value.

Cover or liquidate trades in the pre- and post-market; don't open them.

Never use market orders.

Always use limit orders.

Never chase stocks.

Always look for confirmation among trading signals.

Always know who the buyers and sellers are.

Survive before you thrive.

With most rules that are taught, the lesson usually begins with the consequences for breaking the rule. In this chapter, I will start with the same caveat: "Don't break the rules or else." As I've stated numerous times already, the market is unforgiving of mistakes, and the consequences are clear. The stock market has a natural self-cleansing mechanism built into it by virtue of its capitalistic nature. A trader who continually breaks the rules of market engagement generally starts breaking them in trade entry and stock selection. This individual will then exacerbate the error because he or she will also lack discipline to exit the trade when necessary. Because the stock selection process is perceived to be the most difficult aspect of trading, many new market participants will focus all their energy into this process, with little regard to trade entry and exit means. As a day trader, I believe the opposite is true. Trade entry, the focus of this chapter, and trade exit (Chapter 6) have a greater impact on performance than any other aspect of trading. The skill set a day trader has in finding liquidity with precision execution, married to strong discipline, will be the greatest asset he or she has. Given the many decisions to be made during a trading session, poor discipline will be magnified and will accelerate this self-cleansing process. The advantage, I suppose, for this individual is analogous to a quick death versus a slow death. Because new traders will often begin with less capital, dying a fast death in the market may in fact save them many thousands of dollars. It is the slow-death traders with large capital reserves who suffer most, as they accumulate the greatest monetary losses over the largest periods of time. These individuals, having often been successful in past endeavors, generally possess egos as large as the void that exists in their discipline. While this may sound cynical, it is true of many new traders, and the statistics prove it. Therefore, trade entry skills (and exit skills) must be mastered, which in turn builds discipline.

Markets today are much more complicated than in years past. The "New Economy" stocks have truly changed the landscape of the market. Therefore, when evaluating the market and the stocks to be traded within it, traders must form a perspective about how to engage. In the past, hard work usually paid off in the form of fundamental analysis. Today, that isn't always true. Many amateurs made fortunes on the dot com revolution, while other professionals like Soros got slammed and are nearly out of business at the time of this writing. This is quite a reversal of fortune for those who have not adapted to the New Economy.

The process of evaluating a trade or series of trades is what is referred to as *sizing a trade.* Just as you "size" your competition in a wrestling match or other intimately competitive situation, sizing a trade is much the same. Evaluating risk, capital considerations, time horizons, margin requirements, and portfolio risk are considerations that are encompassed in the process of sizing a trade. But it also includes sizing your competition, which, in day trading, are the market participants who trade your stocks. Before evaluating entry strategies and sizing the competition, it is important to form a more macroview of the trading environment.

Today, markets fall into separate but closely related stages of activity that drive prices. That activity can be defined as money flow in and out of stocks and sectors. The influences in the market that we see today are of the following variety:

1. *Economy-driven environment.* This environment is most often seen when the market becomes sensitized. Periods of correction and volatility are characteristic of this stage since every economic report delivered seems to create uncertainty. Interest rate revisions, employment cost index (ECI) reports, FOMC meetings, and so on all are monitored with extreme focus. The media help to sensitize our market with such news.

2. *Earnings- and revenues-driven environment.* This environment is most characteristic of strong markets where market participants are more reactive to earnings than economic reports because the numbers that companies report reflect their true health at that stage of their business. If they are strong, they build consensus of value

for many traders. If weak, their stocks get crucified. While no one influence is ever completely dominant, a weighting of one influence over the others is ever present. Just listen to the media, and you will hear through the agenda of topics what is weighted heaviest. March, April, and May 2000 were weighted heavily to the economy forces. What will the Federal Reserve Board (FRB) do with rates, what are the economic reports telling us, what will the impact be if they do raise rates? What is the bond market outlook? These questions and concerns are paramount during these times, while earnings seem to have a lesser impact. Other times, rates are increased consistently, while companies like Cisco have great earnings, and the rate hike is completely ignored. It seems during this climate nothing can hold the market down. The weighting in this scenario is obvious.

3. *Momentum-driven environments.* This environment seems to be constant. The momentum players seem to stand alone and smile at the other players in the market, saying: "Hey, you guys fight it out. We focus on the trends of the market. Either way, long or short, we trade it." Momentum markets seem to be gaining dominance. Many predicted that momentum players could survive only in bull markets, and the first correction or crash would shake them out through margin calls and losses. While that is true for many online traders, it is not true of day traders. Momentum traders are now a permanent fixture to the market. They are not going away, and they do move and influence our markets. In fact, they are the best prepared for bear cycles, based on the daily experience gained by actively shorting stocks as well as going long. Day traders are indifferent to market direction and are only concerned with market momentum; hence, they are the best prepared for all market influences and environments.

Traditionally, most factors in the market could be measured from an economic and earnings perspective. This "fundamentally" sound approach has made sense for many years for the longer-term-oriented investor. But today momentum trading has changed the rules completely.

Technicians are not immune either; they have long been the contraside to fundamentalists (direct opposite). Therefore, technicians' decisions are more influenced by patterns that seek to reveal the psychological mood of the market as evidenced by activity. The problem that exists for both sides of this argument is that fundamentalists tend to predict too much based on earnings and economic climates, among other factors, while technicians tend to react too quickly to chart patterns and mathematical averages. In both disciplines, what is often forgotten is how to size a trade in terms of risk/reward and short-term market direction. Because volatility is becoming more apparent in our markets, trading short-term momentum swings offers the greatest opportunity for profit while mitigating systematic risk through time. This view is quite the contrary to what analysts and brokers would tell you, but ask yourself how well this segment of market participants has predicted the future.

Traders today cannot strictly classify themselves as fundamentalists or technicians. In order to size up the market to trade, the three stages of the market noted on pages 86 and 87 must all be considered. Momentum traders perhaps fit this approach best since they utilize methods from all realms, hence making them the most well rounded and multidimensional. The full-breed day trader is who I am talking about, and those who have been delivered into it with little or no background seem to have transitioned the best as a whole. Experienced professionals from the trading floors who have day traded for years would also be included. This very small group of individuals are perhaps the best traders of all.

Sizing trades and interpreting the market mood lends itself to this rule: **No clarity, no trade.** Risk management is as important when opening trades as it is when exiting trades. Once started on the wrong path, mistakes and errors seem to follow naturally, setting in motion an emotionally driven comedy of errors that results in inevitable loses. Positions that are opened based on confusion or a lack of clarity generally result in a continued abandonment of risk management and discipline. For this reason, the rules you follow to determine what stocks to trade and when to trade them are critical. Choosing low-risk–high-reward spectrum trades will be the focus of this important chapter, since once a trade is opened for the wrong reasons, such as a tip, media hype, chat room manipulation, good old-fashioned greed, or the perception that prices are cheap, following the rules for exiting trades will be increasingly difficult. In the preceding chapter, I asked the question: What is the state of mind of traders when opening a trade? The answer is that most amateurs when opening a trade have a level of exuberance and excitement with delusions of grandeur to make big money. Unfortunately because of this excitement stage, far too many trades are opened based on something other than clarity and good rationale. The emotional swing from exuberance to fear and denial is often too much to deal with for the ill prepared who open trades without clarity and supporting data. The likelihood that the rules needed to exit trades will be followed (next chapter) is highly unlikely. Exuberance hindered good behavior when entering the trade; fear and denial will hinder good behavior when exiting, hence the result of the abandonment of discipline will be as damaging financially as it will be emotionally, and that paints a grim picture for a fledgling new trader.

Although total clarity will never be found since all trading activity requires some degree of speculation, clarity and confidence to trade comes from having both a macroview and microview of the market. The macroview gives you the overview of the market, or what Charles Dow metaphorically referred to as the "tides" of the market, representing the overall flow, or primary trends, of the market. Remember what the market really is: All the hopes and fears of all the traders and investors, big and small, playing out their biases as a whole. So how is clarity achieved?

Reading the daily mood of the market begins early, before the market opens. As you start your day, listen to a good market-oriented TV or radio station while enjoying your first cup of coffee. Bloomberg, for example, has a national morning radio program that can alert you to how the overseas markets traded, the Globex futures market, and other premarket indications, such as pending economic news. Monitoring CNBC while reading some key Web sites or reading financial publications is also a good habit to get into immediately. That does not mean that you will react directly to the news; it simply means you are becoming aware of potential market-moving events. How you react to these events will be determined by market forces and indicators as presented during each market session—not by the media, and the strongest indications are seen at the open.

SIZE THE OPEN

When sizing up the market, the opening activity is especially important since a general tone or feel for the opening can be best determined by exchanges such as the futures markets in Chicago, the Chicago Mercantile Exchange (CME), leading to the rule: **Size the open.** Futures trade all night on automated electronic systems (Globex and Globex II) that can have a dramatic impact on the opening of trading. The long bond market at the Chicago Board of Trade (CBOT) is a great leading indicator as well. The bond prices are typically a strong indicator of the direction of the stock market. If bond prices and equity-oriented futures markets are higher in relation to fair value, you should expect to have a bullish bias at least for the open. Naturally, the opposite is also true.

While the scope of this book is not to cover the technical interpretations of these various markets, knowing that these markets are important to follow will help you formulate your watch list of what to monitor every trading day. The appendixes will direct you to many resources and Web sites to learn more about how these vehicles affect the equities market. Let's at least take a brief look at the futures market to pick up on what I mentioned in the preceding chapter. Since the futures market has such a strong impact on the stock market, follow the rule, **Watch fair value.** Fair value takes the current index level, index dividend, days to expiration, and interest rate into consideration. The S&P Futures Contract is the one stock traders track the most, but other financial futures contracts, such as the NASDAQ futures, are also gaining incredible attention. The formula to compute fair value is shown below, but save yourself the work because this formula is relative to the firms that compute it since interest rates, leverage, and the cost of capital to carry the securities are different for all firms. But fair value is very close for most firms and can be found at many different Web sites free of charge:

$$\text{Fair value} = \text{cash} \left[1 + r \left(\frac{x}{365} \right) \right] - \text{dividends}$$

Cash is the price of the actual index at the time of the calculation. Of course, *r* represents the interest rate, and *x* is the number of days to expiration. The term *a futures contract* in the definition means a futures index contract, such as the S&P 500 or the NASDAQ 100.

The importance of knowing and understanding fair value is that, when futures are in an overbought or oversold status relative to fair value, it can trigger program trading. *Program trading* is defined as the simultaneous buying or selling of at least 15 stocks with a market value of at least $1 million.

Large trading houses execute program trades, switching from futures to cash, meaning futures indexes to actual stock ownership, when one has an economical advantage over the other. This can happen at the open or throughout the trading session. These trades are executed at the click of a mouse via the New York Stock Exchange's Designated Order Turnaround System (DOT), automated NASDAQ trading systems, the Globex system, and live trading at the CME, with the simultaneous purchase or sale of futures contracts and the underlying stocks they represent. This type of trading is technically known as *index arbitrage*.

As a trader, knowing the fair value and when it might trigger program trades by several of the big trading firms helps you understand the mood of the market. If a wave of program trading hits, it can have some serious market impact—that is, it can drive prices higher or lower. Normally, the impact of program trading is temporary, lasting a few minutes to an hour or so, while the emotional impact it has on the market can last for the entire trading day. Traders that get burned at the open don't forget it very easily, especially when high volatility occurs due to program trading. Depending on your time horizon and whether the fair value indicates an overbought or oversold scenario, you may want to wait to open or close a position or you may want to scalp its market impact where inefficiency is present. Either way, futures contracts are one of the few leading indicators in the market, and they are closely followed by professionals and active traders.

PRE- AND POST-MARKET TRADING

The next rule relates to the new technologies that allow access to pre- and post-markets. The rule to follow is, **Cover or liquidate trades in the pre- and post-market; don't open them.** I state this rule because the liquidity is not yet vibrant enough as a rule in the pre- and post-market. The cornerstone of a healthy economy is a healthy stock market, and a healthy stock market is found through liquidity. When liquidity is low, volatility is generally very high, as stated in the preceding chapter. Volatility, although potentially very profitable, is also very dangerous when it is matched with illiquidity.

Thin stocks during market hours are characteristic of this volatile condition. Now with the advent of pre- and post-market trading, the same condition is often present, but exaggerated. Pre- and post-market trading are dangerous at this stage because the participation is still not even close to normal trading liquidity, and in my opinion it will not be for a while. I am not saying it is not a good idea, but caution should be employed in engaging this new environment until adequate liquidity or critical mass is achieved.

Liquidating or covering a trade during extended hours is a good idea when the price level is attractive to you (taking profits or covering a loss). In this case, you know where you are willing to trade out of a position, and if the opportunity presents itself in the pre- and post-market, you are taking a known price that you accept. For example, it is not uncommon for a volatile liquid stock like SDLI to trade 10 points higher or lower during extended-hours trading than it did during the previous close or pending open. For the buyer of SDLI who pays 10 points more than the closing print the day before, due to an impatient reaction to seemingly good news, the morning can be quite rough! In this example, the trader has opened himself or herself up to too much uncertainty and often pays dearly for it. Conversely, the trader who liquidates a long position by selling to the impatient trader noted above realizes a 10-point benefit because that trader knew where he or she wanted out!

Certainly there are scenarios where it works out just the opposite, but ask yourself the question, Is that more associated with gambling than trading? I believe it is, and gambling is associated with luck, and the market has no room for luck over sustained periods of time. Eventually, when luck is involved, you will be ground down and spit out of the market through its very pure and ruthless self-cleaning mechanism. Luck rarely survives over time, so don't depend on it. Opening a trade in illiquid markets requires luck for the trade to work out as a rule.

MARKET ORDERS

Never use market orders. That's right: **Never** use them. Some will disagree, but when equipped with the right technology and knowledge, you will always be able to see where liquidity is in issues that you should be trading and have the technology to hit bids and lift offers to enter and exit trades. If I were inclined to use a market order, it would be for the purpose of taking a profit, and certainly not to open a trade at the open.

Market orders are blank checks in effect that you write to professional traders, completely giving all control away in terms of where you will be executed. Consider, for example, our discussion on gaps: The last thing you want to do is give that discretion to a market maker who will use your order to find liquidity at a price he loves and you will hate. That is as insane as swimming in shark-infested waters with a bleeding artery; you will be eaten!

Market-on-open orders are the most frequent market orders placed, and they are placed at the worst time of day, where the largest imbalances occur. If there is strong demand over supply due to an announcement of a stock split, for example, where do you think professionals will try and open stock the next day? As high as possible so they can short stock to the stampeding dumb money crowd rushing in, to take their perceived easy money with market on open orders! Gapping a stock 75 points higher than the previous close comes to mind in the case of

YHOO on one occasion. Amateurs who gave professionals market orders on the open know why this can be injurious to their financial state of being. By shorting stock to the buyers, market makers were in a position to sell high and buy back at lower prices shortly into the day to cover their shorts for a great profit.

You may ask, what about a market order in an emergency. For example, you are in a losing position that is plummeting. You have tried unsuccessfully to get ahead of the price movement by placing leading limit orders, but to no avail because the market is so thin at each price level. Liquidity is hard to find. True, market order will find that liquidity for you, but I doubt you will like the price. If you are in a situation like this, chances are very strong that you're trading a thin stock you shouldn't be anyway.

LIMIT ORDERS

While you should never use market orders, you need to **Always use limit orders.** Limit orders allow you to keep control of the order and determine what price you are willing to trade at. It does not mean you will always get your price, but by knowing where liquidity is through an EDAT system, and by knowing how to use the technology we discussed, traders can fire limit and leading limit orders directly into an ECN to find liquidity. That is control, which is something every active trader needs to learn early in the war of trading.

The use of a leading limit order can be explained by comparing a quarterback to a receiver. The ball is thrown to where the receiver will be, not where he is. Leading limit orders are orders that are sent to the market with room for the order to work. For example, if a Sun Micro Systems (SUNW) is trading strong to the upside and the market is bid 95 by 95⅛ offered and the offers are fading fast since buyers are taking the offer at 95⅛, traders who want to own the stock would lead with a limit order at 95³⁄₁₆ or 95¼. Any sellers at these prices or lower would automatically match or cross with this leading limit bid for an almost instant execution (assuming there are sellers at that price). If there are any remaining sellers at 95⅛ and your order is crossed, you will realize price improvement and get whatever size is left for sale at that price within the ECN you trade on. This is called "cleaning the book," and it is considered an aggressive buy. It puts you in the trade without your giving up your edge as market orders can do. The same concept works for an aggressive seller who wishes to liquidate a long position by hitting a lower bid, as the thinning inside bid (high bid) is fading. As bids would be thinning out on the Level II, due to weakness in the stock, selling at a lower price, perhaps a ¹⁄₁₆ or an ⅛ below the market would make good sense. Avoid chasing the stock lower trying to hit the remaining (and fading) inside bid, which is a common mistake.

Perhaps the following example will illustrate how to use market versus limit orders and how to maintain control using the proper methods of finding liquidity. For example, the quote for AMGN stock is 60 X 60⅛ 2000 X 5000. If you wanted to buy the stock, you should be able to place a limit order to buy at 60⅛ or better and get filled. Exceptions could include if the stock is moving higher quickly and your bid at 60⅛ is not filled because there is stock ahead, meaning that others had orders ahead of yours or if there is less stock for sale at the offer than you are bidding, hence creating what is really a micro imbalance of demand over supply at the $60⅛ price level. By bidding at least ¹⁄₁₆ higher than the lowest offer (60³⁄₁₆ or better), you "step in front" of all bidders at lower prices and take "standing" over their bids by becoming the high bid. Any sellers at $60⅛ would be crossed with your bid, providing you the opportunity for "price improvement." For example, if there are only 500 shares offered at 60⅛ and your bid at 60³⁄₁₆ for 1000 shares is crossed in an ECN, your fill would be 500 at 60⅛ and 500 at 60³⁄₁₆. The benefit is price improvement on 500 shares plus finding liquidity faster than any bids at 60⅛. You are essentially leading the offer slightly to "clean" the book of liquidity on any offers at or below the 60³⁄₁₆ bid.

By understanding the Level II, you have a portal to see much of the market in a given issue, and this defines a form of market transparency. By understanding transparency, traders gain insight into where to execute orders proactively with execution tools using limit and leading limit orders. Chasing a stock lower or higher before finding liquidity creates an unnecessary market impact cost (MIC). For example, suppose you owned stock at 60 3/16 and wished to sell the stock since it began to look weak. As the buyers at the bid begin to dissipate from the bid side of the Level II at 60 1/8, the seller tries to offer his stock for sale with other sellers at the ask of 60 3/16. The imbalance of supply (more sellers at 60 3/16) over demand (fewer buyers at 60 1/8) suggests strongly that this seller should have hit the 60 1/8 bids while they existed, instead of trying to sell at the offer or ask where many sellers are also in line to sell at 60 3/16. The result would soon show a seller reducing the price from 60 3/16 to 60 1/8 while the bidders are no longer willing to buy there. Instead, bidders are willing to buy at lower prices such as 60. The seller is caught up in a vicious cycle of chasing stock on the way down by trying to sell at retail prices (the offer) instead of hitting bids. As the perception of a bearish move exists in the market for this given issue, the bids continue lower as buyers become more and more elusive. The seller in this example finally catches up with a buyer at a much reduced price such as 59 11/16, for example, causing him to suffer a loss much higher than necessary by not understanding the Level II screen, transparency, and liquidity.

What could have been a small loss by hitting the 60 1/8 bid while buyers were present, or even 60 1/16, turned into a bigger loss, and the seller lost much more by being greedy or uninformed, trying to sell the 60 3/16 offer when the imbalance of sellers over buyers indicated weakness. Why would buyers step up to the plate in a declining market for this issue and buy from the seller at 60 3/16 when other market participants are selling to them for less at 60 1/8? They wouldn't, and this is the reason the seller in this example never got filled at the 60 3/16 offer. The market impact cost is defined as the difference between the 60 1/8 the trader should have sold at while buyers were present at the bid and the 59 11/16 price he or she finally did sell at when the stock hit a probable support level.

Proactive traders who understand liquidity and where to enter and exit trades can substantially reduce market impact costs. Reactive traders and investors give the control away to professionals with market orders. So remember, MIC is far more expensive than commissions and more of a nemesis to an uninformed trader's success than most other reasons.

CHASING STOCKS

This leads us to the next rule: **Never chase stocks.** This often occurs when a stock is moving higher or lower rapidly. The amateur tries to get a better fill than he or she deserves by attempting to lift a fading offer price, which is quickly moving higher. The market maker on the offer (ask) has 17 seconds to refresh the offer to sell before having to execute another order. When the offer is refreshed, the stock may trade a ¹⁄₁₆ higher or more. If volume is high, the Time & Sales (TAS) screen may not be keeping up with the market makers, especially if they take the full time to post a new price. Furthermore, that new price may be higher, putting a limit order outside the inside market. Thus, you do not get filled.

It is common for new traders to keep trying to lift the inside offer and not get filled. Often, when they do get a fill, the stock has reached a resistance area where buying has subsided and selling pressure has increased. The move may well be over, and the trader is too late. The more experienced trader leads the market in this situation, anticipating the next price level and leading above the inside offer price as an aggressive buyer before chasing the stock to resistance.

CONFIRMATION

When opening trades, another rule critical to follow is to **Always look for confirmation among trading signals.** Too often, new traders seek to employ only one indication of price activity. This narrowly focused approach leads to the largest number of trades with the highest degree of risk. The importance of confirming indicators goes far beyond the obvious benefits of increasing the odds for a profitable trade, as they also influence the emotional aspects of trading in terms of confidence and conviction.

The level of confidence and conviction you have in a trade and the range you believe the price of that stock is going to move determine your time horizon and how you enter the trade. For example, the scalper acts on very short-term momentum signals and even instinct. He or she sees a minor increase in volume and thinning overhead selling pressure (OSP) and immediately buys

1000 shares of Applied Materials (AMAT). If AMAT pops up a ⅜ or a half dollar, the scalper is often out. If AMAT drops ⅛ or a ¹⁄₁₆, he or she is also out. This style suggests a very short time horizon with less conviction and a lot of trades per session.

Some day traders look for longer-term moves, holding positions for hours (range trading). Swing traders take positions for days. Both of these traders must have stronger convictions. Their time horizons are longer, which means they must decide if they are aggressive buyers or passive buyers (or sellers) when entering these trades.

In other words, do they go after the market or do they wait for the market to come to them? Aggressive buyers lead the market. If AMAT is at 40⅛ X 40⅜, they may go ahead and lift the offer of 80⅜; if they are passive, they may join the bid at 80⅛ and wait for the market to come to them. The point is, the confirming indicators you use should be consistent with your time horizon in the trade. Day traders will use fewer confirming indicators but will be more aggressive while entering trades, while swing traders generally are more passive, using more confirming indicators.

THE AX

Not all market participants are worth monitoring and following. Some market makers will show a strong conviction for the stock, and others will not. Therefore, you must **Always know who the buyers and sellers are.** Market makers lead the way in most stocks. In fact, the most heavily traded stocks with the most activity are traded by the best market makers in the world. Because they trade the most active stocks, they provide day traders the opportunity to read their intentions. Even if an active stock you are monitoring is not a stock you want to trade, finding an "ax" can tell you a lot about not just an individual stock but even a group or sector. A trader is trying to determine if a market maker has strong or weak hands in terms of sentiment. There is a considerable difference between the Island ECN being on the inside market, either bid or ask, or a major market maker, like Goldman Sachs & Co. (GSCO) or Merrill Lynch (MLCO). Large market makers, like GSCO, trade for their customers, which are often very large institutions or mutual funds, and for their own considerable inventory. You will see market makers stay at the inside market holding their ground when they have a large need to buy or sell stock. Therefore, they show you more about the strength or weakness of a stock than ECNs or smaller market makers or firms that handle more retail order flow. Monitoring strong market makers is what I call *shadowing the ax*. The message here is to recognize who is dominant in a particular issue and monitor their appetite for the issue closely. If their appetite is strong and you are scalping or day trading, going long is the trend; if their appetite for the stock is dissipating and other indicators in the market confirm weakness, shorting is the bias. Looking for an ax to follow is the rule for active day trading.

The rules covered in this chapter carry varying weights. Some are considered critical because they can help manage downside risk, while others are more associated with strategies that can uncover opportunities. All are important, but before entering a trade, what is most important to remember is that active trading is about taking control of your own order flow. Keeping that control while continually gaining skill through experience is the fine line or edge that makes a dramatic difference in performance. Just as the average difference in scores on the PGA are very narrow, so are the statistical advantages that profitable traders enjoy over unprofitable traders. The real difference will come from experience and engagement in the market, since a book or class will take you only so far. Only trading will truly teach one to trade; therefore, I will close this chapter on the most important rule: **Survive before you thrive.** Only good discipline in selecting your criteria to open trades will allow you to survive long enough to cross the fine esoteric line that so many aspire to. Our next chapter will pick up where this leaves off by covering the rules of exiting trades.

RULES FOR EXITING TRADES

Rules of the Trade

The market will lead the way.

Know why you are in a trade, and where you will exit.

Know how to route your order to reach your objectives.

Set mental stops.

Stocks tell their own story ahead of the news.

Don't expect to squeeze all the juice from the orange.

Exit on reaction, not price.

The market is unfair at times.

When in doubt, get out.

The rules of exiting strategies are very much the same as for entering strategies, with only minor differences. In both cases, **The market will lead the way.** Emotions should never be the beacon for trading. If an emotion, such as exuberance, is setting in due to a profitable situation, your tendency will be to sell too soon. Conversely, when despair is setting in due to the wrong decision, the tendency is to stay too long, hoping for a recovery. Marrying a position or trade is the most common mistake traders make. From an active trading perspective, trades that are held for prolonged periods of time are usually losers. You can generally spot losing trades by their size. When you see positions of 1000 shares or higher or a high percentage of the account value tied up in one or a few trades, you can bet that most of those trades are losers, and the trader is waiting and hoping for a break.

Perhaps the best way to illustrate the rules that dictate trade exit strategies can be answered through an actual trade scenario which highlights many events that converge to form not just a sound exit strategy but also an entry strategy. Knowing how to combine strategy with mechanical skills to enter and exit trades comes from executing trades and using analytical data to support holding a position or exiting one. The example I share is meant to illustrate the mindset and rationale for decisions that impact and motivate both trade entry and exit. This actual trade scenario illustrates many of the rules we have covered thus far and helps convey what must be followed at all times.

I was long and heavy in Amgen (AMGN) to the tune of 10,000 shares, which I scaled into over the course of 2 days. My criteria for entering the trade was based on two key trading ranges that AMGN was trading within over the course of 10 days. I had been actively day trading the stock long and short during this 10-day period, and I would never have seen the patterns that revealed themselves had I not been day trading the stock every day. I think I saw every tick and print in AMGN during this period, and I began to form a clear idea of its price levels based on my active trading experiences with it. Through day trading, I knew where the stock was "hot" and where it would "cool" down, in terms of the price levels of support and resistance. I believed that if the stock could hold certain price levels, it would likely break out hard, making a higher high, then come in a bit, making a higher low, and then make a higher high once again.

As these levels were day traded, I could also feel the liquidity at certain prices to detect the strength and weakness of certain market makers over the course of days. From the microtrading approach of day trading, I also could not help but form a broader swing trade feel for the stock as well. I had been net positive in the 10 days of day trading, but as time went on, I was getting progressively more and more profitable since my instincts for AMGN grew keener as the result of my strong activity in the stock. As my profits grew, so did my confidence, but not to the point of becoming cocky or overconfident; I simply felt I had greater clarity as the days passed for these key levels. On the eleventh day, I told myself that if AMGN pulled back to 56⅜ (it was trading at 58¾ at the time), I would press heavy into the stock since I knew the range around 56⅜ was a strong support level based on the patterns revealed in the preceding days. Sure enough, after remaining patient, the stock came in, and I purchased 3000 shares between 56⅜ and 56¾. My expectation for profit was 2½ points based on the consistent honest range it had shown me time and time again during the previous 10 days. I also felt if AMGN could break 59, it would break higher and likely make a new higher high and a new 52-week high as well. I decided that not only would I not liquidate my 3000-share position but also I would lean even heavier into it, if this occurred. At 59¼, I watched AMGN catch on fire, and I purchased 5000 additional shares between 59¼ and 60⅜. Within the next two hours, AMGN pulled back to 59 and acted very strong during this pullback. That may sound contradictory, but relative to the biotech sector, NASDAQ, and the futures at that time, AMGN was very strong (relative strength). The biotech sector pulled back almost twice as much as AMGN did and indicated AMGN had great support. I bought another 2000 shares at 59, buying weakness, meaning that I bid for the stock at the bid price level on the Level II and let sellers hit my bid. I was able to save the spread because I provided liquidity to the market by bidding for stock while there were still sellers in the market. The point here is that I knew where I wanted in and didn't mind buying some stock at this price. I also felt there was good subscription from two market makers who were net buyers for the day and who were also buying weakness at that time (shadowing the ax market makers).

In the next two days, the NASDAQ continued to sell off by over 110 points, and AMGN never broke down through 59. I knew my stock was acting strong in the face of a minor two-day tech selloff, and I let my position stand, knowing that if AMGN could hold this level, it would advance quickly relative to the market, once the market took off. Additionally, economic news was being released, and an FOMC meeting was being held with an expected 50-basis-point rate hike. I felt that the rate hike had a strong chance of moving only 25 basis points higher and that if I were right, the market would surely surge. Additionally, I had already had some unrealized profit in AMGN and had some room to work with if the market responded poorly to the economic news and if the rate hike exceeded 50 basis points. You see, the selloff in the market the preceding few days was already building in the expectation of a 50-basis-point rate increase; therefore, even if that had been the case, I felt there would be more upside bias than downside bias since once again the market had begun correcting for it in advance of the FOMC news (the market trading ahead of news). If it increased only 25 basis points, I had tremendous upside potential; therefore, my speculative risk was a low-risk–high-reward spectrum, since I was long a stock with good relative strength within its group and sector. The combined market condition, as I just noted, including my unrealized profit in AMGN, gave me strong conviction to let my trade work and wait for the news to release.

Sure enough, the FOMC increased rates by only 25 basis points, even though I was comfortable with a 50-basis-point hike relative to my position. AMGN ran 7 points that very day, and I began to sell into strength taking my profits when it was up around $5, scaling out completely when it was up around 5¾ at 65.

While my story is a good one in this case, it cemented once again in my mind how rewarding the market is when you know why you are in a trade and when you should be out. My day trading activity highlighted this swing trade to me based on my price level recognition. Having a broad view of the market as well as my bias for the stock relative to its industry and index further confirmed the reason I stayed with the trade. While I did not sell the perfect top when AMGN traded up 7 the day I sold, I sold into strength for a good bit of the move and never regretted it for a second! The moral of the story is also the rule: **Know why you are in a trade, and where you will exit.**

While not all trades are winners such as this one, and I feel compelled to share a few hard lessons I have learned—the story illustrates how exit points can be determined. Had AMGN sold off even near 58, I would have leveled the entire position and controlled the downside risk. Knowing where key levels are in price and more importantly market psychology will more determine exit points than any other factor. Paying attention to this will naturally guide you to letting profits run while cutting losses quickly, hence allowing the market to lead you in and out of trades.

A final point regarding this trade. While my position was large for a swing trade, I averaged my winners as AMGN rallied, which afforded me more risk tolerance. Additionally, because of the discipline I have, I was prepared to exit the trade at a predetermined price level.

MECHANICAL EXIT STRATEGIES

The often-asked question "When is the right time to exit a trade?" is best answered not only through the numbers and the data the market presents through the tools but also through the interpretive skills a trader possesses.

The speed and ease of market access today often lead to spontaneous trading, which can be a fatal mistake. Fools rush in, and in today's environment with the ability to bypass brokers and trade the hot technology sector, greed and gambling have become commonplace. I often ask traders "Where is the liquidity at the moment? If you had to get out of this trade fast, how would you do it?" "What price is your threshold for pain?" If I do not get solid answers like "I have Island's book up and it's stacked with buyers!" or "Look at the Level II, the ax is buying everything in sight!" I give them our stop-loss/liquidity talk. It is imperative that traders know where they are right and wrong about a trade before they enter it, and they must have the mechanics to find liquidity for a fast exit should that become necessary.

On the mechanical side of exit strategies, there are various phases that a trader will be in, given the time horizon and strategy he or she employs. For example, a day trader will be fighting for every ⅛ while a swing trader may be less focused on fighting for the same ⅛. The day trader working with greater size is also concerned with finding greater liquidity at each price level, while the swing trader is inclined to allow for more price discretion and movement. In the case of a highly capitalized professional trader who will scale into a large position over days, the same liquidity issues will arise. Therefore, regardless of the time horizon of the trade, consideration for liquidity must be accounted for in both trade entry and trade exit. Because of this, day traders and traders that trade larger size need to know when to be aggressive or passive. This determination is best made based on the micromomentum of the market and the stocks they are trading. For the purpose of this discussion, I will use an exit strategy example from the long side, but the same theory applies when covering short positions (buying).

Aggressive sellers, in this context, get the best price possible while exiting trades in the most expeditious manner. Sellers want the best price possible; therefore, the momentum of the stocks they are trading is most important to find the best price with the most liquidity. Selling into a rally is very effective and desirable. Conversely, if the momentum is showing signs of weakness, aggressive sellers find liquidity at or below the bid. Aggressive sellers hit the inside bids placed there by market participants or even hit bids below the inside market when liquidity fades at the inside bid. Passive sellers will offer their stock at the offer price or even above the inside offer as seen on Level II when upside momentum is present. The risk for the passive seller is that no buyers may be willing to lift their offer, causing the passive seller to remain in the trade. If a stock saturates at this price level, this risk is realized, causing many passive sellers to become aggressive sellers, hitting bids at or below the inside market. The swing in price from a passive seller to an aggressive seller can be extreme, such as a ½ point or more, which amounts to serious capital when trading larger size like many traders do.

Often the need to shift from a passive seller when there is perceived upside bias to an aggressive seller is real because when stocks truly roll over, selling motivation far exceeds buying motivation. This is when the risk of chasing stock is greatest, which can for even the experienced trader yield a very high market impact cost (MIC). The reason that even an experienced trader can get caught when these reversals occur is that emotions do kick in, and emotions are the nemesis of the trader. For example, if a stock like Juniper (JNPR) is 165 X 165¼, 500 X 2000, and a trader is long 3000 shares, if JNPR finds resistance at the offer of 165¼, this trader better act fast as an aggressive seller. In a scenario like this, I wouldn't hesitate to hit the 164⅞ or bid even lower depending on how strong the selloff was. Getting out of a trade quickly in a situation like this is far more comforting than waiting to see where things turn out. Most amateurs will not learn this until many painful lessons are taught.

The other risk associated with the seller in this scenario is that the probability that other sellers are in the market at this saturation point is very high, hence making it more likely that the selloff will be severe. The possibilities in this example are almost endless, but the example illustrates the subtle nuances of momentum trading to determine aggressive or passive strategies.

Once you decide how aggressively you want to sell, you must **Know how to route your order to reach your objectives.** This was touched on in Chapter 2 briefly, but we will go into deeper detail now in determining which execution system to use. Selecting the right ECN, SOES, SelectNet, or other means will prove invaluable considering that time will be wasted in sending a futile order, which can prove to be quite expensive. By the time you receive your cancel alert and change routes, even given the speed of an EDAT system, a volatile stock can really hurt you.

The first thing an ECN attempts to do is match new orders with ones that it already has on its system. Its inventory of unfilled orders is simply called its "book," meaning book of open orders. Traders love it when they get an "instant cross," as it is called. Fills can come back to you in nanoseconds when crossing orders, and knowing how to cross orders and which systems to use to get such a fast fill is imperative. If the ECN does not have a match in its book, it does one of two things. One type of ECN holds the order in its book and waits for a match. The Island ECN (ISLD) is the archetypal example. Just like its name, it is an island unto itself. But it will post orders it cannot fill to Level II or its internal book of liquidity. If the order becomes or joins the best bid or offer (BBO), the order will display on Level II. The limit-order protection rule of the exchange provides for this. Otherwise, if the order is away from the BBO, the order will be placed in the internal book of liquidity of the ECN. This way an individual trader becomes a de facto market maker, without having to make a two-sided market in the stock. Like a market maker, the world sees your order once it is on the Level II.

The second type of ECN routes orders it cannot immediately match to other ECNs for a match. The Archipelago ECN (ARCA) is a prime example. Like its name, it represents a group of islands or books of liquidity through a "proactive" algorithm that attempts to find a contra to fill an order. The Speer Leeds and Kellogg Redi system (REDI) is also such an ECN.

The decision traders face when selecting between these two types of ECNs is which one will get orders filled faster and at the best price. With the Island ECN, unfilled orders go into its book, which is very liquid in most actively traded stocks. If the unfilled orders are near the inside market and the market is moving in the direction of the unfilled orders, they will get filled. Archipelago, on the other hand, searches for liquidity if it cannot fill an order. This takes time as it sends and resends the order to other ECNs and market makers through either a direct route or what is called a *SelectNet preference*. Where Island represents only its own liquidity, Archipelago can find liquidity within the NASDAQ market (listed stocks are also included). Experience teaches the electronic trader that each type of ECN can be useful. It depends on where the liquidity you are seeking is for a specific stock. In other words, either type can be your better bet depending on your strategy.

The listed and regional exchanges have their own electronic routing systems as well. The New York Stock Exchange and American Stock Exchange have SuperDot, while NASDAQ has the famous Small Order Execution System (SOES) and SelectNet system.

Another big consideration is what types of orders will these systems accept. For example, ARCA accepts only round lots of 100 shares or multiples of 100 shares, while ISLD accepts odd lots. Let's say you are buying 500 shares of Biogen, Inc. (BGEN), and you get a partial fill of only 425 shares from an SOES order. You could not sell the remaining 75 shares through ARCA, while ISLD would take the order. Additionally, although not recommended as a rule, you might place a market order in an emergency, which you can do on ARCA but not on ISLD. These nuances must be known, and you can expect them to change. For instance, ARCA will most likely accept odd lot orders in the future as well as allow listed stocks to trade through it; therefore, the dynamics of the market and the tools we use must be continually studied.

ELECTRONIC AND MENTAL STOPS

In addition to understanding the mechanics of trading systems and how aggressive or passive to be while using them, another rule required of all traders is to **Set mental stops,** which is imperative prior to ever even entering a trade. This rule requires that you program your mind before programming your computer.

The two methods for setting these stop levels are mental and electronic. Mental stops are simple price levels you set in your mind that, once met, prompt you to exit or enter the trade. This is the mechanism of most professional traders who monitor their positions closely throughout the day and don't want to reveal to the market where their entry and exit points are.

A stop-loss price represents the worst-case scenario for getting out of trades when things do not go as planned—it represents your threshold for pain that you are unwilling to exceed. The reason for mental stops is that, as in poker, you never want to show your hand. Think of market makers and online firms that sell order flow to wholesaling market makers as "secret handshake" poker partners. They love to know your buying and selling intentions so that they can trade against them or provide liquidity with them. Telling a market maker where you want to trade your stock is showing your hand. Many argue "What's the difference? I wanted to trade at that price anyway." The problem is that there is little to be known about the market condition at these literal price points where stops are set, since stops usually represent the market condition at some time in the near future. I would much prefer to analyze the market condition once my stock reached this price point to decide if it is to my advantage to make the trade. Relying on stops, without being present when this price criterion is met that triggers the stop, to me, is like getting up from the poker table and telling your opponent to pick up a king of hearts for you while you are getting a drink. What transpires in hands while you are away will affect you dramatically if you still want the king of hearts, not to mention the fact that you told your opponent where you want to trade cards. In the market the same is true for a day trader. I don't want some market maker to know where I want to buy or sell stock until I show it to them as I hit their bids or lift their offers. This is why mental stops are important. I program my mind where I want to buy, such as the case with a buy stop, or where I want to sell, such as the case with a sell stop. Obviously, limit-order protection can be added to stop orders if stops are to be used.

Electronic stops are now available on EDAT systems that allow the trader to set these limits on his or her own PC without sending the order to a market maker or broker who may trade against them. The local PC holds the order electronically and fires the order when the conditions that you set are met. This keeps the order safe and sound on your PC without any possible manipulation. The risk with these systems, though, is that *prints away from the CMV*—defined as trades that are printed to the market that are not representing the current price in a given stock—could trigger a stop order due to a bad print. This can occur for several reasons such as late prints or trades being reported out of sequence. While the situation is relatively infrequent, it is a real possibility and the reason why I am apprehensive about using electronic stops.

The reason stops can make sense for you when used properly is that they give you the benefit of what I call "imposed discipline." For example, if you are going long 3 Com Corporation (COMS) because you expect a bullish move based on Merrill Lynch & Co.'s upgrading it to a buy from a hold, where will you get out if that move does not materialize? You know in advance how much heat you are willing to take, and the electronic stop makes sure you follow through. If COMS does not break out and instead stalls or reverses relative to your position, you automatically have a defensive strategy programmed, and you should always be defensive in your trades. Offensive when getting in, defensive when getting out! Remember, the right trades will pretty much take care of themselves; it's the losses that require your most disciplined attention. Electronic stops impose that discipline on you by preprogramming the stop limits into your PC.

THE MATURATION OF HARD AND SOFT DATA

While mechanical understanding is invaluable in terms of which tools to use and the strategies to employ while using them, market psychology, technical indications, and experience will also greatly contribute to exit strategies. A cliché I introduced in Chapter 3 has such widely followed acceptance that I have made it a rule: **Stocks tell their own story ahead of the news.** While this rule is true and applicable for entering trades as well as exiting, recognizing and reacting to key market indications to exit stocks gives a trader an edge that most new to trading don't recognize exists. Increased market maker activity, new support or resistance levels over key moving averages, and so on are all clues that some kind of news or impact is about to occur. The news could be a new development in the biotech sector or an increased consensus of professional traders or even increased activity of day traders, but the point is, whatever the reason, stocks tell you what is happening before the media and even analysts can generally explain it. Therefore, traders must learn to read the signs first and then to react to them with some degree of speculation or uncertainty to take advantage of the impending news as others follow suit on the discovery of the same information or media coverage (certainty). In terms of Dow's wave theory, you are on the wave that trends one direction or the other before the masses; hence, you benefit from the move and possibly avoid downside risk. By the time the news is well known, you will know whether to stay away from the trade or go the other way. Either way, chaos is generally the result once the public and the media get a hold of some market-moving news, and chaos is difficult to trade regardless of your experience level and time horizon.

In fact, discipline is not defined by controlling downside risk through cutting losses in terms of literal prices but by recognizing indications that illustrate that weakness is setting in and then acting on the information by liquidating (long positions) or covering (short positions) prior to the associated price change. Price is again a lagging indication. The events that can be seen prior to the associated price change can cause you to be a more proactive trader, which is incredibly important for active trading.

The ability to adhere to your strategy, and the rules associated with it, is really what defines discipline, not literally cutting every loss at a ⅟₁₆ or ⅛ for day trades or ½- or ¾-point downturns for swing or longer time horizon strategies. The key is to know what indications correctly identify imbalances in supply and demand as well as volume and to monitor when such indications present clues as to when to exit the trade. The discipline to act on the information will automatically reward the proper behavior.

Think of this philosophy as the "invisible hand theory." In macroeconomics Adam Smith used this term to describe the natural force that guides capitalistic free markets. In trading, the term could be adapted to describe the natural force that if the right activity is employed and the discipline to follow the rules associated with the strategy are followed, the positive results will be delivered as if an invisible hand gave you the results you desired.

TAKING PROFITS

As indicated at the beginning of this chapter, a fine line exists between selling profitable positions too soon and hanging on too long. As a rule, **Don't expect to squeeze all the juice from the orange.** This simply means that the trader who can be satisfied with a lower net return by taking less profit will reduce his or her risk for the exchange of acting early and exiting, while the masses provide the liquidity needed to exit the trade. More traders lose in short-term trades, day and swing trades, by staying in trades too long. If you get out of a trade with a profit and the trade continues to run in what would have been your favor, do not look back in regret. For example, you visualized a trade making a 1-dollar move. It did that, and you exited the trade, only to watch it move up another dollar.

Did you leave a dollar on the table? No! That is 20/20 hindsight and not good mind food. While we want to let our profits run based on the indicators we follow, we cannot punish ourselves for not selling the tops or buying the bottoms. That is not the essence of trading. Trading is about taking consistent high probability trades often, and moving to the next trade, even if in the same stock. This is not a cause for self-recrimination. It is a time to enjoy a dollar-per-share profit.

Exit on reaction, not price. This rule becomes even more important to traders who trade size. Traders who move 20,000 shares at a time, for example, need more outlets and liquidity to stay nimble. For example, when trading into a trend, I would prefer to trade within the middle 50 to 60 percent range of a move. (See Figure 6.1.) The lower-risk zone exists within this middle range, while providing higher consistency, as opposed to trading the edges of a trend at support and resistance where the risk of reversal is much higher. If I am trading trend reversals, and fading the beginning of the end of a trend, whether up or down, then I want to buy near the support level and sell near the resistance. (See Figure 6.2.) Those that think they must top tick the trade when selling and bottom tick when buying miss the point and are at a distinct disadvantage since they increase their risk dramatically while being "whipsawed" out of trades the most as they realize they cannot pick tops and bottoms.

THE MARKET IS UNFAIR

The basis of this rule, **The market is unfair at times,** requires you to remember that mechanical understanding is somewhat easy; it just takes time to study and practice the theory. Mechanical understanding in the grand scheme of things is in my opinion no more than 10 percent of trading. But the psychology of understanding how to use the indicators to open and close trades as well as developing the discipline to follow such indicators is

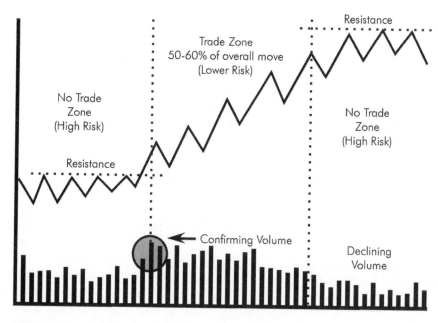

FIGURE 6.1   Trading into a trend

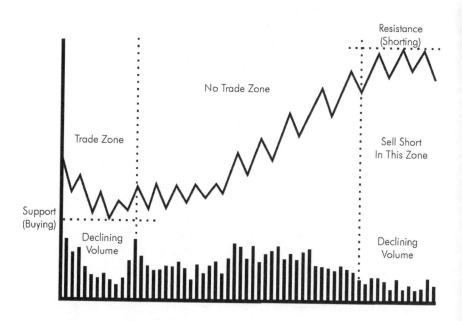

FIGURE 6.2   Trading trend reversals

what really separates professionals from amateurs. The psychology of trading is a journey that continually evolves, and that makes up the other 90 percent. Exiting trades is tougher for most not only because timing is so critical but also because emotions seem to run the highest when exiting a losing trade. Every rationale will enter your mind trying to convince you to stay with the trade on the belief that the stock will come back. Think of that voice in your mind as the little devil on your left shoulder, telling you it will be OK. Doing the right thing may not seem easy at first, but once you form the habit of cutting losses quickly, it becomes quite routine and very gratifying. Taking the devil's advice will prove very damaging very fast, but in time you will not hear from him anymore because you won't be trading! It is very easy for even experienced traders to exit too early on profits and too late on losses. Of the two, early with a small profit is far better that late with a loss. On the other hand, no trader wants to leave good money on the table or get whipsawed. The latter occurs when you enter a trade, and it moves against you. You exit only to watch the stock move in what would have been your way had you not exited the trade. You were head-faked out of a winner.

If you beat yourself up about exiting too early, you set yourself up to exit future trades too late. That is the risk. Worst of all, the world's greatest traders cannot time the market with impunity. So accept this fact of the market and incorporate the right behavior so that when it occurs, it is the exception, not the rule. The market may seem unfair at times, but never lose your statistical advantage by letting that destroy your discipline.

CHANGE YOUR PERSPECTIVE

When swing trading, I will often use that time to study my trade from other perspectives. I will ask myself what I would do if I were in a day trade or even if I were longer-term oriented. I perform this function by studying the charts when other signals are not totally clear to me. I ask myself questions like the following:

- What are the profit takers and contra (shorts) side traders seeing?

- Why would someone take profits or short your stock at this price?

Price charts of the stock being traded from different perspectives provide useful indications that, while they will not give me the clarity I am looking for, will expand my perspective in terms of time horizon. Let's say you are looking at a one-minute intraday chart. What does it look like set at 5-minute intervals? Or what about a weekly view? Or monthly, quarterly, or 200-day charts? Run some technical studies at these different time intervals. Every once in a while, take a look at how other traders see the same market you are trading. From someone else's perspective, you might see different trend lines or major support and resistance levels that explain why they are trading against you. At this point, as always, you evaluate the supply and demand issues but from a longer time perspective. These questions will never be totally answered, but they do present perspectives that will influence your bias, especially when used with other indicators to form an overall opinion. When that bias is against your position and you no longer feel the stock is acting well relative to it, this is a good exit indication. You certainly want to use hard data and indicators to support this bias, but in the end, your feel (soft data) generated by experience and multiple time perspectives will help lead the way. If clarity is still elusive, follow this closing rule: **When in doubt, get out.**

RULES FOR HEDGING RISK

Rules of the Trade

Understand options contracts.

Acquire options experience.

Some market participants traditionally defined as professionals, such as market makers, specialists, institutions, and active traders, have created a paradigm of trading that is narrowly focused on just one financial vehicle. But with the accessibility to the market available today, traders must incorporate a multidimensional approach to provide an opportunity to reduce risk and hedge equity positions while allowing profits to continue to run.

One of the most powerful ancillary and complementary financial vehicles to understand and marry to equity trading is an options contract. While options trading has gained tremendous popularity since the inception of organized and standardized options markets in 1973, many engage this market segment for the wrong reasons and with the wrong strategy. While options can be a great speculation vehicle and they should be incorporated as a strategy in time, hedging risk with options is a more important topic to begin with. This chapter will focus on strategies that will help the electronic swing trader hedge risk through options contracts as a complementary strategy to trading stocks. The rule is simply **Understand options contracts** to hedge risk and produce income. There will not be many rules in this chapter regarding options; instead, I will focus on strategies that will enhance your trading dramatically as you evolve into a more sophisticated trader.

I will not focus on all the mechanics of options basics in this chapter since I assume that you either already have an understanding of options or will acquire it. I recommend two books as resources that provide an excellent opportunity to get started toward this knowledge and reinforce options basics. The first book, *All About Options,* was written by my friend, Thomas McCafferty. The second book I suggest reading is *McMillan on Options,* by Lawrence G. McMillan. Both books are strong introductions to options trading. Although these books are unevenly biased to options trading and cover very little in the way of equities trading, they do a good job explaining both the mechanics of options trading as well as the strategy.

OPTION BASICS

You can buy a call option to gain the opportunity to buy stock at a lower price in the anticipation of its appreciation, or you can buy a put option in the anticipation of the stock's decline. Thus options can be used in an almost unlimited fashion in conjunction with stocks to limit risk while leaving some upside. Whether your strategies are centered on making money from volatility or stability in the market, in all scenarios, options married to equities create synergistic opportunities to make money in virtually all market conditions. Bull markets, bear markets, stable markets, or volatile markets together make up the landscape of our markets today. Therefore, the intellectual assets a modern trader must possess must include options. Certainly, options apply to many financial instruments, not just individual stocks. Options have application in indices such as the S&P 500, the Dow Jones Industrial Average, industry-sectors, and indices such as the Oil Index, the Internet Commerce Index, as well as other optionable securities like financial futures.

Many people have an incorrect perception that futures are the same as options, but they are in fact very different instruments. As a quick side note, *futures* are standardized contracts (like options) that call for the "delivery" of a specific quantity of a commodity on a specific date. *Options* do not create an obligation on both sides of a transaction as is the case with a futures contract—hence, the very large difference between the two vehicles. While much more time could be spent on each vehicle, my focus is to assure you that using options contracts in concert with equities at times makes strong sense. Before discussing a few popular options strategies, let's focus on the market forces that most influence options price. As the name implies, stock options are options that give the option buyer the right (not the obligation as in the case with futures contracts) to exercise. The seller of the option contract is obligated to fulfill the contract by either buying or selling the underlying asset (stock). Therefore, the price of the underlying asset will have a huge impact on the derivative product, called an *option*. Thus, stock prices will most influence option prices. The method used to measure this impact is called *delta*. Delta is the change in options prices due to the change in the price of the stock that the option is based on.

The next largest influence on options is the *strike price*— that is, the price at which an option is exersizable between the option buyer and seller. For example, if you purchase the AMD March 45 calls at $3, your strike price is $45 because this is where you may exercise to buy the stock from the call option seller. You paid the call writer (seller) $3 per share for the right (not the obligation) to buy AMD at $45 by the end of the third week of March. Obviously you anticipate AMD to trade higher than $45 by that time, thereby giving you the right to buy it at $45 when the stock may in fact trade higher than that price at or sometime before the expiration date.

The next two important factors that influence option pricing are volatility (*vega*) and the time left until option expiration (*theta*). Theta and vega are important, since theta erodes premium over time while vega increases premium over time. The rationale is simple: because option contracts have a limited life cycle due to time expiration, they lose time value over time. In terms of vega, volatility inflates premium, because the likelihood that the underlying will have the range to meet the strike price is greater. The combination of these market forces has an impact on the pricing of options, which clear through the Options Clearing Corporation (OCC). Knowing this, we can now discuss how this information can be used to form strategies that can help the trader hedge risk while leaving upside potential.

To establish additional rules for trading, let's use another metaphor: the 80/20 principle. This principle states that 80 percent of the results are produced by 20 percent of the people. The same theory can be applied to the market in that 80 percent of a market's move will tend to occur during 20 percent of the trading day. While this is not meant to be read too literally, the concept does hold merit because price action occurs during limited periods of time since the reaction from the market participants is generally centered on an event. The event can be news, price breakouts and breakdowns, or other criteria that cause a reaction.

Once the news or action in the market becomes known, it tends to cause people to react, hence effecting a change in price directly correlated to the imbalance of supply and demand that occurs due to the reaction leading to the associated price change. If positive news enters the market, demand through buying creates an imbalance that will result in a temporary move in price over a limited period of time, which is why this 80/20 principle also applies to market movement in many situations (though not all). This is why it is so important for traders to react quickly to take advantage of large moves (80 percent) within short periods of time (20 percent).

To further support this theory against actual market activity, let's move back to options to apply this concept and evaluate what the impact on options prices will be while price moves occur during this limited 20 percent time horizon. This theory is well supported by the fact that option premiums often become less expensive prior to larger moves. The stable nature of a stock will tend to depress option premiums (historical volatility) during periods of stabilization and consolidation. The lack of activity depresses option prices as a rule, while volatility tends to increase option premiums (implied volatility). Traders should know what moves prices in both stocks and options and know when to avoid volatility, which will inflate option premiums. These inflated premiums can work well for the option seller, but work against the option buyer.

When news strikes, overreactions often occur resulting in overbought and oversold conditions. The activity that leads to these conditions is volatility, and, as stated, volatility leads to rich pricing in options premiums.

The way in which market volatility benefits a day trader engaged in options trading is the same way that equity traders benefit from volatility. The ability to gain additional advantages as an options day trader through time value and volatility further benefits the sophisticated trader. Amateur call option buyers will often rush in to buy a stake during volatile markets and hence pay a higher price to option sellers. Equity traders who own stock have an opportunity to sell or write option contracts on their underlying assets to the option call buyers who are willing to speculate on the anticipation of price appreciation. Because options offer so much leverage, they seem to attract the least prepared and undercapitalized speculators. This is an advantage to the option seller. As volatility increases, consider selling call options to buyers to receive premium in exchange for granting the right to the buyer to buy stock at what would be a favorable price, called the *strike price*. *In-the-money options* are options with intrinsic value, meaning that the options already have intrinsic value at the time of the transaction. A call option is in the money when the strike price is below current market value of the underlying asset, and a put contract is in the money when the strike is above the current market value. All options have some element of time value prior to expiration. The greater the time, the greater the value. Selling in-the-money options yields higher premium since the option already has intrinsic value if exercised. As a seller of an option, you become an insurance company, or the "house" in the sense that you are being paid premium in exchange for accepting the obligation to sell for calls and the obligation to buy for puts.

THE COVERED CALL

Receiving premium is a form of hedging that can be best explained by an example of what is known as a *covered call* or a *buy-write*. A buy-write is an open long equity position with another leg added to the position where calls are sold against the long position in stock. Buy-writes normally are done when the equity moves in your favor and calls are sold against the position. For example, suppose you purchase 1000 shares of AMD at $50 and the current market value of AMD is trading at $50. The market in AMD has been volatile, and you decide to sell calls on the underlying stock. By selling the AMD 50 calls, you receive $4 premium, bringing $4000 into your account, hence lowering your cost basis from $50 to $46 due to the premium income. By writing the covered call, you have limited the upside because in the event that AMD surges above $50 at expiration, the call buyer will exercise, forcing you to sell your position; but at the same time in this example you have also ensured a $4000 profit, plus any profit on the underlying stock over the cost basis. If AMD remains stable or even retraces in price, you make the $4000 premium and still own the underlying security, enabling you to write the calls again for the next expiration month to further reduce your cost basis in the stock, or hold the stock with no option position, leaving the upside and downside.

The point is that by using an option in conjunction with the equity position, you provide options for yourself that can lower your cost basis. The downside of a covered call occurs when the underlying security drops in price by more than the protection provided through the premium. For example, if AMD drops in price to $40, the trader loses more in market decline than the $4000 premium he or she received even though the call option will not be exercised. The other disadvantage is that when the price accelerates above the strike price, it can cause the option to move "deep in the money" and be exercised by the call buyer, limiting participation in the upside. But even in this scenario, the covered call writer still profits even though the profit is limited from the move. This strategy provides downside protection for the call writer equal to the premium received at the cost of limited upside potential; therefore, this strategy is good for the stable stock or slightly bullish stock. Another variation to this strategy would allow the trader to trade around the underlying stock with options. I call this strategy *trading around a post.*

TRADING (DANCING) AROUND A POST

This strategy is a variation to the covered call, allowing the trader to speculate with less risk by comparison to a pure stock trader. The strategy here is to sell calls against the position (the post) during rallies and to buy back the calls on pullbacks. The act of day trading options around the "post" underlying position, is like "rainmaking" or dancing around the position to continually lower the cost basis in the underlying stock position in this example. This is a particularly good trade when a stock is volatile and the calls are sold when there is time value left in the premium. This is best accomplished by selling calls three to four weeks from expiration. This way, sudden volatility will not immediately cause you to be called out of your position, and second, as the call seller, you enjoy the premium of time and volatility value that the call buyer pays for. The premise with this strategy is to have a bullish bias on a stock you know well based on trading patterns and familiarity you acquire through active trading (specialization). Here is an example:

Suppose in the AMD example cited, you sell the AMD 50 calls at $4, as stated above. You sell the calls during rallies in the stock, which in turn improves the premium (delta). During the day, the stock comes in a bit and retraces $3. Because of this, the calls are selling for $1½; therefore, you buy them back and cover your short position and make $2½. The post is the underlying stock, and by day trading calls around the position, you gain the ability to protect more downside risk while benefiting from volatility. Your biggest risk is limited upside and extreme downside, which you have anyway when owning stock. In fact, because your downside is mitigated to the amount of premium received from selling the calls, trading around a position that is volatile is a good way to day trade while controlling systematic risk and benefiting from the premium. The numbers are working toward your favor as the seller, on the backs of the option buyers. In a sense, options have a unique way of automatically separating dumb money (buyers) from smart money (sellers). The exception to this is the professional trader who understands when buying options (weakness) makes sense.

THE PROTECTIVE PUT

Another strong strategy that supports the rule to understand options strategies is the *protective put.* This scenario is quite popular for the stock trader who believes there is substantial upside potential but at the risk of substantial downside as well. Purchasing a put option in conjunction with an equity position allows the trader to protect downside without limiting upside potential.

The protective put allows the put buyer to "put" stock to the put seller at a predetermined strike price in the event the underlying security falls hard. For example, suppose you suspect strongly that a biotechnology stock will move from phase I testing to phase II testing for a new drug. You realize that if the drug passes to the next phase successfully, the stock will soar and you want to participate in such a dramatic move. At the same time if the drug does not pass testing, the stock will fall hard, and you do not want the exposure. By purchasing the put option at a strike price slightly below the price you bought the stock for, your total downside risk is limited to the difference between the stock price and the strike price of the put option you purchased plus the price you paid to buy the option. If the stock passes testing and runs much higher, your profits are unlimited and are affected only by the price of the premium paid for the put option. This scenario reminds me of buying a new house (compatible to the stock) and buying protection for it like fire insurance. Yes, you pay for the protection, but your downside is substantially eliminated, while the home can still appreciate. The same is true for the protective put.

Many ask, "Why not use a protective stop?" It is a fair question, but a protective stop has its limitations. For example, suppose your stock retraces to the stop level and "stops you out" but then continues much higher. In this scenario, you would be out of the trade and not share in the upside, where the protective put will be exercised only by you if, at or near expiration, your stock is still lower than the strike price. This strategy gives you the time between your option purchase and expiration date to work, which you can predetermine based on the anticipated testing of the drug in question. Here the protective put makes strong sense by comparison to the protective stop.

This strategy works well also with news events that can be anticipated such as earnings events, stock split pay dates, and economic news events that directly impact sectors and stocks within the sectors.

The strategies that can be employed for the "short" side of the market work equally as well. Suppose, for example, you short stock on the belief the stock is overbought. To protect against follow-through where the stock may continue higher, the trader in this scenario would buy a call option in association with the short position. This is the exact opposite of the protective put, and it is called a *protective call*. The trader has the ability to "call in" the stock, forcing the call seller to sell the underlying stock to the call buyer at a strike price that is generally slightly above the price level where the underlying security was shorted.

HEDGE BEFORE SPECULATING IN OPTIONS

As you can see, the options strategies discussed in this chapter have been more associated with hedging risk than speculating. While many opportunities exist for speculation with options contracts, I suggest you speculate with equities and hedge with options due to the time decay that is inherent with option buying. As your sophistication grows, you can speculate with options through option buying or selling or through synthetic options positions, which is the process of combining calls, puts, and stock to create equivalent positions. This is in fact a popular tack for experienced traders who understand complex strategies and who also have an interest in predetermined risk management.

One popular example of a synthetic position used by options traders is the spread, which can take the form of a bullish or bearish outlook. Spreads are created when you are long and short an option of the same type (calls and puts) at the same time on the same underlying security (stock in our example). For example, a bull spread would be a synthetic position that has a bias to the upside and can be achieved using call or puts, where with calls you create what is called a *net debit position,* and with puts you create a *net credit position.* Most bull call spreads that are opened are what are called *vertical spreads* since, stacked together, they match in terms of expiration month, underlying security, type, and size. Refer to Figure 7.1

When using call options, the trader is creating a weighted bias toward buying calls but offsets the cost or premium of the call buying by selling (writing) out-of-the-money calls in conjunction with buying in-the-money calls. To buy an in-the-money call will cost more in premium since an in-the-money call has immediate intrinsic value defined by a strike price below the current market value of the underlying stock. At the

Size	Security	Expiration	Strike	Type	Prem
Buy 10	XYZ	October	50	Calls	$7
Sell 10	XYZ	October	60	Calls	$3

FIGURE 7.1   What the call bull spread would look like

same time, the trader would sell out-of-the-money calls and receive a credit or premium for selling the calls. The calls sold will draw less premium since they are out of the money, but what money they do draw will help offset the cost of the in-the-money calls purchased. This strategy creates a net debit spread because there is a net cost to the overall position by buying calls for more premium than what is received for selling calls. The net effect is a synthetic position that mimics a long position in stock that cost premium to put on the trade for a bullish outlook on the stock. Synthetic positions such as this limit risk by the net debit paid at the cost of also limiting upside as well. Here is an example: Suppose a trader has a bullish outlook on XYZ when XYZ is trading at $55, and he or she decides to buy 10 October 50 (in-the-money) calls at $7. The cost would be $7000 since 1 contract represents 100 shares of XYZ stock, and the trader bought 10 contracts, which represents 1000 shares of XYZ stock at a premium of $7 per share. At the same time and with the same expiration month, the trader wants to reduce his or her cost of the option and is willing to cap his or her upside by selling 10 XYZ October 60 calls (out of the money) at $3, bringing in $3000 premium. The net debit position is $4000 paid to put on this synthetic "call bull spread" ($7000 − $3000 = $4000).

As the P&L graph shows, the maximum gain and loss are limited. The maximum loss is limited to the net debit paid to put the spread on, and the maximum gain is limited to the difference between the strike prices less the net debit paid [($60 − $50) = $10 less $4 = $6 (10 contracts) = $6000].

Obviously the end result is that the trader is buying a right to purchase XYZ stock at the strike price, which is favorable (under the CMV) to your position, while limiting the upside since, if the stock continues higher to the strike price of the call sold, the call buyer will exercise and call you out, forcing you to sell the position that limits any further participation in the upside move. This is best seen on a profit-and-loss graph as shown in Figure 7.2. The point is that options in conjunction with equities and even options by themselves give the electronic trader the ability to hedge risk and maintain control of market conditions that otherwise would be outside his or her control. The most common use of spreads that I see and implement in my own trading style is for trading size. I like spreads that create a

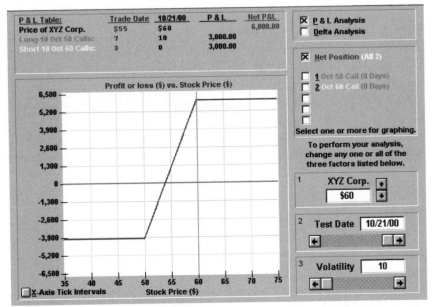

FIGURE 7.2 This profit-and-loss graph was created with tools provided by the "Options Tool Box" available free at www.cboe.com. This is an excellent tool that I highly recommend using.

good risk-reward ratio where I can risk perhaps $1 to have an opportunity to make $4. If in this scenario I could have a net debit on a bull call spread of $1, I can afford to trade much larger size such as 500 contracts. In this scenario, I spend $50,000 to make the trade and have an opportunity to make $200,000. If I am bullish on a stock, this is an example of a trade I would make using a spread. Of course, many different spread scenarios exist for going long and short as well.

There are many other scenarios and positions that can be built to complement the electronic trader. There are six synthetic positions that can be created to simulate positions using the actual underlying security (assuming stock):

1. Synthetic long stock = long call/short put
2. Synthetic short stock = short call/long put
3. Synthetic long call = long stock/long put
4. Synthetic short call = short stock/short put

5. Synthetic long put = long call/short stock
6. Synthetic short put = short call/long stock

THE ZERO-SUM GAME

By understanding how these scenarios interrelate to each other, you gain creative ideas about how one can hedge or speculate using options. The number of scenarios is almost infinite, but by grasping a solid understanding of options and how to apply the knowledge to equity trading, you will gain additional control that most amateur traders will never work toward. With the incredible increase in online trading, the market is poised for growth with plenty of amateur money to take advantage of. Although that may seem a bit aggressive, it is reality.

I won't say the stock market is a zero-sum game because stocks in fact create and add value to the market and investors. One person's gain is not another's loss with equities, as is the case with derivative products like options and futures. But the shorter the time horizon in equity trading such as day trading, the closer one gets to a zero-sum game. The same argument can be made with the laws of supply and demand. The more active one trades, the more your focus on this law must be, looking for rapidly changing releases of the forces of supply and demand. Therefore, the moral of this story is to recognize that as you trade equities more actively and combine derivative positions with equity trading, the more you must poise yourself to compete with the market as if it were a zero-sum game. The more dumb money in the market, the more opportunity for the professional, educated trader.

I included this chapter on options with the purpose of exposing you to options, not to teach you all aspects of options trading. That is why my rule **Acquire options experience** is so important. The only way to truly understand options and stock is to trade them. The first step is to gain a solid foundation of knowledge; once that is achieved, you will start to find what strategies appeal to you the most. Not all concepts will. For example, I do very few spreads since I do not like to limit my upside, which is what spreads do. When I do trade spreads, it is again with size. I am a more aggressive trader than most should be as beginners. As traders find experience and success, many of them grow in aggressiveness at times in their journey of trading, and some do not. The point is that you need to find your own propensity for trading through as much exposure to the markets as possible with the most flexibility. Options add opportunities through true synergistic growth potential. By adding options trading to your equity trading, the opportunities exceed the sum of the parts. Equities plus options equates to an almost infinite number of scenarios that can be adapted to your risk spectrum. With this knowledge, there is no need to trade outside your own personal parameters. There is no need to take a stock tip, no need to assume, no need to gamble. Certainly there will always be a degree of speculation when trading financial instruments—without it there would be no opportunity for substantial gain—but adding options continues to put the statistical advantage on your side as opposed to giving up your edge to the unforgiving market that will eat you alive given the chance.

I truly believe that anyone with the ability to learn and apply these concepts can capture this statistical advantage and consistently beat the S&P 500. The S&P 500 has long been the benchmark barometer for mutual funds and private money managers. And statistics have shown that close to 80 percent of fund managers do not in fact beat the S&P 500. Sound familiar? The 80/20 principle at work again? I think so. So what separates the two groups? How do you become a 20 percenter? How about a 10 percenter or even a 1 percenter? Not only do you obtain the knowledge, but you combine that knowledge (through hard work, continuing education, research, reading, and adaptability—all driven by your passion) with execution. Like a good business plan, without equally good execution of the business plan, they are just interesting ideas. Traders need to execute learned strategies through trading to gain the intangible attributes that are also required. Those attributes include feel, intuition, and confidence (along with some healthy fear) to complete the circle of awareness that well-rounded traders have. When the maturation of these qualities occur, I have confidence that you can beat the S&P 500 handsomely. No book like this or any other can provide you with the intangible skills you require. Going into battle with a solid understanding of what it will take to defeat your opponent (the market), combined with the right conditioning through hard work, will always put you in a position to score. Enter with anything less, and you may be forced to cheat. In this business, the only person you cheat is you, so ignore the shortcuts, tips, IPOs, and other seemingly sexy fast cash, and hunker down, do the work, employ what you learn, expect minor failures, and ultimately you will win.

RULES FOR THE TECHNICIAN

Know the range within the time horizon you are trading.

Day trade the ranges and swing trade the trends.

Always use indicators to confirm charts and patterns.

Never replace instincts with technical analysis.

Never ignore volume regardless of your trading style.

Don't make it rocket science, 'cause it ain't.

Stay grounded.

Technicians of the market are a unique group. They form opinions based on a common belief system called *technical analysis,* which is a way of looking at the market through chart formations and mathematical formulas designed to find and uncover patterns that have a high likelihood of either repeating or changing. The theory stems from the belief that all factors in the market are built into the psychological patterns in which market participants (professionals and nonprofessionals) trade stock. Market events, such as earnings, R&D developments, and sector rotation, cause people to react. These reactions are manifested in the way people buy and sell securities to reflect their up-to-the-minute perception of the market and stocks. Because of this perception, the purest technicians are not at all concerned with market-moving news because the impact of such news will play itself out in the bid, offers, and prices of securities, which can and will be reflected on charts. These charts, therefore, are the foundation of all technical trading. Charts allow the technician to read the psychological behavior of the market as a whole, often referred to as *market psychology* or *sentiment,* as well as individual views.

Because so many people have an opinion of the market and stocks, and most times those opinions are unfounded and with little merit (hence the reason to run from stock tips), technicians are not interested in these opinions. This explains why news and media attention are of little value to them. Technicians pay attention only to the opinions of market participants that act on how they feel about the market or stocks in terms of how, what, and when they trade. Therefore, do not confuse market sentiment as read through the media as the sentiment technicians track through the charts.

The value of patterns and charts goes far beyond the literal meaning of what they are designed to reveal. It is important to understand these patterns, but it is even more important to know when to rely on them. This is perhaps the greatest question to ask: When do you rely on chart patterns? I would encourage you never to completely rely on them! Technicians like to believe that each trade or series of trades with a time stamp (1 minute, 5 minutes, and so on) is a battle between the bulls and bears of the market, and the winning side moves the stock price in its direction. While this is true at an elementary level, the focus must go deeper, using the tools of real-time data. The application of these tools in concert with charts is where true utility is found, and this will be the focus of this chapter. Let's begin with ranges that reveal themselves in the market every day.

TECHNICAL RANGES

Perhaps the most popular chart formations among market participants are channels. My rule is **Know the range within the time horizon you are trading.** Trading ranges are established by repeatable patterns of support and resistance (for a more detailed understanding, refer to Appendix C for a list of books to read). Support and resistance are the most followed technical indicators among amateurs. Because of this fact, these levels can create self-fulfilling prophecies as participants rush in to buy at support and sell at resistance. By knowing these perceived levels, I like to day trade at these price points. I day trade them because imbedded in them are the ingredients that I need to formulate a day trade. First, there is generally good liquidity due to the perceived levels, and second, when reactions do occur, the trends, although often short-lived, are often more easily recognized. The third reason I trade support and resistance is that professional bias can also be more readily seen. Because professionals also know what I just stated, they think of these opportunities the way fishermen think of a hot new fishing hole. Expect them to come and drop a line.

By anticipating increased market activity at support and resistance levels, the day trader must stand ready to go long and short, since it is at these points that price capitulation is at its peak. When these support and resistance levels change, I perceive that to be a turning point and a good indication of a new trend line. For example, when a support level is breached, it is called a *breakdown*. This indicates a propensity for stocks to decline. Conversely, when resistance becomes support, it indicates a breakout and a propensity for stocks to go higher. As these new levels form, many amateurs are caught on the wrong side, buying at support when they should be shorting and shorting at resistance when they should be buying. The fact that new levels are being formed is a good indication that the professionals are taking the stock higher or lower at these levels. Keep in mind that *professionals* here are defined as the participants with knowledge, experience, and the capital to move these stocks. They do not only represent market makers and specialists. As these new trends form, they create a good opportunity to find liquidity to not only open trades but also to open them at favorable prices. For example, if at resistance a stock is breaking higher or at least showing signs as such, many amateurs are selling, not buying. This gives you an opportunity to buy stock from sellers who perceive weakness, not strength. Therefore, it is easy to bid stock at lower prices and still attract sellers. The opposite is true when support is broken, forming a new resistance level where many perceive strength and will buy while professionals are selling or shorting. Once again, more favorable prices can be acquired from a day trading perspective due to the liquidity provided from the amateur crowd.

In the preceding discussion, I do not mean to suggest that perfect bottoms and tops will be traded. Good traders have indicators that support the idea as mentioned earlier in this chapter and the conviction to give the trade a chance to work by accepting some heat as the amateur crowd dissipates. Once buyers begin to diminish, selling pressure will take over, pushing stocks lower during breakdowns or down trends. When selling pressure diminishes, buying will take control, driving stocks to rally as new support levels are formed on up trends. Trading support and resistance levels will leave clues where these levels are being formed. By paying close attention to liquidity issues such as when stocks get thick and thin, stocks that get thick relative to where they were (thinner) become less volatile and highlight where support or resistance may be building. Just remember, when support levels don't hold, there is a greater propensity for stocks to trade lower, changing the prior support level to resistance. This would indicate an impending down trend. When resistance levels do not hold, this would indicate a stronger propensity for rallies, causing the prior resistance to form a new higher support level, hence an up trend. Learning to pay attention to the ranges within which a stock trades allows you to either trade with the range by selling at resistance and buying support or to recognize a change in the pattern and use other indicators to trust a new trend line being established. Either way, the best way to trade ranges is to know the stock's habits and characteristics, and that comes only through close observation. This argument supports the wisdom of becoming a specialist in a few stocks and getting to know them intimately through real-time tools like Level II and the tape, as opposed to surfing the market, trading everything that makes the news.

A simple rule to remember and practice and one that I subscribe to is **Day trade the ranges and swing trade the trends.** This is a good rule because when stocks break ranges, they form trends, which tend to create new ranges that last for longer periods of time. Trading ranges tends to be more honest in the sense that it statistically pays you to trust resistance and support within trading ranges and therefore to day trade the range over the time horizon you select, assuming it is intra-day. But once a stock breaks the range and sets out on a new trend, it pays to have more risk tolerance with these trades and ride the wave. The offsetting practice of lowering share size when trend trading for longer time horizons is very important.

Because charts and patterns are the foundation to so many traders' strategy to the market, another rule that must be adopted if technical analysis is to be utilized is **Always use indicators to confirm charts and patterns.** An indicator is a mathematically driven tool that adds much more objectivity to a chart formation. Charts use pictures of the past to attempt to predict the future. While charts have merit, they represent only one leg of the stool. To use them alone without confirming indicators could make for an uncomfortable throne. Too many self-proclaimed gurus like to rely on the complexities of chart-reading, because they are literal and can fill page after page in explanation. The problem is that this level of focus on chart-reading draws too much attention to looking for explicable market activity at the expense of instincts that can only be developed by trading. That said, many indicators exist that you can employ to complement a technical approach. Moving averages are one such indicator that most all technicians agree must be utilized while trading. Some would say moving averages are lagging indications of price movement and, therefore, not very helpful; others see it differently. A moving average (simple) measures average prices or volume over certain time horizons. In that sense, it is lagging, but when stocks trade above their moving average, there must be a reason for them to do so. Good stocks trade higher with good reason and poor stocks trade lower for good reason, and it is called, once again, supply and demand. When a stock begins to break above its moving average, it definitely feeds me more positive sentiment than negative. I then look for other subscriptions to confirm my bias, such as a Level II where I can see who is buying and selling. I will then follow the ax and see if that market maker or specialist tips his or her hand to me to help me further confirm my bias or refute it. Many traditional technicians would argue that when using a moving average, it is best to buy at or near the moving average price, but I completely disagree, especially in regard to technology stocks that are often trending. When tech stocks rally and trade above their moving average, I like to look at three to four periods of time to measure it against, but, in the end, I tend to trust trades more that are above a moving average as opposed to trades that are at or below. Moving averages come in many forms, and when they are combined, they can form good trend following indicators.

I would suggest paying attention to the simple and exponential moving averages in particular. They are the most followed moving averages, and in the momentum-driven market that we are in, I believe they are the most predictive. While many other averages are more complex, remember the principle that supports TA. The psychological patterns of those who subscribe to this belief are fairly predictable. Some traders will fade these patterns on the belief that the masses will rush in at key levels as identified on the charts, and others will trade with the pattern. I have come to the belief that day trading the patterns on a short-term basis makes sense, as long as risk is mitigated by not staying in trades too long. I like to fade these same patterns from a swing trade perspective as the pattern becomes more known, on the belief that the pattern will lead to saturation points of the trend, which will lead to reversal. The simple and exponential moving averages are in my opinion the best "timing" indicators to use. Always know that the shorter term the moving average is measuring, the more sensitive—hence why day traders trade directly with the trends that moving averages reveal and why swing traders look for reversal patterns as moving averages begin to show signs of strength or weakness. The exponential moving average gains more value over time, since this MA automatically becomes more "smoothed" over time due to its less-sensitive nature, as well as the way it is calculated. Exponential moving averages are weighted moving averages, but they are based on a series of simple moving averages. A good approach to understanding these indicators is to first understand the mathematics behind them. Suggested reading for this would include the *Technical Analysis of Stock Trends* by Robert D. Edwards and John Magee. Originally published in 1948, I believe this book is still one of the most complete explanations of technical analysis.

Other popular tools used by technicians would include oscillators, which are mathematical methods that measure momentum and rate of change. When measuring rate of change, oscillators are your best bet from a technical perspective. The theory is that as market participants react to news and events, they act on emotional impulses that can cause a rapid change in market condition in a given stock. As the saying goes, "haste makes waste," and that is my feeling on violent reactive moves caused by hype and overreaction that are often associated with news. Although this indicator is a very valuable tool to supplement your trading style, I would suggest avoiding it as a single decision support tool since on its own it tends to be a short-lived indicator.

The most popular and well-followed oscillator would be the *moving average convergence divergence* (MACD). MACD is composed of three moving averages (exponential), which are shown on a horizontal chart indicating where equilibrium exists for the moving averages. Simply put, when the moving average is at equilibrium, the indication is muted and of little or no value. When the indication is below the equilibrium line, the signal is bearish, and when above, bullish. The theory is simple. As a shorter-term exponential moving average (EMA) is in control, hence pulling up the average, the indication shows that short-term strength is pulling up the average and is, therefore, a good indication of short-term upside bias. If the short-term EMA is lagging behind the longer-term EMA, it is pulling the average down, and therefore it is bearish. I prefer to read the tape and Level II to look for price levels and patterns that support the indication, as opposed to using oscillators as the sole reason for making a trade. Additionally, I feel the best way to measure market strength on a short-term basis is to put some bait in the water in the way of trading. You can tell from the way in which your orders are executed how passionate the contra is that is buying from you when you are selling and vice versa. As a day trader, I feel that this is a better indication of the strength or weakness of a stock when measured from a very short-term perspective.

A final word on indicators like moving averages and oscillators: Always remember, in the final analysis, stocks either move up or down based on supply and demand imbalances. Therefore, when a trading range compresses between support and resistance, it indicates a thickening stock in terms of liquidity, as well as stability in stock prices and its moving average. In the most simple form, this just means that buyers and sellers are getting evenly matched with no real dominant force. As these various signs all show "compression," it is good to think of these indicators as springs. As these springs compress, pressure builds, and when this pressure is released by the emergence of a dominant force (supply/demand), it tends to release with great force represented as large relative movement in stock prices. Therefore, it is the compression points where opportunity and risk are greatest.

HARD AND SOFT DATA

While many other confirming indicators exist, one cannot forget that feel, intuition, and the pulse of a stock cannot be ignored. Technicians rely heavily on "hard data" to formulate ideas, but as I stated throughout the book thus far, "soft data" play an even more important part as mechanical understanding grows. The best traders I know all seem to settle on this point, which I believe is a rule: **Never replace instincts with technical analysis.** The hard lesson to learn here is that instincts cannot be taught. Just as in sports, you've got to "get in there," as a fellow trader I know likes to say. And he is 100 percent right. Now when taking the other side of this argument, hard data like Japanese candlesticks seem to reveal all kinds of clues. For instance, the body of the candle indicates the open and close of a stock within a given period, while the color of the body tells if the stock was up or down within the measured period in terms of the opening and closing price. Then come the "wicks" on the candle, representing the high and low of the stock within the measured period. This all seems fascinating, and the lessons could go on and on, but the point to be made here is that just because stock price activity can be graphically illustrated does not mean it can have predictive powers on its own. The feel one develops while trading and monitoring a stock as it opens and closes within a time period or makes highs and lows within that period cannot be substituted by any technical tool. The psychology behind this information is what really matters, and that is why traders still pay for a seat on major exchanges. They witness reaction, psychology, body language, momentum, and the like on the floor reading more about the supply and demand equation than what an object on a computer screen can tell them alone like candlesticks. While I am not minimizing the value of tools like candlesticks, I am making the point that they are still minor contributors in comparison to the instincts you will develop by mastering trade entry and exit strategies when used in conjunction with the tape, Level II, sector/indicie strength (weakness), and overall market trend within in a given day. To sum up this point, I don't think you or I will predict tomorrow's market movers, but I know we can give ourselves a statistical advantage by reading today's momentum stocks through the eyes of experience, monitoring the indications stated. Therefore, never replace instincts with technical analysis.

To illustrate this rule, I can't help thinking of a trade I made based on a phone call from my partner, Jack. Jack is not a day trader, although he has been in the market for many years. He called me one day and said, "Did you see BGEN sell off today?" I replied, "Yeah, it seemed pretty severe." Jack said with a certain tone in his voice, "It was!" I know Jack has traded and held BGEN for many years as well as other biotechs, and he knows the biotech sector very well. I felt through my own intuition about the way Jack expressed himself about the selloff that he felt the stock was oversold. Although he never gave me a tip, nor would I have accepted one, I read through his voice his strong sentiment for the stock to the long side (that provided the soft data to look closer). The next logical thing to do was to pull up a few charts with varying time perspectives and compare the chart formations along with some important simple moving averages that I still subscribe to. After the charts suggested there was good support for the stock, I then watched BGEN trade during the open the next day on Level II and noticed that CS First Boston (FBCO) had a strong appetite for the stock by buying heavily on the bid and selling in a very shallow way when on the offer. Finally, the biotech index as well as the NASDAQ composite and futures seemed to be coming off a support level as well, and since I knew that BGEN was part of the NASDAQ 100 and a strong leader in the biotech sector, I bought the stock aggressively. I knew the stock was well correlated to the indices I just mentioned, and there were several strong indications to buy BGEN. These indications formed an alignment where all indicators (objective and subjective feel) showed me a low-risk–high-probability trade. Over the course of that day, I bought BGEN on every pullback. The stock was up for the day over 6½, and I had three or four opportunities to buy it as it came in a bit on light volume at "higher lows" for the day. I held a position going into the close, and I covered ⅔ of my position near the close. I carried the remaining shares overnight because I liked the way the stock was acting. The next day BGEN gapped to the upside, and I sold in the premarket to close the position. This trade illustrates how soft data and feel can lead to trading ideas, but why it is also important to balance the idea with technical analysis and other tools that exist today (hard data) to formulate an overall opinion. Many traders today subscribe to just one discipline and theory of how to trade, but that methodology is much too narrowly focused and one dimensional for an experienced profitable trader. In this sense, like most endeavors, trading is not completely black and white. It takes the maturation of ideas, technical objective data, feel, discipline, and the ability to act to complete the list of attributes a trader needs.

VOLUME

The final indicator I will cover is the best in my opinion: volume. Volume measures market participation, sentiment, momentum, and the passion of bulls and bears.Therefore, volume is thought of as a lagging indicator, but for active trading, volume is also the best indication of impending market activity as well. Volume is an indication of what is happening and what is about to happen, and therefore a critical rule: **Never ignore volume regardless of your trading style.**

So many traders seem to be looking for the magic that will lead them to success in the market—that elusive crutch to lean on to support the weak legs of confidence that many new participants have. Technical indicators, because they are tangible, seem to receive disproportionate praise and are given more value than they deserve, causing participants to ignore the obvious signs of market activity, such as volume.

Day traders like to read volume right off the Level II and the Time & Sales screens. Perhaps this sounds too simple to be an effective market analysis tool, but when the activity on these tools is fast and furious, volume is increasing and indicating activity. Once that is known, all that is left to determine is the directional bias of the issue being traded. It is that simple. The other technical tools that are invented and implemented are often made overly complicated with the belief that the more complicated the formula is, the more value it has. I have studied and traded using most of these indicators, and I have made the mistake of having an overweighed bias toward these indicators. In the end I have come away with the belief that making the market more complicated than it needs to be is a mistake. Therefore, I will highlight a few volume indicators that I believe offer the best balance of level-headed practicality and technical analysis that leads to impending price change. I have formed these opinions based on actual trading experience, putting capital at risk in the market based on the reliance of these tools and techniques, and I have come to this opinion that is also a critical rule: **Don't make it rocket science, 'cause it ain't.** Keep a level head, and never ignore good old-fashioned common sense. Metaphorically speaking, when signs of precipitation are present, you don't need Doppler radar or a "sling sychrometer" to know it. After all, what do you think traders on the floor are keying in on? Why are they there? The answers and the solutions to these questions are all related to volume. Traders key in on, monitor, and participate on the floor activity to recognize imbalances in supply and demand to speculate on the directional bias of the market. The act of monitoring what traders buy and sell in real time on the floor is how they read volume. You don't see many floor traders walking around with a laptop computer running complicated mathematical models to know that others are trading actively in a given issue or security. Although technology has made its way to the floor, most of what that technology is used for is to receive and execute orders, not to make trading decisions or read direction. That said, let's focus on a few technical indicators that can mimic the psychology of the market that floor traders read through human interaction.

High-Volume Pullbacks

When volume is strong during a pullback relative to a given measured time horizon, what you are seeing is actually the action of sellers in comparison to buyers. Sellers in this scenario are simply more motivated to sell, whether opening shorts or liquidating longs, than buyers are motivated to buy, whether opening longs or covering shorts. This is simply a supply side imbalance over demand measured through increasing volume. Many technical tools exist to measure these increases in volume, such as accumulation/distribution (A/D) and moving average on volume. Both are available on EDAT systems and are easy to use, but again, it is not within the scope of this book to teach the mechanical application of these studies. However, I can highlight what it is that you are reading through the study and explain what to follow and what to dismiss. The moral here is to pay attention to high-volume pullbacks and expect the pullback to initially follow through. To open a long position during this scenario is a high-risk–low-probability trade and a mistake. Instead, waiting for selling pressure to subside with lighter volume would be the intelligent decision before even considering going long.

High-Volume Rallies

The same logic stated above holds an inverse relationship in terms of price movement with this scenario. Buyers are more motivated to own stock and securities than sellers are motivated to sell. This indication suggests that the rally is likely to continue and offers a good risk-reward scenario for long trades. Think of this as a breakout over a previous resistance level. Conversely, if volume shows no clear increase within the time horizon being measured, the likely result is that the stock being measured will not break out and instead will return within the accumulation range. Therefore, in the absence of breakout volume at resistance levels, a short play is statistically stronger. I define breakout volume when average volume is 15 percent greater than the previous average within the time frame it is measured against. Without breakout volume, I have a greater bias that the rally will stall and return to the trading range prior to the rally. If the volume is truly stronger, I have a greater bias toward a breakout and expect the rally to follow through. I use 15 percent based on my own experience. I know that many old-school technicians would look for a higher percentage, but in today's new economy, the beta on stocks in the technology sector is much higher. Beta measures the sensitivity of a stock in terms of its propensity to move in either direction, by comparison to the overall market. For example, if a stock had a high beta such as 1.8, that would suggest that the stock would change bullish or bearish with little prompting, whether that prompting were economic news, industry news, or especially stock-specific news. Technology stocks generally have much higher betas than traditional thick large cap stocks. These sensitive stocks have a "hair trigger"; just breathe on the trigger (volume) and it "fires," and the prices change in response. The 15 percent increase in volume is a very sensitive trigger and therefore indicates an impending price change. Thick large cap stocks need to trade very heavy volume at each price level before they move. Volume increases have varying effects on stocks depending on the nature of the issue; therefore, do not try to apply a literal percentage increase in volume to all stocks.

Low-Volume Pullbacks

By now, you should be able to anticipate where this scenario leads. When a stock "comes in" or pulls back on lighter volume, generally it has begun to find support. Stocks will often come in a bit after a strong rally on high volume and take a small breather before restarting an up trend. This breather is the low-volume pullback and is considered a buying opportunity. Refer to Figure 8.1. As you can see, buying pullbacks along an up-trending line is a good strategy for day traders and swing traders alike. Remember that the trend line is relative to the time horizon being measured. The success percentages change from stock to stock, but buying low-volume pullbacks is a high-percentage trade. Always remember, these concepts are guidelines, not literal interpretations. Traders who trade literally without confirmation through indicators are making costly mistakes.

Low-Volume Rallies

You may be aware of the technical analysis concept of waiting for the pullback before opening a trade that is breaking out or down based on technical chart formations. The concept is supported because when shorting stock during a low-volume rally, the idea is to wait for a stock to break down through support and then to wait for the issue to reverse temporarily on a low-volume rally. This creates a resistance level where support used to be

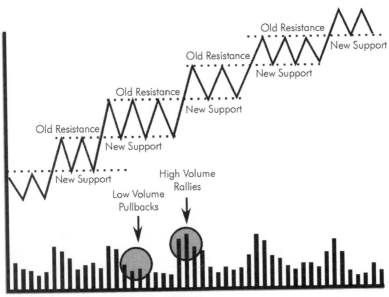

FIGURE 8.1   Low-volume pullbacks

(remember how support became resistance during breakdowns). This resistance level is formed above your short entry point because most traders believe that you should not short the first rally or pull back after a breakdown because you want to test if in fact the price level below the support is in fact a real breakdown. Waiting for a low-volume stock to rally after the perceived breakdown makes sense to confirm a new resistance level is put in place above where you will short the stock. This means you will not sell the perfect top of the breakdown; but the gain to be had by waiting and confirming that the breakdown is real far outweighs the few price ticks above where the first short would have been opened, assuming the breakdown is real. After the first rally following a stock trading below support, you want to look for the next lower-volume rally, indicating that there is no real passion of buyers. This second rally is a great signal to open a short position or exit a long. Waiting for confirmation that a true breakdown is present limits risk dramatically.

Relative Volume

The final word on volume is that what you measure volume against is what creates a relative indication of increasing and decreasing levels. I think of this relational value the way an arbitrageur will look at the futures market in comparison to the equities market. It is not only where the price levels are that impacts the futures and equities market but also where they have come from. If the S&P 500 futures contract is down −13 at midday but coming off of its lows for the day, the relative indication can show strength as opposed to the obvious weakness as read one dimensionally from the net change.

Volume should be read very much in the same way. How strong or weak is volume relative to where the stock you are trading has been within the time horizon being measured? Consider earnings, for example. While events like earnings usually bring increased activity to an issue, that increase does not mean that volume will help you pick the overall trend of that security. This is an example of how temporary increased volume can send a false signal, jading the more important volume averages that have been created over longer periods of time. For this reason, I choose to rely on technical indicators for measuring volume (and price action for that matter) over longer, broader-based time frames rather than shorter-term time frames such as day trading. The reliability of technical information is much greater with a broader perspective. Conversely, while day trading, I read volume through the tape and where volume is relative for the day. For example, if CMGI has traded 8 million shares after three hours into the session and the volume is low compared to its average volume for the last five days (assuming the absence of news), I factor this in and don't need technical indicators to know that. On the other hand, if I am studying stock trends over longer periods, such as weeks, I will rely more on technical tools like charts, moving averages, and A/D.

So much more can be said about technical analysis; in fact, this field of study is almost endless. I believe the rules stated in this chapter should give you a fair perspective on how to use technical analysis with the right balance of other tools. Therefore, my final rule on the subject is **Stay grounded.** Multidimensional trading requires a field of view that allows for other possibilities and tools that will help confirm and defeat ideas you have. Trading with a narrow focus of any one style is not advised, and the best traders I have ever met have a multidimensional approach. The funny thing is that most don't think of themselves that way. They do what they do subconsciously based on years of experience. In that sense, many great traders have become competent by doing the right things without too much analysis. In that sense, I believe "ignorance is bliss," and being consciously competent is unnecessary. Results are what matter, and when you can let the market tell you what to do as opposed to your inflicting your beliefs and attitudes onto the market, your trading will take on a new level of positive performance. The caution I use is similar to the advice I gave my son Zachary when he received his first toy hammer. Don't be so anxious to use your new toy that everything in the house begins to look like a nail! Take that same perspective while gaining technical skills as a trader. Don't be so anxious to make a trade based on some chart formation or indicator you learned about, that every chart starts to show you patterns that you are anxious to find. The market will show you the way if you maintain an objective, logical, and commonsense view of it. If you cross the line that many technicians do where they see the market as some mystical aberration of nature, you need to put away your spyglass and reevaluate. The best way I have found to snap yourself back into reality is to take a good look at your trading activity and P&L. Most who find themselves in this place trade far less than they should and have many more opinions of the market than results. To me, that is the telltale sign of the unbalanced market technician.

RULES FOR EVALUATING PERFORMANCE

Know thyself.

Inspect what you expect.

Update and review weekly.

Don't lie to your spouse or significant other.

Unfortunately, for most, by the time a trader realizes that it is important to evaluate results, he or she is generally in a state of confusion or dismay. In most cases, the challenges that trading produces yield a confused outlook since this is the very reason that the trader is evaluating performance in the first place. When traders are making money, most will not take steps to evaluate how the results were achieved. As I stated in Chapter 2, they are in the unconscious competent stage of development. Unfortunately, this stage is most often temporary, and in order to progress to a stage where continuous growth is possible, the trader must learn how results are achieved. This can only be learned through two things: trading and evaluation of personal trading patterns. The evaluation process I am referring to is not as much about profit and loss as it is about the psychological evaluations that all traders need to go through to move forward. Think of this step as a checkpoint on the journey of trading. Most traders do not want to stop at this checkpoint, but those who do because they realize the importance of it are already much further ahead than those who do not.

We have all known people who have experienced early success at something, only to gain a cocky attitude in the process. Ultimately, that type of overconfidence can lead to very unpleasant results. The rules I cover in this chapter are geared toward the other group of people, those who believe these checkpoints are necessary—those who have learned to check their egos at the door before entering the trading arena—that is, those who believe that continuing education is imperative and can admit without hesitation, "I don't know something." These are the attributes of winners in this game of speculation, and, I would argue, most everything else in life as well.

The self-evaluation stage is generally reached at the most critical stage of one's trading career. While trade evaluation should begin immediately, self-discovery of this critical process is usually manifested through dismay. It is a stage where questions like the following will be raised:

- "Is trading really for me?"
- "Is profitable day trading possible?"
- "How much longer can I survive?"

This is the self-doubt stage, the very point when most will quit. Some, when they reach this point, will place blame on impersonal factors such as high commissions, bad technology, or poor market conditions. This is the stage that every trader must pass through. In Chapter 1, I spoke extensively about the need of a trader for a mentor, that is, a trusted advisor who can encourage and teach at the time of greatest need. The time when one is faced with the process of evaluation is that time.

While you should be evaluating your performance on a daily basis through your journal cited in Chapter 1, taking a broader view of your trading patterns will reveal other characteristics of your trading style that cannot be seen on a microscopic, day-to-day basis. A broader review will convey psychological patterns in trading that can reveal how well one handles emotional issues. While emotions are not friends to traders, they are not going to be completely eliminated, especially when traders are just beginning. How one deals with loss, failure, and success are areas that should be explored. Going through a process that helps address emotions is certainly not baseline mechanical education that most will employ when beginning to trade, but for those that take this aspect of trading also very seriously, the benefit is easily seen. As a form of baseline evaluation for novice and experienced traders alike, the quiz that follows is a great beginning toward the first rule of trade analysis: **Know thyself.**

THE TRADERS' QUIZ

A strong start with or without a mentor or trading coach is to ask yourself some questions that relate to your personality. Although this self-evaluation does not extend to trading results, it does begin to reveal whether you have the attributes and mental control to trade in the first place. Being proactive and responsible by performing such an evaluation before engaging the market says something about you already—that you have some of the qualities I believe you need for consistent profitable trading.

As a day trader, your job is to take money from others who will not only strenuously resist your best efforts but will likely be better funded and more experienced and will have the same motives you have, to take money from you. When your hard-earned capital is at risk, emotions like fear, anxiety, stress, and apprehension can run wild. The way you handle risk, emotions, and the inevitable losses you will incur is as much about trading as the stocks you trade. Your electronic equipment and financial resources are a given and probably on a par with that of most other day traders. What will set you apart is your psychological makeup—that is, your self-confidence, your ability to exercise grace and cool thinking under fire, the way you deal with setbacks, and the steadfastness of your determination to make day trading work for you. Some of us will even need to learn how to keep from snatching failure from the jaws of success and to accept, without self-sabotage, the financial rewards that can be won in this arena.

The stock market is a picture of human emotion and crowd mentality in action. You have seen a stock fluctuate wildly over an hour or two or longer. These fluctuations have little to do with the underlying value of the stock. Rather, they are reflections of how market participants see the stock through the twin lenses of fear and greed. Emotions and psychology are important components in the market. Your ability to read and deal with emotional factors, yours and those of other market participants, will determine your success or failure in trading.

The following questionnaire is an invitation to examine your emotional assets, as well as potential risk factors, in order to optimize your chances of success before putting your capital at risk.

Please read the following statements. None of them has a right or wrong connotation. They either apply to you or they don't. Try not to spend too much time in thinking about the "right" answer, but rather, let yourself have the response that occurs to you spontaneously. Then enter the appropriate number into each box in accordance with the following point scale:

Section A

Never   = 4
Rarely   = 3
Sometimes = 2
Often   = 1
Always   = 0

1. (   ) If my plans go wrong, I stay angry with myself for quite a while.
2. (   ) I tend to worry a lot about money.
3. (   ) I know that having a lot of money will finally make me happy.
4. (   ) I need people around me to be able to work effectively.
5. (   ) I find it difficult to work in disorganized situations.
6. (   ) When things suddenly don't go according to plan, I lose my concentration.
7. (   ) Little things tend to upset me.
8. (   ) I tend to be critical of myself.
9. (   ) I have a tendency to second-guess myself.
10. (   ) I trust luck more than skill.
11. (   ) I tend to gamble and take big risks, and I cannot control this habit.
12. (   ) I tend to use drugs and/or alcohol to make myself feel good.
13. (   ) I have major financial problems.
14. (   ) I feel dissatisfied with myself and my life.
15. (   ) I often feel overwhelmed by problems.
16. (   ) In trading, I will be pleased only with above-average profits.
17. (   ) I need the money I will make in trading to solve several major life problems.
18. (   ) I buy lottery tickets all the time.

19. ( ) When I make an error in judgment, others will look down on me.
20. ( ) I like having things my own way.
21. ( ) I don't like rules and prefer to do things my own way.
22. ( ) I want to do things perfectly the first time and get angry at myself when I cannot.
23. ( ) I blame the market when my trades do not go well.
24. ( ) I get carried away by the feelings of the moment.
25. ( ) I take failure very personally and tend to think about it for a long time afterward.
26. ( ) I have had a problematic relationship with money.
27. ( ) I don't like making decisions until I feel totally sure that I am right.
    ( ) TOTAL

Section B

Point Scale:
Always   = 4
Often   = 3
Sometimes = 2
Rarely   = 1
Never   = 0

1. ( ) I believe I can become financially secure by hard work.
2. ( ) My life is good and successful.
3. ( ) I feel confident in myself.
4. ( ) I get nervous under stressful situations, but I usually recover quickly.
5. ( ) I enjoy working hard.
6. ( ) I am happy with how successful my life has been and is.
7. ( ) I feel in control of my life most of the time, and I know where I want it to go.
8. ( ) I believe I can find solutions to most problems life presents to me.
9. ( ) When I am in pursuit of an important goal, I can be very patient and determined.

10. (   ) I believe that one of the keys to success in trading is to always take responsibility for the consequences of my decisions.

11. (   ) I can focus for hours on things I am interested in.

12. (   ) The market never ceases to fascinate me.

13. (   ) I can easily work by myself and don't need anyone to direct me.

14. (   ) I am by nature an optimist and have a positive attitude.

15. (   ) I believe in the saying that the harder I work, the luckier I get.

16. (   ) I think that failure is just another word for learning experience.

17. (   ) I love learning new skills and working on challenging situations.

18. (   ) I feel that I have sufficient training to start trading.

19. (   ) I would not like to lose my initial trading stake, but if I did, it would not be the end of the world.

20. (   ) I have a clear understanding of the trading process and can navigate the software with ease.

21. (   ) When I enter a trade, I have a clear picture in my mind about when to exit and how.

22. (   ) I see management of loss of trading capital as the most crucial discipline in trading.

23. (   ) Having begun to trade, I adhere rigidly and invariably to my mental stops.

24. (   ) I have committed myself to make trading work for me and will provide the necessary financial and time resources for myself.

25. (   ) I believe an up or down market will provide daily trading opportunities so vast and bountiful that I cannot ever exploit them all.

26. (   ) When I feel stressed, I have a routine in place that will help me cope.

27. (   ) I have a good social support system that includes other traders with whom I exchange ideas on a regular basis.

28. (   ) I read financial publications and books and keep a trading journal in order to improve my performance and to
document what works.

(   ) TOTAL

Congratulations! You have finished the questionnaire
except for the scoring and the interpretation of your score.

Point Range

Group A	224–168
Group B	168–112
Group C	112–56
Group D	56–0

Interpretation

Those of you who scored in the 224 to 168 range have superior
prospects of doing well in day trading. Your attitude is excellent
as are your motivation and commitment to the process. Whatever
obstacles you encounter, you will likely overcome fairly easily
and quickly. With more than sufficient emotional, technical, and
financial resources, your outlook is indeed bright.

The prospects for those scoring in the range of group B are
obviously not as good as for the higher-scoring group, but you
have a more than fair chance at doing well. There are some issues
concerning motivation and emotional stamina, but you ought to
be able to overcome them with practice, training, and some guidance. You may want to examine some of your basic attitudes
about your life—emotional issues and the way in which you handle feelings and stress.

Group C scorers show some serious problems in the areas of
self-esteem, money, and conduct of life in general. It would be
wise to resolve these before you start trading seriously because
you may find it difficult to deal with financial losses and their
impact on your life. In this group, as in the others, motivation,
practice, and determination can still produce gratifying results.
Guidance and mentoring would nonetheless be helpful and perhaps even mandatory.

Group D is going to be in a difficult situation. In spite of motivation, there are serious limiting factors in the areas of personality style, excessive expectations and risk taking, lack of flexibility, and difficulty in handling the emotional and stressful aspects of high-speed and intensely charged market situations. Extreme caution is advised before proceeding with any trading.

The Trader's Quiz courtesy of Dr. Peter Berndt.

TRADE ANALYSIS

With computers it is possible to amass large amounts of data, and with the data it is possible to construct information. That is exactly what the technology is designed to do, to produce useful information. Data collected and not interpreted are useless; but the opposite is true when data are formatted into information, which can be learned on an ongoing basis. What follows is a sample of what a database of trading activity can produce for traders. The data are captured each day, but the information that is produced is capable of saying a lot about a particular trader that will help him or her grow toward his or her ultimate goal. **Inspect what you expect** is a critical rule to follow once trading has begun.

This process has led to many small discoveries about a trader's preferences and confidence levels. This is one of the easiest and surest ways I have found to understand yourself and your trading. I have observed patterns of success related to the time of day trader trades or the amount of time a trader remains in a trade. For example, many traders do extremely well from the opening to midday. In the afternoon, they often give back their profits. Why? Was it fatigue, boredom, or something else? Who knows for sure, but the cure is often to take the afternoons off. To address this set of circumstances, the *Trade Analysis* software program shown in Tables 9.1 through 9.3 was designed to quantify the trading patterns of traders. This allows us to show traders objective analysis of the type of trades that are profitable and unprofitable. This, of course, is not a shortcut to success—there are none. It is just another tool to help you put your trading into perspective. You, as an individual trader, can do it for yourself if your firm does not provide such services, and I recommend you do it at least for the first year because the practice of collecting the data is as valuable as analyzing it. To get you started, I would suggest you look at the following:

- Type of trade (long or short)
- Number of shares traded (less than 200, 500, 1000, etc.)
- Price per share (less than $10, $50, $75, $100, $150, etc.)
- Term of trade (day, swing, midterm, or long term)
- Minutes in trade (0 to 5, 6 to 15, 16 to 30, 31 to 60, 61 to 120, over 120)
- Trades by stock symbol (AOL, CSCO, EBAY, VRNS, MOT, etc.)
- Trades by industry group (electronics, financial services, internet, manufacturing, etc.)
- Time of day
- Profit or loss (and how much)
- Emotional factors (fear, greed, indifference, etc.)
- Number of losers and/or winners
- Best trade in each classification
- Worst trade in each classification
- Percent of gainers and/or losers
- Average gain and/or loss in each classification

Once this information can be created, it can be interpreted with objectivity as well as from a psychological perspective. In the end, I see the psychological dynamics of trading the same way I see the laws of supply and demand. They are the precursors or the cause that must exist before the effect can be seen or realized. What your mind believes, your body achieves, such as a strong profitable month; hence, the mind is a precursor to results just like supply-demand imbalances are precursors to movements in stock prices.

To drive the importance of trade analysis home, I have profiled three actual traders from our firm. While the names remain anonymous, the utility of the analysis is clear.

The first trader we will explore wishes to be a "plunger." A plunger trades heavy size, therefore the confidence level of this type of individual must be high. His or her winning percentage must also be strong. While this trader is not very active in comparison to the day trader who takes no overnight positions, it does indicate that results can be found with many methodologies.

Trade Analysis 1. The Plunger

I call this trader *the plunger* because he finds an idea and trades it very heavily in terms of share size (see Table 9.1). The following is known about this trader:

1. He is really good. He is correct 91.5 percent of the time. That is incredible.

2. He likes the long side of the market more than the short, but he is multidimensional and will go short.

3. This trader, being the plunger that he is, trades less frequently, and he definitely has a swing trader style, but he also participates in day trades. It could be said this trader picks his trades very carefully and is not emotional at all. A cold hard logician. It also proves that overtrading is not necessary to profit. This trader averaged only one round turn per day (two transactions).

4. This trader also trades with options in conjunction with the underlying equity, another strong attribute.

5. Finally, this trader is definitely a tech trader, with a wide variety of interests, including health care and biotech, computer hardware, electronics, software, and wireless communication.

6. The improvement opportunities for this trader are few, but as the analysis shows, there was one large loss on an options position that could have been cut sooner. When I interviewed the trader about this, his response was fast and clear. He said, "That was a covered call, and the profit on the underlying far outweighed the option loss; therefore, I was hedged." All I could say next was, "Great Job!"

TABLE 9.1 Trade Analysis for Anonymous Plunger

(From January 2, 2000, through May 2, 2000)

	Trades	Gains	Losses	Profit	Best Trade	Worst Trade	% Gainers	Avg. Trade
Long vs. short								
Long	65	61	4	$355,443.34	$159,803.25	-$48,530.42	93.8%	$5,468.36
Short	17	14	3	$18,594.10	$24,311.55	-$104,001.74	82.4%	$1,093.77
Shares traded								
Less than 200 shares	19	16	3	$41,052.66	$24,311.55	-$104,001.74	84.2%	$2,160.67
201–500 shares	1	1	0	$1,442.02	$1,442.02	$0.00	100.0%	$1,442.02
501–1000 shares	26	26	0	$34,062.67	$8,360.58	$0.00	100.0%	$1,310.10
More than 1000 shares	36	32	4	$297,480.09	$159,803.25	-$48,530.42	88.9%	$8,263.34
Share price								
$1–$10	17	15	2	$141,098.25	$24,311.55	-$4,125.81	88.2%	$8,299.90
$10.01–$25	9	7	2	-$88,291.90	$9,996.00	-$104,001.74	77.8%	-$9,810.21
$25.01–$50	11	11	0	$46,051.98	$14,787.66	$0.00	100.0%	$4,186.54
$50.01–$100	39	36	3	$270,386.88	$159,803.25	-$48,530.42	92.3%	$6,933.00
$100.01 and up	6	6	0	$4,792.23	$1,251.71	$0.00	100.0%	$798.70
Term of trade								
Day trade	32	31	1	$26,628.36	$4,465.36	-$250.61	96.9%	$832.14
Short term (1–3 days)	24	22	2	$136,963.63	$21,970.18	-$5,250.23	91.7%	$5,706.82
Midterm (4–10 days)	16	14	2	$89,223.32	$17,811.39	-$4,125.81	87.5%	$5,576.46
Long term (10+ days)	10	8	2	$121,222.13	$159,803.25	-$104,001.74	80.0%	$12,122.21
Minutes in day trade								
0–5 minutes	10	9	1	$2,672.19	$637.50	$250.61	90.0%	$267.22
5–15 minutes	7	7	0	$4,104.35	$917.60	$0.00	100.0%	$586.34
16–30 minutes	3	3	0	$3,676.16	$2,797.89	$0.00	100.0%	$1,225.39
31–60 minutes	5	5	0	$8,814.34	$4,465.36	$0.00	100.0%	$1,762.87
61–120 minutes	3	3	0	$1,984.78	$1,251.71	$0.00	100.0%	$661.59
More than 120 minutes	4	4	0	$5,376.54	$2,279.14	$0.00	100.0%	$1,344.14
Not a day trade	50	44	6	$347,409.08	$159,803.25	-$104,001.74	88.0%	$6,948.18

	Trades	Gains	Losses	Profit	Best Trade	Worst Trade	% Gainers	Avg. Trade
Trades by industry group								
undefined	18	15	3	$41,002.88	$24,311.55	–$104,001.74	83.3%	$2,277.94
Electronics, semibroad	7	6	1	$189,048.27	$159,803.25	–$48,530.42	85.7%	$27,006.90
Drugs, biotechnology	26	25	1	$88,883.39	$21,970.18	–$2,131.67	96.2%	$3,418.59
Drugs, drugs, other	5	4	1	$9,783.06	$5,085.34	–$602.62	80.0%	$1,956.61
Internet software and services	3	3	0	$1,447.77	$742.80	$0.00	100.0%	$482.59
Internet service providers	1	1	0	$2,493.46	$2,493.46	$0.00	100.0%	$2,493.46
Electronics, semi int cir	1	1	0	$624.59	$624.59	$0.00	100.0%	$624.59
Computer soft and svcs, biz software and services	2	2	0	$715.38	$637.50	$0.00	100.0%	$357.69
Drugs, diag substances	1	1	0	$1,038.53	$1,038.53	$0.00	100.0%	$1,038.53
Computer hardware, netwk and communication dev	1	1	0	$497.76	$497.76	$0.00	100.0%	$497.76
Computer hardware, PCs	3	2	1	$697.95	$698.80	–$250.61	66.7%	$232.65
Computer hardware, Periph	1	1	0	$1,436.75	$1,436.75	$0.00	100.0%	$1,436.75
Electronics, semiequip and mat	4	4	0	$16,815.05	$8,360.58	$0.00	100.0%	$4,203.76
Computer soft and svcs, application software	2	2	0	$1,944.45	$1,575.77	$0.00	100.0%	$972.22
Telecom, processing systems and products	1	1	0	$1,060.58	$1,060.58	$0.00	100.0%	$1,060.58
Telecom, wireless	1	1	0	$1,442.02	$1,442.02	$0.00	100.0%	$1,442.02
Electronics, diversified	2	2	0	$2,871.31	$2,279.14	$0.00	100.0%	$1,435.65
Diversified svcs, research	1	1	0	$8,517.28	$8,517.28	$0.00	100.0%	$8,517.28
Computer hardware, divers systems	1	1	0	$778.25	$778.25	$0.00	100.0%	$778.25
Telecom, long distance	1	1	0	$2,938.71	$2,938.71	$0.00	100.0%	$2,938.71
Totals	82	75	7	$374,037.44	$159,803.25	–$104,001.74	91.5%	$4,561.43

Trade Analysis 2. The Day Trader

This analysis (see Table 9.2) shows the classic active day trader, grinding out profits every day and cutting losses short, with minimal overnight positions.

1. This trader is almost perfectly balanced between the long and short sides of the market. This indicates a true day trader at work, completely indifferent to the market. This is a strong attribute for a day trader.

2. This trader is fairly active, averaging approximately 35 round turns per day and 70 transactions. This again indicates the purest day trader.

3. Notice that this trader is only correct a little better than 50 percent of the time, yet this trader is still profitable, netting over $68,000 for the month. While not yet highly profitable, this trader is very disciplined for a new day trader.

4. The analysis shows that this trader trades good liquid stocks as evidenced by the share price. Stocks in the range of $50 or more is where this trader lives, and that spells liquidity and another strong attribute to his success.

5. There are very few overnight positions as evidenced by the term of his trades; in fact, 95 percent of this trader's trades are closed the same day. This way the trader saves the high cost of margin interest and the higher cost of market risk.

6. The length of time in the majority of trades is also quite impressive. This trader is a skilled "tape reader" and gets out of trades within 15 minutes in the majority of trades.

7. Finally, the analysis shows this trader has found his niche in trading, averaging only $93 per trade, but limiting market risk with limited time in trades while grinding out an attractive living.

Trade Analysis 3. The New Trader

This trader is having some trouble; his losses are big, and he appears undisciplined (see Table 9.3). The problem is not his ideas or even his ability to trade, but rather his discipline to cut losses. This trader has potential, but a long way to go:

1. This trader has good activity and is quickly gaining experience through transactions, which is the best way to learn. In fact, the trader is also very balanced in terms of longs and shorts.

2. Another positive to be seen is that this trader is trading in lower share size while he learns. Most of his trades are between 200 and 500 shares, which makes it more difficult to profit from short-term trades. The fact that this trader is willing to lower his size to learn and understand his emotions while trading is a strong attribute.

3. I also like that this trader is trading stocks with good liquidity. His stocks range from $50 and above which is also a good sign.

4. "New trader" is also doing a good job as a day trader since he does cover most trades intraday, which is what he set out to do. But as further review will reveal, this trader has trouble cutting losses, and the losses are what he takes home when he does keep an overnight position. This is a mistake that is costing this trader money.

5. By reviewing the "best trade" and "worst trade" columns, you can see this trader has a problem with losses. Some of these losses are huge and simply inexcusable. If this trader can control his emotions better and cut his losses sooner, he will be well on his way to making a good living trading.

6. As you can see, this trader averages only $8.62 per trade. You may say that it is crazy to try and make a living on that kind of margin, but remember, with high activity, traders don't need to make huge profits per trade; instead, they need to be consistent at cutting losses and the numbers will work. The day trader in the second example is proof of that phenomenon.

TABLE 9.2 Trade Analysis for Anonymous Day Trader

(From April 1, 2000, through April 30, 2000)

	Trades	Gains	Losses	Profit	Best Trade	Worst Trade	% Gainers	Avg. Trade
Long vs. short								
Long	397	213	184	$51,391.57	$7,067.54	–$14,713.38	53.7%	$129.45
Short	334	164	170	$16,609.78	$8,109.19	–$10,554.04	49.1%	$49.73
Shares traded								
Less than 200 shares	42	23	19	$5,978.67	$8,109.19	–$14,350.04	54.8%	$142.35
201–500 shares	185	94	91	$15,625.88	$4,227.41	–$3,362.78	50.8%	$84.46
501–1000 shares	373	191	182	$45,627.69	$5,497.73	–$2,050.49	51.2%	$122.33
More than 1000 shares	131	69	62	$769.11	$7,067.54	–$14,713.38	52.7%	$5.87
Share price								
$1–$10	72	35	37	–$5,530.74	$8,109.19	–$14,713.38	48.6%	–$76.82
$10.01–$25	19	11	8	$381.56	$3,535.17	–$7,870.34	57.9%	$20.08
$25.01–$50	121	69	52	$27,453.65	$7,067.54	–$1,622.26	57.0%	$226.89
$50.01–$100	431	228	203	$51,829.36	$6,077.18	–$3,177.16	52.9%	$120.25
$100.01 and Up	88	34	54	–$6,132.48	$4,058.91	–$10,554.04	38.6%	–$69.69
Term of trade								
Day trade	696	357	339	$71,659.90	$5,497.73	–$3,362.78	51.3%	$102.96
Short term (1–3 days)	26	17	9	$24,040.00	$8,109.19	–$10,554.04	65.4%	$924.62
Midterm (4–10 days)	6	2	4	–$1,554.88	$2,642.32	–$2,203.47	33.3%	–$259.15
Long term (10+ days)	3	1	2	$26,143.67	$2,919.75	–$14,713.38	33.3%	–$8,714.56
Minutes in day trade								
0–5 minutes	404	187	217	$10,719.94	$4,091.65	–$1,747.84	46.3%	$26.53
5–15 minutes	205	120	85	$44,974.15	$4,227.41	–$3,177.16	58.5%	$219.39
16–30 minutes	42	23	19	$4,159.39	$5,497.73	–$2,756.48	54.8%	$99.03
31–60 minutes	24	14	10	$6,406.37	$2,847.36	–$3,362.78	58.3%	$266.93
61–120 minutes	12	7	5	$3,156.22	$3,183.51	–$2,914.28	58.3%	$263.02
More than 120 minutes	9	6	3	$2,243.83	$1,567.90	–$1,468.20	66.7%	$249.31
Not a day trade	35	20	15	–$3,658.55	$8,109.19	–$14,713.38	57.1%	–$104.53

	Trades	Gains	Losses	Profit	Best Trade	Worst Trade	% Gainers	Avg. Trade
Trades by industry group								
Undefined	24	15	9	$7,429.58	$8,109.19	−$14,350.04	62.5%	$309.57
Computer soft and svcs, business software and services	174	114	60	$44,958.92	$7,067.54	−$1,853.71	65.5%	$258.38
Drugs, biotechnology	3	1	2	−$836.47	$584.27	−$741.80	33.3%	−$278.82
Internet, software and services	29	11	18	$374.78	$2,001.63	−$688.87	37.9%	$12.92
Electronics, semibroad	1	0	1	−$77.85	$0.00	−$77.85	0.0%	−$77.85
Computer hard, peripherals	6	4	2	$2,832.73	$1,922.55	−$886.26	66.7%	$472.12
Drugs, manufacturers, other	43	22	21	$7,890.61	$5,497.73	−$2,203.47	51.2%	$183.50
Health svcs, specialized	2	1	1	$198.60	$549.06	−$350.46	50.0%	$99.30
Computer hard, diversified systems	1	0	1	−$1,726.99	$0.00	−$1,726.99	0.0%	−$1,726.99
Wholesale, computers	1	0	1	−$123.80	$0.00	−$123.80	0.0%	−$123.80
Internet, service providers	1	1	0	$2,002.85	$2,002.85	$0.00	100.0%	$2,002.85
Computer soft and svcs, application software	176	81	95	$2,683.35	$4,058.91	−$10,554.04	46.0%	$15.25
Materials and const, heavy construction	197	98	99	$17,732.62	$6,077.18	−$2,914.28	49.7%	$90.01
Tobacco, cigarettes	3	3	0	$5,832.19	$3,535.17	$0.00	100.0%	$1,944.06
Elect, semiequip and mate	1	0	1	−$14,713.38	$0.00	−$14,713.38	0.0%	−$14,713.38
Elect, semimemory chips	2	0	2	−$355.09	$0.00	−$290.42	0.0%	−$177.54
Elect, semispecialized	57	23	34	−$4,446.92	$1,396.26	−$2,756.48	40.4%	−$78.02
Internet information providers	7	3	4	−$678.62	$586.13	−$990.10	42.9%	−$96.95
Elect, semiintegrated cir	3	0	3	−$975.76	$0.00	−$777.19	0.0%	−$325.25
Totals	731	377	354	$68,001.35	$8,109.19	−$14,713.38	51.6%	$93.03

TABLE 9.3 Trade Analysis for New Trader

(From April 1, 2000, to April 30, 2000)

	Trades	Gains	Losses	Profit	Best Trade	Worst Trade	% Gainers	Avg. Trade
Long vs. short								
Long	89	38	51	-$20,683.16	$669.37	-$7,362.81	42.7%	-$232.40
Short	66	35	31	$22,018.68	$8,423.13	-$13,427.40	53.0%	$333.62
Shares traded								
Less than 200 shares	7	3	4	$457.87	$485.59	-$239.41	42.9%	$65.41
201–500 shares	139	65	74	$8,352.40	$8,423.13	-$7,362.81	46.8%	$60.09
501–1000 shares	7	5	2	$9,005.69	$8,105.41	-$3,884.69	71.4%	$1,286.53
More than 1000 shares	2	0	2	-$16,480.44	$0.00	-$13,427.40	0.0%	-$8,240.22
Share price								
$1–$10	1	1	0	$7,906.93	$7,906.93	$0.00	100.0%	$7,906.93
$25.01–$50	7	1	6	-$613.36	$99.78	-$231.48	14.3%	-$87.62
$50.01–$100	84	46	38	$10,234.47	$8,423.13	-$13,427.40	54.8%	$121.84
$100.01 and up	63	25	38	-$16,192.52	$1,116.32	-$7,362.81	39.7%	-$257.02
Term of trade								
Day trade	142	67	75	-$4,780.96	$1,637.28	-$1,988.11	47.2%	-$33.67
Short term (1–3 days)	10	5	5	$6,764.36	$8,423.13	-$13,427.40	50.0%	$676.44
Midterm (4–10 days)	3	1	2	-$647.88	$2,612.41	-$3,053.04	33.3%	-$215.96
Minutes in day trade								
0–5 minutes	71	31	40	-$5,883.70	$1,116.32	-$1,954.57	43.7%	-$82.87
5–15 minutes	48	23	25	-$103.12	$1,637.28	-$893.94	47.9%	-$2.15
16–30 minutes	12	8	4	$1,000.86	$1,118.28	-$425.63	66.7%	$83.41
31–60 minutes	6	2	4	-$1,855.68	$166.48	-$1,988.11	33.3%	-$309.28
61–120 minutes	3	1	2	$441.87	$917.20	-$429.03	33.3%	$147.29
More than 120 minutes	2	2	0	$1,618.81	$1,387.76	$0.00	100.0%	$809.41
Not a day trade	13	6	7	$6,116.48	$8,423.13	-$13,427.40	46.2%	$470.50
Trades by industry group								
Elect, semiintegrated cir	67	31	36	$300.27	$7,800.26	-$3,884.69	46.3%	$4.48
Elect, semimemory chips	18	9	9	$418.14	$669.37	-$455.65	50.0%	$23.23
Computer soft and svcs, business software and services	4	1	3	-$709.68	$284.47	-$362.24	25.0%	-$177.42

170

	Trades	Gains	Losses	Profit	Best Trade	Worst Trade	% Gainers	Avg. Trade
Undefined	4	0	4	–$1,281.52	$0.00	–$549.37	0.0%	–$320.38
Internet, software and svcs	11	5	6	–$790.08	$544.17	–$794.93	45.5%	–$71.83
Computer hard, periph	16	6	10	–$3,715.07	$574.58	–$3,053.04	37.5%	–$232.19
Internet info providers	3	3	0	$783.86	$328.17	$0.00	100.0%	$261.29
Elect, diversified	4	2	2	$301.06	$352.65	–$56.96	50.0%	$75.27
Drugs, biotechnology	1	0	1	–$550.84	$0.00	–$550.84	0.0%	–$550.84
Telecom, communication	3	2	1	$91.68	$356.08	–$526.73	66.7%	$30.56
Equipment								
Elect, semispecialized	24	14	10	$6,487.70	$8,423.13	–$13,427.40	58.3%	$270.32
Totals	155	73	82	$1,335.52	$8,423.13	–$13,427.40	47.1%	$8.62

THE JOURNAL

All the traders discussed above are real, and so are the results. All have taken important steps: They've captured and evaluated data about their trading patterns. Their work, however, is not finished. As I stated in Chapter 1, traders should maintain a daily journal. The journal allows traders to talk to themselves in an honest, private way. The best method I have found is to buy a bound, blank journal and create columns—which allows for the date, security and size traded, strategy, price, and comment area to describe your emotional state each day. Like working out, some days you are heavy and tired, while other days you just want to tear it up. What may have motivated these emotions is useful to journal, especially in the beginning. Emotional and psychological forces and how they work for or against you can provide tremendous insight. This will help you decide which emotions to trust and which to fade.

Sound too detailed? Too programmed? Too boring? That is up to you, but I can tell you this: It cannot hurt you! It only has upside, and I like scenarios with limited downside and substantial upside; they usually form great trades.

Use these numbers to determine how efficient you are. For example, if you cancel a large percentage of your orders, it may denote indecision or lack of conviction on your part. Looking back on how the trades worked out may indicate that you should trust your instincts and convictions. Because the software available lets you see every trade, cancellation, and order, even if unexecuted, you will know exactly when you placed the order when you backtrack to your analysis.

If your conviction is weak, that really means your confidence is weak in the trade, and you may need help improving your skills in reading the Level II and Time & Sales windows or other tools you utilize to formulate trading ideas. Studying figures like these and reviewing them with your mentor will help you.

FREQUENT REVIEWS

This rule, **Update and review weekly,** is perhaps one of the most neglected practices of traders. Having a trade plan is your map; looking at it weekly is the only way to steer a true course to your objectives. I recommend that you do this each week, perhaps on Saturday or Sunday. You should be able to obtain a profit-and-loss statement from your firm, or better yet download it from their Web site, since all the trades are matched, and, therefore, they should be databased. If your firm does not have a readable file that you can import into a good database like Microsoft *Access,* then find one that does. This information is too valuable to ignore. The P&L report isolates each round-turn trade and includes a list of open positions as well. This should be done after all your trades are booked for the week. You then can print it out and use it to make sure you are following your plan.

THE BUDDY SYSTEM

If you don't have a significant other in your life, you can still benefit from partnering with another person. A practice that works for many is the same principle that works for physical fitness: the buddy system. If you have a weightlifting partner, for instance, and you agree to meet each morning at 5:30 a.m. at the gym, you will feel what most reasonable people feel—what we call *imposed discipline.* This simply means that your obligation to show is imposed on you by the other party and your respect for the other party. Not showing after your buddy drags himself out of bed at 5:00 a.m. to get there on time is not going to be well received, believe me! The same theory works well regarding your trading plan. Have your partner review your plan while you review his or hers. Any breach of discipline brings accountability to each party and will be a good source of support. I have seen this relationship work well with husbands and wives, brothers and sisters, friends, and so on.

SPOUSAL SUPPORT

I know people who get their spouses involved, not always to trade but to support the trader of the house with detailed analysis like this. The patterns that can be seen from another perspective can be invaluable to you. Additionally, what a great way to get your significant other involved with not just your trading but your life. Remember, trading is one of your passions, which means you will spend a good bit of time engaging and researching the market. Wouldn't it make sense to include the most important teammate you will ever have?

I work with my wife, Tracy, and I have done so since almost the beginning of my career. She has worked in my office for the past 10 years, and she has a huge impact on my success. I can tell you that having your spouse involved with every aspect of your life is very gratifying and rewarding—not just financially but also emotionally. If you are reading this and feeling nauseated, perhaps you have some bigger issues to deal with before you try to conquer the mind game of trading. Of course, this close interaction with your spouse or significant other is not for everyone. I know many great traders who do not share this aspect of their lives, but for many others the experience is quite rewarding. As a caution, I will tell you never to hide your trading results from your spouse. One day I had a crushing day in the market, and I neglected to share it with my wife even after she asked how my day was. I thought I could trade my bad day away, and she would never need to know. That was a huge mistake because not only did that put increased pressure on me the next day but I felt even worse when my trading pattern for the week worsened. Finally, I selfishly had to unload my poisonous lie that was killing my trading to just get my attitude back. My wife was very obliging to the losses because she has confidence in me but very upset for the lie through omission. She threw a few insulting blows my way and reminded me that we were a team. Of course, I write down my true feelings here, but during the spat I instead employed my foolish wit and replied to her, "It is these problematic qualities I possess that kept me from getting a better wife!" You can guess where that got me. So here is another rule worth following: **Don't lie to your spouse or significant other.** With all fun aside, your spouse can also be a great mentor, coach, or team player.

Taking the patience and time to evaluate your progress toward your goals and how well you are adhering to the rules you set for yourself is often seen as a mundane task that new traders are reluctant to engage in. But I can tell you that I still enjoy running my trade analysis and studying my patterns as well as writing in my journal. The effort pays many dividends, both financial and emotional, and those traders who embrace the process will not regret it.

10

RULES FOR TECHNOLOGY AND THE INTERNET

Know your technology.

The more bandwidth, the better.

The cleaner the connection to the Internet, the better.

Your system is no stronger than its weakest link.

Spending too much time on hardware, software, or Internet connectivity tends to be counterproductive to trading.

Never walk away from a live order.

Always know your positions and the funds in your account.

Use redundant systems to access your brokerage firm. Ping before you trade.

As a rule, serious traders concentrate on trading, not on knowing how a computer works or how to write brilliant programs that select stocks complete with entry and exit points. For the record, there are no magic programs that can do your trading or thinking for you. Technology is a tool that aids the electronic trader; it does not replace him or her. This explains why the market making systems still exist today and are bigger than ever. Human beings still drive the market, and trading takes guts as much as brains. It is as much intuitive as cerebral.

Nevertheless, whether you are implementing a program trading system as an institutional trader or connecting to an EDAT brokerage firm, technology is taking a larger and larger role in the world of trading. As an individual trader or investor, one of your most important considerations is establishing a solid Internet backbone, whether you are an online trader or an EDAT trader. Therefore, my rule **Know your technology** is critical because of this one important point: Technology providers will not always tell the truth. Strong statement? Absolutely. True? Absolutely. Electronic traders don't have the luxury of excuses, so don't accept any from your providers.

Internet service providers (ISPs), telephone companies (telcos), and even hardware providers make up the subcomponents that complete the loop that successfully connects you to the market. Many factors can go wrong within these many links, and I have found that if you cannot understand the language in the technology and Internet world, many providers will take advantage of your ignorance. When technology fails—and it will since there are potholes in the information superhighway—you must be able to diagnose the problem yourself or at least understand the excuses that will be given to you about why things are not working out. In the defense of technology providers, technology has grown so fast that the management of human resources is a very difficult challenge for providers. The ability to acquire, train, and retain competent people in the technology field is actually a bigger challenge than creating the technology itself. Therefore, your ability to take control to understand the systems that you will employ will allow you to gain the respect required from the technical support personnel of these providers. Not only will you find much faster solutions to your problems but you will also realize the benefits of knowing the technology, which will contribute to your trading performance. Additionally, by understanding technology better, you can help yourself to establish opinions of various sectors and companies, and that is very useful to the trader and investor as well.

Remember, technology for the electronic trader is considered "mission-critical" systems and data. Without a high-quality system, delays in data handling and downtime will cost you. This could be considered a *technology impact cost* (TIC), meaning that cost in trading performance due to kinks or flaws in the system. A low-bandwidth connection that slows down your access to critical information, especially price quotes in heavily traded stocks, will prove far more expensive in your trading performance than paying for a high-quality system in the first place. "Pennywise and pound foolish" comes to mind when we see new participants ignore this point by taking the low-cost alternative.

A good basis for determining your bandwidth and hardware needs is to use the market itself in terms of volume. Remember that volume often spikes just when you need price quotations the very most—when the market is making major moves up or down. These are instances when you most need timely quotes. Active markets create opportunities for active traders, and active markets require vibrant connections to the Internet.

The Internet is an incredibly complex system, with information flowing from one end of the system to the other—with thousands upon thousands of computer systems linked together. The larger the bandwidth capacity between one computer and another or between a computer and an information routing device, the faster more information can be conveyed. As market activity swells at critical times of trading, the bandwidth capacity must grow accordingly.

As a trader, you rely on the ability to get inbound information and send outbound messages. You must know the inside bid and ask at a very minimum. To execute an order to hit the bid or lift an offer, you must be able to send your order to your broker or place it directly in the market through an ECN or other EDAT system. Knowing how much bandwidth and computer capacity you will need to trade is critical. Therefore, the rule **The more bandwidth, the better.** As a general rule, you should always opt for the maximum bandwidth available. The more bandwidth you buy, the higher the cost. There are three basic types of trading systems, and each has its own bandwidth requirement, ranging from modest to extensive. If you are only going to be using a system requiring only the modest bandwidth requirement, that is all you should buy. There is no need for you to invest in 2-inch-diameter pipe when you need only ¾-inch pipe. This would be the case for the online investor who makes occasional trades but does not rely on real-time information.

The three types of trading platforms are the Web-based, hybrid, and EDAT. In each case you get your trading software from a broker-dealer. No matter how you place a trade, it eventually goes through a brokerage firm that has made arrangements to clear your trades. *Clearing* simply means the trade is matched with the other side, referred to as the *contra*. Buys must be matched with sells and vice versa. Also keep in mind that the price quotations you receive can be live (real time) or delayed. If they are live, fees must be paid to the exchanges. You pay the exchange fees directly as part of the software fee or indirectly via the commissions you pay your broker.

The Web-based trading system is the most common. It is what is generally known as *online trading*. The trader accesses the trading platform via his or her Internet browser. The key elements of the system are the ISP, the line from the Internet to the computer, the modem, and the computer. This type of system operates satisfactorily with a regular telephone line, a 56K modem, and almost any computer manufactured in the last few years. The reason is that only modest bandwidth is required.

As the systems become more complex, more bandwidth and computer power are required. The more complex the system, the more sophisticated the trading becomes. The online trader only observes the research and information that is made available to him or her on the brokerage firm's Web site or other sites he or she visits. This type of trader cannot create his or her own charts, run technical studies on them, or conduct proactive analysis in real time. On these online trading sites, the depth of the price quotation information is limited. For example, on most systems you can request only one quote at a time, and you see only the inside market. These are the reasons the bandwidth requirement is low.

The hybrid trading platform offers the basic features of the online system plus some of the functionality of EDAT trading. The software now resides on the trader's computer, rather than the Internet. On this system, you may have access to a single Level II window and a more advanced charting package. It might include direct access to one or more of the ECNs, as well as allow you to place orders by e-mailing your broker's order desk. Your bandwidth requirement is higher because you are receiving a lot more quotes, and high-quality real-time data and quotes can be bandwidth hogs. Also, the software resides on your computer, so the hardware requirements increase.

The most advanced system for the individual trader is the EDAT platform. You can create as many Level II windows as your computer system can handle. Very active traders usually have four or more open to track the stocks they expect to trade that day. Because an EDAT platform has all the bells and whistles, it requires the most bandwidth. It must draw huge quantities of data to populate multiple market maker windows, time and sales information, charts, and numerous decision support windows. This system requires more attention and is irreplaceable to day traders and active traders.

In all cases, a very reliable Internet connection is a minimum requirement. Since the need of the EDAT trader is the most complex, let's study the schematic in Figure 10.1 to see how your computer connects to the Internet and what makes up the backbone. You have several options to hook up your computer to the World Wide Web:

- POTS: Plain old telephone system—that is, copper wire transmitting at about 56K per second at a cost of about $15 per month. This can work fine for online trading, particularly if the line is clean, meaning that it has not been split and there is little or no interference. It may not be enough for the EDAT trader. But if you have a current version of Microsoft *Windows,* you can use its

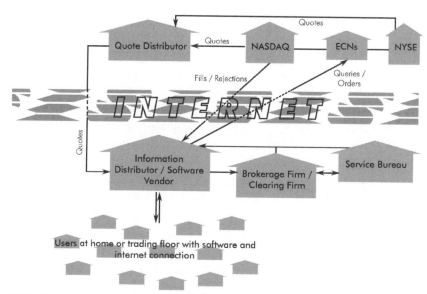

FIGURE 10.1   Connecting to the Internet

multilink feature to bind two or more modems or POTS together and get increased capacity. This is often referred to as a *shotgun modem.*

- ISDN: Integrated services digital network. This is an entirely digital signal that runs through existing telephone lines and jacks. Being digital, there is no need for a modem to convert the regular analog telephone signal to a digital format to be used by a computer. This speeds up the process and increases the bandwidth from 56 kilobits to 2.0 megabits per second. The cost varies by geographic location, but it is usually around $500 for installation and $150 per month to lease the line.

- DSL: Digital subscriber line. This allows you to use your regular telephone line for digital data transmission without interrupting your regular analog telephone calls. The speed of digital transmission determines your monthly cost. For 256K per second, it might run $35 to $40 per month. If you boosted it up to 7.0 megabytes per second, it could run considerably more. This alternative is very favorable if you can qualify for it since its cost per connection speed is about as low as it gets at the time of this writing. DSL is "distance sensitive" in that it uses old copper technology already in the ground. There is a distance requirement from your access point in your area that needs to be evaluated. Your local phone company can test your line with one simple phone call.

- Cable: This is fast becoming a popular selection, as more and more cable companies are forming relationships with telephone companies in order to provide both services. You get your Internet access along with your cable TV signal. A cable modem can provide 10 megabytes per second of bandwidth or more and is therefore a very favorable system.

- Satellite: This is the choice of traders in remote locations that do not have access to any of the above-listed advance systems. A digital satellite dish receives the data, and a regular modem converts them to a digital format for use by your computer. This means there may be some lag time when sending and receiving data. You also must be aware that some weather conditions, like heavy cloud cover or snow, can disrupt transmission. But if you live in a remote location, a South Seas island, or on top of a mountain, it may be the best and only choice.

- T-1: This is the choice of the most serious of traders, where cost is not an issue. This is the type of system you will find on trading floors and in institutional trading firms and places where serious full-time traders trade. It is a frame relay circuit providing a full trunk of 23 phone lines with a point-to-point dedicated connection to the ISP. This system is not required to use an EDAT system, but is more associated where multiple users are required. Investment clubs that share office space are an example of those people who may consider a T-1 connection.

I have not mentioned the possibility of a wireless connection. In time, we feel it will become a contender. At the moment, it has not shown the reliability to provide the connectivity you need to trade nor the speed. Nevertheless, there are some wireless devices for the online trader that might be considered, but test them first before using one in a live trading situation.

Once you have decided what type of connection to go with, you must choose an Internet service provider (ISP). There are two kinds. One is directly connected to the Internet and the other is indirectly connected. This means the latter must access the Internet via one of the former. As a rule, **The cleaner the connection to the Internet, the better.** You can find out if the ISP you are considering is directly connected to the Internet by asking one of its representatives.

But this is only one consideration. More important is the number of lines per subscriber. The ISPs do not expect all their subscribers to be connected at one time. Therefore, they have fewer lines than subscribers. The ratio is important. Look for a ratio of 1 to 5 or less. You will find this out by asking them or reading their Web site, since ISPs are required by law to publish this information.

Also ask if there is an "idle" policy. Some ISPs will drop subscribers from the system if they have not accessed the system for a period of time once they are connected. All the ISPs are trying to do is free up lines for other subscribers if one subscriber has left his or her computer hooked up and has been distracted by another activity. The problem to you as a trader is that if you are monitoring price quotes and are intently watching a trade you are in but have not accessed the system by sending a signal, the ISPs may interpret this lack of activity as idle and kick you off the system. All of a sudden, you are disconnected. This *is* a problem. Many cases exist in which a trader could not immediately log back on, and we do not need to explain how this can cause problems for the market participant. You need to know the idle policy of your ISP before opening an account. Some software will periodically send a signal to your ISP while you are connected to prevent this from happening. Many national providers have this policy; therefore, we have found that local providers are often a good alternative. Many local ISPs have more capacity than subscribers due to their limited exposure and can have excellent subscriber-to-line ratios. Business-oriented ISPs are also excellent resources, such as backbone providers like MCI/WorldCom's UUNet, Level 3 Communications, Sprint, EPIC, and others. The reference in the back of the book provides a good list.

The last thing you want to learn is how good is the technical support you will receive when you need it. Is it 24/7? This can be important if you live on the west coast when the market opens at 6:30 a.m. If their customer service does not come up until 8:00 a.m. local time, you could have a problem. Our recommendation is to use a local, well-staffed, well-equipped, and well-financed provider. It also is not a bad idea to have more than one ISP as a backup if it is not cost prohibitive.

Okay, now that you've learned how to connect to the Internet, it's time to focus on the type of system that you will use. The rule here is **Your system is no stronger than its weakest link.** You need a good computer, composed of a CPU, RAM, hard drive, video card, sound card, monitor, and input devices. Since trading does not require much sound, just about any sound card is sufficient. As far as input devices are concerned (primarily a keyboard, mouse, and CD-ROM), almost any available on today's machines will do fine. Some traders prefer the trackball type mouse devices because they are more comfortable over long trading sessions. The other components need a word or two.

- CPU: This is the brains of your computer. If you are buying a new computer, do not take the cheap alternative on the central processing unit (CPU). Buy the fastest one you can afford. You might get by with 266 megahertz, but you will be happier with one in the 400 to 600 or better range.

- RAM: This is the random access memory. The more RAM you have the less time your computer spends retrieving data from your hard drive. This is not an area to try and save money. 128 megabytes provides far superior performance to just 32. You will be pleased with more, and in the trading world this is a minor expense by comparison to the technology impact cost mentioned.

- Hard drive: Today's trading programs are memory hogs. The reason is the outstanding graphics. But as long as you have 3 to 6 gigabytes or more, you will not have any problems. If worse comes to worse, it is one of the easier components to upgrade.

- Video card: Due to the explosive demand for computer games, video card technology has blossomed. You should not have a problem on any new computer with this component. With multiple monitors, an expanded video card is necessary.

- Monitor: Here is another key component. It must be large enough to accommodate all the windows you will monitor while trading. This could be 4 to 10 or more Level II (market maker) windows, a Time & Sales screen, plus charts, order entry, order tracking, tickers, and other windows. The other key attribute is picture quality. The serious trader may be viewing the screen 7 or more hours in a day. If advanced technical studies are overlaid on price charts, like Gann lines or MACD, a very sharp picture is required. If you need crisp text and images, pick a dot pitch of 0.28 millimeters or less.

Depending on which software packages are used for decision support, we have found quite a few traders who prefer using multiple monitors. Multiple monitors give the trader increased flexibility to view market data. For example, I like to read a good bit of data at one time since I actively day trade; therefore I have three monitors on one CPU at the time of this writing. I know traders who are more active than I am who utilize as many as six monitors. The caution I offer is to avoid putting more data in front of you than you can absorb. As time and experience grow, so will your propensity to absorb data. As this occurs, add additional technology to support the information you require. When trading becomes an integral part of your life, the cost of technology is not a real consideration. In fact, it is one of the cheapest considerations. Consider the trader who trades 50 times per day on average, at an average ticket cost of $15 per trade. In the course of one month, that trader will spend $15,000 in commission. Over the course of a year, this compared to a $10,000 system makes the hardware cost less. Therefore, buy the best technology you can.

Once again, don't try to get too deeply involved in the mechanics of computer selection. Use a professional. A trader's job is to trade. But have adequate knowledge and understand the language of the providers you will use. We have found that those students that have an inordinate interest in the technical side of the systems tend to get buried in them. My rule is that **Spending**

too much time on hardware, software, or Internet connectivity tends to be counterproductive to trading.

After you've connected your computer to the Internet, what happens next?

You log onto your EDAT trading software. A link is established between your computer, your broker's back office, the over-the-counter market (NASDAQ), the New York Stock Exchange, and a variety of ECNs, depending on which ones your broker is affiliated with. At the same time, your software company is linked to all the exchanges via a price quotation vendor. Direct prices from the exchanges are processed and sent to your brokerage firm or software company. It converts them into a format that fits the software package you are using and transmits them to your computer. And all this happens in seconds.

When you place an order, it is sent to the exchange or ECN you select. Instantly it is recorded in the back office of your broker-dealer. This is important because if you lose your Internet connection, you can call your broker and find out if your order was filled or canceled or is still pending. You do this with one of your redundant systems, which you have because it is critical that you have immediate access to your firm's back office.

When your orders are filled, the price immediately "reports" on your computer screen. On most systems orders are color coded. Typically, a live (unfilled) order is red. When it gets filled, it either turns green for a purchase, purple for a short sale, or blue for a liquidation of a long position. Cancellations generally are shown in black. This color coding makes it easier to spot open orders, so that you do not leave them open when you shut down your system. Powering down your system does not automatically cancel an order, and because live orders can be filled even after traditional trading hours through many of the ECNs that offer extended hours, I strongly suggest that you **Never walk away from a live order,** unless you have set stop levels with predetermined exit points.

Because electronic trading gives you the control of your execution and order routes, it also requires responsibility; therefore, **Always know your positions and the funds in your account.** The Internet is a complex system. Combine this complex network with a complicated broker/dealer network like NASDAQ and the NYSE and you have potential for problems. As you help pioneer the future of electronic trading, your responsibility is to know all your trades and not to rely solely on technology to monitor your trading activity. Traders take this responsibility very seriously since many have learned expensive lessons from ignoring position management. Keeping a trade journal is a natural solution to manually recording trades. Not only do you create another record of all activity, but the act of recording your activity reveals patterns and emotional influences that will help you grow.

Another critical rule regarding technology is, **Use redundant systems to access your brokerage firm.** If your telephone line or Internet connections are interrupted, a cellular phone is a good choice and a cheap investment in comparison to the potential for loss in trading blind while your system is down. Work with firms with accessible trade desks that have qualified registered personnel who can get you in and out of trades when situations do occur. Not only is it important to have a medium through which to contact the trade desk of a firm but it is also equally important to be able to speak to a resource who can answer questions and put a trade on without your having to mess around with automated response systems. This is not the time for technology. When a problem occurs with technology and you need to speak to someone, "high touch" takes precedence over "high tech." Too many firms today have lost contact with their customers because they have attempted to replace personnel with new technology, as if the two were mutually exclusive. The reality is that when technology fails, people still need to be the layer of insulation between reasonable frustration due to technical failures and infuriated anger due to incompetence or inadequate redundancy that can be easily provided by a trade desk. A good electronic firm sees all orders or positions you have on/pending on their back-office computer system, and it can liquidate them and cover them as you see fit.

The final rule regarding technology relates to what you can do to be proactive to test how your connectivity is pulling the needed data to trade. Before citing this rule, always know that another fact of life is that live data or real-time price quotations are, in reality, only near real time. There is no way to replicate on your computer the price activity that takes place on the floor of an exchange as it actually happens. It must be gathered, digitized, edited, reformatted, transmitted to your software-broker, and delivered to your computer. That takes time, perhaps only nanoseconds, but time nonetheless. That is why the best system available in your budget is the minimum requirement.

Knowing that, the rule is **Ping before you trade.** Your firm should allow you to "ping" the servers that you receive data from each day to test how clean your connection is to the servers that serve the data to you. This test path of the connection for accuracy and speed is called a *trace route.*

Through the trace route you can send a signal to a beacon located at the source of your data. Whether you use a service bureau that sends the data to you or you receive the data from a proprietary network provided by the brokerage firm you trade with, testing the number of "hops" it takes and the time it takes to get to the beacon will allow you to pinpoint where problems or potential problems in the form of bottlenecks may exist. A ping test will quantify how many router portals you will travel through to reach your data destination. Because the Internet is rapidly growing, hubs and portals are constantly changing, and that does not always mean for the better. Hubs can become saturated through activity and subscriptions in a given area, which causes delays and strains on subcomponents of the path you take to your data source. These strains or bottlenecks will be the places in your trace route that weaken the connection; hence, the reality that you are only as strong as your weakest link. Trace routes will show you how fast data are received and sent at each hub to help highlight where potential problems may exist. Although there is little you can do about this due to the fact that these hubs are each multi-million-dollar networks, you can at least attempt to connect through another service provider that will most certainly have different trace routes.

For example, you may ping the data source from which your real-time data come (decision support tools) and find that it must pass through 12 hubs before it reaches you. You may find that each hub delivers data at very high speeds such as 95 milliseconds. But as time goes on, a certain hub may begin showing higher and higher times, such as 300 milliseconds (slower throughput). Although these times may not show noticeable differences in the data you receive immediately, this is a good indication that a given hub or series of hubs along your trace route is beginning to show signs of saturation. Given that scenario, you may want to test another ISP service to compare times and trace routes. Moving from one service to the next makes sense during this rapid-growth revolution in technology and bandwidth if you can reduce the number of hops you take with associated faster speeds. Your ISP won't like it, but who cares—you are not running for mayor here. You're giving yourself every advantage to receive mission-critical data on time. If your ISP is falling behind in the new world of survival of the fittest, drop them like a bad habit and move on to the next best service.

So the rule is this: Test your trace routes often, and always look for new innovative companies that are providing new solutions to Internet connectivity. The biggest is not always the best. New companies like Level 3, Epic, and Enron are emerging companies that are getting into this fascinating communications networking business, and they are providing great new solutions that often surpass the known players. Don't ignore their presence; they have great futures in connectivity. On a side note, companies like Enron are best known for their energy and oil affiliations, but they have for the past few years built an incredible fiber-optic network while digging trenches to lay pipe. "Why not throw some fiber in the hole while the ground is open and build a network of our own?" was obviously the foresight of the Enron executives who created this formidable new player in the world of telcos and connectivity. I mention this because not only will it help you with your technology but also it relates to my rule to get knowledge of new-technology companies that may have the potential to become the next CSCO or MSFT of the world. Technology is the reason for our new economy. Embrace it, because it is the future.

RULES FOR MONEY AND MIND MANAGEMENT

Be humble and admit mistakes.

Never let emotions control you.

Avoid stock tips.

Never take home a loser.

Open trades on the anticipation of news; offset positions on what actually happens.

Define the strategy, and match the discipline to it.

Allow for more heat.

Exclude commission costs from your exit criteria.

Never let your confidence exceed your skill.

Know thy tax law.

Contemplate before you speculate.

Lose the labels.

Learn to pace yourself.

Follow your instincts.

Find your own game or recipe for success.

Learn to lose.

Make trading a habit.

Never let your attitude suffer.

The market is always right.

The rules I want to begin with for the first section of this chapter will cover the gamut of errors that occur frequently with both new and experienced traders regarding managing money and market risk. Instead of laying them out in a linear fashion, I thought the rules would best explain themselves through a true story. As I take you through this story, I will offer along the way strategies that could have been used to mitigate much of the risk. Finally, for the second half of the chapter I will list rules for the mind that every trader should follow. When reading a recent article, I encountered a story written by a reporter who described his own experience while trading a few high-tech Internet stocks. The author was quite brave to share his experience, and my intention is not to fire shots at him. Instead, I commend him for the candor. He makes no claim to be a trading expert, and his story teaches the first rule of risk management: **Be humble and admit mistakes.**

Unfortunately, the mistakes that follow are all too common for many traders and investors. The story reflects how media hype mixed with excitement and inexperience can lead to an expensive lesson. What made this story particularly interesting to me is the ironic way in which the reporter himself fell victim to his own reporting.

After reporting on high-tech firms for five years, a reporter decided to trade a few high-tech flyers. He bought an updated computer and opened an online brokerage account. He opened four positions buying shares of the companies that made his new computer, manufactured the chips in his computer, provided his Internet service, and developed his Internet browser. The earnings reports of all four companies were about to be released when he bought each of the stocks. As he says in the article, "I braced myself for winnings." However, he had not prepared himself for losses, and while in the trades, he had a difficult time admitting his mistakes. With no exit strategy in the event of failure, when the computer and the chip manufacturer missed their earnings targets, he realized his mistakes quickly, but he dealt with them poorly. Additionally, the browser company announced that it was giving its software away, which was received negatively by the market, while the Internet provider's stock was the only gainer. Three out of four were losers.

Undaunted, this reporter charged forward into new trades, breaking the next most common rule: **Never let emotions control you.** He turned on his television as a source of additional research. It alerted him to a "hot" IPO just hitting the market. As soon as it hit the secondary market, he broke two rules noted in Chapter 5 by *placing a market order* and *trading IPOs*. Emotions are the most plausible reason why anyone would use a market order to buy an IPO. Greed and excitement are the emotions that lead so many amateurs to financial ruin.

The IPO skyrocketed from $15 to $60 the first day, eventually closing at $50. He thought he was happy until he got his confirmation, which showed that he paid the high of the day at $60. Not knowing what to do, he relied on hope and waited another day before exiting the trade, eventually getting out at $30 per share.

As if he had not received enough punishment, he joined a chat room for $75 a month. He read a biased discussion that appeared to be a conversation between a bull and a bear speculator on a particular stock. It fascinated him. Eventually, the bear conceded that this $4-per-share tech stock was poised for a major move up. This reporter blindly jumped in to buy the stock. The stock bolted to $5½ on thin volume with very few shares trading at this price and then quickly fell to $3. Due to the light volume at $5½, he either wasn't able to sell or just didn't put in an order. After taking his losses, he learned that the bull and the bear were the same person and that the chat room trader had front-run the stock. (*Note: Front-running* is the practice of buying stock ahead of other orders, which are expected to have substantial market impact. In other words, the front-runner profits from the buying of other parties. This is an illegal practice for licensed stockbrokers and should be for everyone in my opinion when associated with manipulation through chat rooms or any other medium.) Hence, the rule: **Avoid stock tips.** Maintain control of your trading by making your own decisions; don't react to the hype and potential manipulations of chat rooms and stock tips.

As a trader, you can maintain absolute control of just a few risk factors in the market, such as the number of shares you trade, the stock you trade, and the amount of time you are in the market. That makes these factors that much more valuable, so why give away control? Any departure from this control takes you closer to gambling.

Finally, our high-tech trader just kept getting in deeper and deeper by breaking this rule: **Never take home a loser.** If a trade goes sour, dump it as quickly as you can; ignore this rule and the "judge" of the market will drop its gavel on you, sentencing you to financial execution. Sound a bit extreme? Maybe, but I can't think of many reasons to take a losing overnight position. Hope of winning and fear of losses take control of the amateur mindset, putting the trader at a significant disadvantage. Perhaps the irony of this real-life story is that this reporter traded these stocks as literally and predictably as the media who report market events and try to explain every move and reaction in the market. The reality is that the market cannot always be explained, and those members of the media or amateur crowd that believe and wait for everything to be explained discover this lesson very quickly.

The rules our reporter friend broke while embarking on his new trading venture remind me of the paths we take in life. It is all about making the right choices from the beginning. He started off on the wrong track, a move that can often be the beginning to the end, resulting in the breaking of one rule after the next. This is equivalent to a juvenile delinquent's starting out on the wrong foot and then later growing up to become a frequent flyer on the parole officer's most active list. He had been reporting in the industry for a while, and he felt he knew it. But I do not think he knew much about how the stock market functions; he merely had some background knowledge regarding the tech industry.

Unfortunately, the reporter made no attempt to learn how the market functions, or, at least, he did not mention it in the article. If he did, he would have learned a critical rule regarding news: **Open trades on the anticipation of news; offset positions on what actually happens.** Instead, greed and excitement proved that, in this case, his confidence exceeded his skill, and the juvenile delinquent of trading was born.

A lot can be learned from studying where another trader goes wrong, but when it comes to managing trades for yourself, the lessons can become more complex and difficult to learn. The real lessons begin by asking yourself less obvious questions. Reviewing how you handled the trades you opened during the day is an exercise that some consider mundane and time-consuming, but the result of doing so will be a foundation of discipline. Questions you begin to ask yourself, such as, "Did I act with clarity, conviction, and discipline?" are important questions for your journal. If you can answer yes to these kinds of questions and you still get punished by the market, learning not to beat yourself up for doing the right things but to learn from the experience instead will help you frame the proper mindset of a trader. Over time, you will be rewarded for such discipline. Micromanaging your daily activity is a good "cooldown" for each day. Unfortunately, this type of discipline cannot be taught completely; much of it comes instead from your own personal choice to control risk and take responsibility for your own trading. These are just a few of the considerations you must address when you engage the market. Unfortunately, every day people are introduced to the market through the same emotions to which the reporter fell victim. Thousands of amateurs who neglect what should be called commandments never have the opportunity to embrace the passion within them that may have been present. Ponder how many people begin trading simply by buying a computer, an Internet connection, and a fresh new online account, driven by the next IPO or other market event that elicits emotions like greed and excitement. Next, ask yourself what their success rate will be. I think you can decide which methodology makes the most sense.

Neither this book nor any other can completely teach you the "art of trading" nor that which I believe to be the cornerstone of this art, controlling your downside risk. Therefore, make the decision right now that whatever trading discipline you aspire to, or work at, you will stay within the parameters of the trade you set prior to entering the trade. The rule is, **Define the strategy, and match the discipline to it.** Discipline cannot be explained for all trade scenarios. Again, we are faced with the reality that the market is not that literal. Discipline cannot be defined as cutting losses at ⅛ or a ¼ point. There are many occasions when it pays to be more risk tolerant (such as shorting), and other times to be purely disciplined. Instead, discipline is defined by your ability to determine the risk-reward relationship before opening a trade and then to have the fortitude to stick with your plan once the trade is opened. Otherwise, if you have a literal definition of loss tolerance, you may be the victim of another form of risk, "whipsaw risk." Traders who have no conviction for trades often fall victim to whipsaws, whereby they liquidate and cover trades too soon, only to have the stock move back in what would have been their favor. In other circumstances, discipline may determine that if the trade works against you the slightest bit, you cover. So let's explore the circumstances in which it pays to be flexible, or what I call *risk elastic,* based on solid criteria, and those in which it pays to be a "cyborg," acting with pure disciple.

Pure discipline is required when you are trading more actively, such as day trading. For example, suppose you are trading SDLI to take a very fast incremental profit. The stock is showing upside momentum, and you decide to "lift" an offer with SOES. You get filled immediately, and suddenly SDLI is showing signs of weakness with offers building rapidly. Your decision to enter the trade was based on pure momentum strength, and your decision to trade the stock was not based on pattern recognition. Therefore, in this scenario, you *must* exhibit *pure discipline!* You must trade like a cyborg, with no emotion whatsoever, and cover the trade. Your motivation was to time the market and take a small profit based on perceived upward strength and an imbalance of demand exceeding supply. Obviously, in this case you were wrong and your timing was off. Emotions, hope, or blind faith can never play into your decision-making process, and the trade must be covered immediately.

Other times, it pays to be more risk elastic. One such occasion would be when you are shorting stock. That does not mean you will be undisciplined; it simply means you will need to give a short a chance to work, without hesitation.

Rules for going short are unique due to exchange rules that require an uptick. In NASDAQ issues, upticks are measured when the current inside bid in the market is higher than the bid prior. When trading listed securities, the uptick is measured as a trade that takes place higher than the previous trade. Because of this rule, when shorting stock, the rule **Allow for more heat** is imperative. Expect it. If the bullish sentiment is in the market to create the uptick while day trading, and I sell the offer short, I have the bias that the stock is near a top or resistance level for the time horizon I am trading. If buyers are lifting my offer, I expect the stock to trade higher. That bullish sentiment will often follow through and carry stock prices perhaps a price level or two higher than your short entry point. Don't expect to sell the perfect top due to the uptick rule, but at the same time, you must know where you are wrong if the stock continues higher. Shorting stock requires perhaps more conviction than any other trade strategy. Therefore, buying to cover the first price level or two above your short entry point without confirming indications that the stock is getting stronger is a mistake. Shorting provides substantial profit opportunities, but requires a higher propensity to take risks.

Exiting a trade should be a purely mechanical process, because the mental decision to get out should have been made once the criteria and market conditions violated the trading limits you set. The logical side of your mind should kick in, prompting an immediate exit. Emotions should have little to do with trading, and only trading enough over time will allow you to divorce yourself from them. In the interim learning stage, use "emotional hedges" by setting rules for each trading strategy before getting in, while implementing discipline to follow the rules once in the trade, regardless of the situation.

As you are beginning to see, the determination of when to be purely disciplined and when to accept more risk is based on many different events and strategies. Determine and define what risk tolerances you will accept prior to entering trades, and survival will allow you to develop instincts that will serve you well going forward. In the absence of such considerations, most new traders never survive long enough to find out what potential they may have had. Discipline is different for everyone, and you must define that for yourself, but all traders need to employ it.

MONEY MANAGEMENT

Money management must include the topic of commissions, since they are part of active electronic trading; therefore, let's separate some of the myths and realities about commissions. An important rule for maintaining the integrity of your mental stops is to **Exclude commission costs from your exit criteria.** While keeping track of commissions post-trade is important for evaluating your overall performance, the desire to squeeze a little profit out of a weak trade in order to cover the commission costs of that particular trade can quickly lead to accelerated losses and market impact costs that far exceed the commission. If a trade is affected by the commission in terms of profit and loss, then the risk-reward spectrum is too tight, and the trade is not worth the risk. All traders will encounter losing or marginal trades that trigger their criteria for an immediate exit. Yet some traders, rather than exit the trade immediately, up or down a $\frac{1}{16}$ or at breakeven (scratch), will hold on to the trade, hoping to get an extra $\frac{1}{16}$ or $\frac{1}{8}$ point to cover commissions. But then they find that the stock continues in the wrong direction, leaving them faced with substantial mounting losses that far exceed the commission. Put another way, when evaluating a particular trade, commissions should simply be thought of as a sunk cost; the rules for when to exit that specific trade should operate independently of the existence of commission costs. While commissions on an aggregated basis are an important consideration, if you allow commissions to affect your trading habits on an individual, trade-specific basis, the market impact cost from remaining in undesirable trades will far outweigh any perceived benefits.

Money management in good times also needs to be considered. Learning trade mechanics will take time but is elementary compared to the art of trading. Learning about ECNs, limit or market orders, keystrokes, liquidity, and so on are all a matter of time. You can use a simulator for practice until you are proficient with the mechanics. But the art of trading is about your own psychology, and understanding it will be a lifelong learning process. Some traders' worst days have come right after some of their best. Hence the rule, **Never let your confidence exceed your skill.** When your confidence exceeds your skill, you're in trouble. When trading strong, trade more aggressively but stick with your rules. For example, I will tend to make more trades because I am in tune with the market or sector I am trading, but I will fiercely engage the rules of trading. Trading within the rules is always critical, but after a profitable spell, it is even more important since subconsciously you may be taking risks that you would never have taken had your recent trades not been so profitable. Simply put, you consciously or subconsciously become "cocky." Some call it "self-sabotage" because your subconscious psyche doesn't feel you deserve the success. All I can say is, whatever causes irrational trading behavior, the best solution is to be aware of it and be more focused on your rules.

As your understanding of the market grows through trading, confidence will replace your fear. Greed and excitement are strong emotions and can often jade your recognition of what all traders need: a healthy respect for the market. Healthy respect and even some fear forces you to gain more knowledge and understanding before embarking into the unknown, while excessive fear paralyzes action. Before you know it, you become a victim of the stock market, left with a jaded view of its tremendous potential because your fears were realized through damaging losses.

Another rule regarding money management is less interesting but still important: **Know thy tax law.** There are some special tax advantages available to the active trader. I am not a tax accountant or lawyer; therefore, I will only alert you to what is available. You will need to contact a competent tax practitioner for professional consultation if you think you are eligible for any of them. I have included the Web site of a CPA firm familiar with this specialty in Appendix C.

MIND MANAGEMENT

Traders need to maintain a clear focus, and that comes only with a clear head. The rules that could be listed for this topic are as broad as the subject of psychology. Therefore, I will focus on some of the more common mistakes I see new traders make.

The rule **Contemplate before you speculate** is one that many ignore, including the reporter at the beginning of this chapter. The cost of trading must be considered from numerous perspectives. Lost income if you plan to trade full time and anticipated trading losses are just a few of those considerations. Can you afford to become a full-time trader? Or are you going to trade part-time? These are questions that you must address with your spouse or partner if necessary. Making these decisions alone when others are involved is a mistake and only adds pressure to your state of mind during this learning process if you do not address this issue before beginning. We have seen the results of abandoning this advice. Upset spouses and a lack of support are not positive elements to deal with, so set your foundation right from the beginning and do not avoid this dialogue between you and your partner in life.

Another rule for the mind is **Lose the labels.** Market participants don't need titles. You're trading your capital on your electronic system with no one to answer to except you and your significant other. Those that give themselves titles like "technician," "expert," or "guru" are implanting false signals into their own minds. Why limit yourself by calling yourself a technician? Many market events can lead to successful trades that are fundamentally driven, psychological indications through the tape and Level II, and so on. Labels pigeonhole your mind into a narrow focus that constricts broad-based thinking rather than enhancing specialization. Those that have ego-driven motives are the first to use labels; unfortunately, the paradox is that they often earn the label of failure or loser because of those very qualities. My advice is, walk softly and carry a big stick. If a label is really important, though, how about "student?" Become a student of the market; there is always something new to learn.

Another critical rule of trading is, **Learn to pace yourself.** A word of caution: good times can still be dangerous. When almost every trade you put in works and your account is growing rapidly, slow down; you do not have the Midas touch. The risk now is overtrading. Jumping into higher-risk trades because you are doing so well is common and a mistake. You need to take a cold shower and review every trade based on the rules you have developed for yourself. That is one of the big reasons you must put your daily plans on paper—so that you can go back and make sure you are doing what you are supposed to be doing. When I am hot, I have learned to cool myself down. I know arrogance and overconfidence usually lead to a lesson in humility. This has not only made me a better trader but also a better judge of my own behavioral patterns.

This understanding of your own psychology will teach you to **Follow your instincts.** Nobody, not even Freud or Maslow, can fully explain what is in your head; hence the revelation from Freud, "The best psychologist is within your own head!" When trading, you are attempting to foretell the future. This is obviously impossible. This is what makes your instincts such an important tool, your sixth sense. Find out early on if you have good instincts for the market or not. That is important because it is your instincts that you will often rely most heavily on.

Learn to be totally honest with yourself. When your instincts work in your favor, imprint those feelings in your mind. It's like making a perfect swing with a golf club. When you feel the groove, you must imprint it in your mind so that you can repeat it. On the other hand, if you take a profit totally by accident, be able to separate this feeling from the feeling you had when you honestly followed your instincts. Accidental incidents are not repeatable, but instinctual ones are. Big difference: Instincts are not mystical; they are instead ever-changing and evolving attributes that you should not ignore, but rather embrace. Instincts are developed over time and through experience, and surviving the market first will allow you to thrive in it later.

Another rule that is much more important for the mind than people think is to **Find your own game or recipe for success.** As I mentioned earlier, a sound financial and educational base is imperative and makes for a great beginning, but that is all it is: a beginning to a journey. At some point, the more you search for answer from others, the more you divert yourself from finding that understanding of yourself. Learning from others is imperative, but relying on others is a mistake. There is a difference.

As you develop your own unique trading style, you also must consider a reality for all traders. This rule for the mind has a low acceptance rate; but remember, the best traders are in the minority, and the best traders, **Learn to lose.** Day trading is "riding the edge," pushing the envelope of your capability. The extreme! The ultimate crescendo to trading. The most aggressive and exciting realm of market engagement.

Because active day trading is "on the edge," one of the truly difficult psychological barriers to accept is learning to accept losses. It is a major component of active trading and simply part of the endeavor. With the acceptance of this fact, traders see losses differently, knowing that every loss has a lesson within it. Traders must embrace losses and see them as a cleansing process to rid them of the mental anguish that losses bring. The deeper the loss, the greater the burden, and the losses can weigh on you like useless cargo that has no value or upside. By developing such a paradigm, you begin to train your emotions and your mind to cut them quickly, moving you ever closer to understanding trading.

This brings us to the next rule—**Make trading a habit.** Do not try to trade when you have a minute. You always need focus. You always must be at your best. You always must be able to concentrate 100 percent. Set a regular trading schedule. If you cannot devote the necessary time to trade, don't, because the market has no room for luck or incompetence. As I said, the market is both unforgiving and very rewarding. Mistakes are rarely tolerated, but hard work and the adherence to these critical rules are usually rewarded. If for some reason you are not able to make this kind of commitment, wait until you are able to become a trader. A false start in this business rarely allows for a second chance. Better to be patient and begin wisely than to be exuberant and destroy your most valued asset, your attitude toward trading. Which leads to the next rule for this chapter:

Never Let Your Attitude Suffer. Trading is not a profession for the depressed or moody. Most active traders during the 1000-trade learning curve lose on more trades than they make. It is simply a fact of trading. One of the most important keys to psychological health and trading success is that you accept this fact and realize it is part of the tuition we all have paid. The earliest signs of failure I see are from those who do not accept this fact or responsibility. These individuals seem to be in the majority and have a propensity to pass the blame of losses during this very normal learning process. Once you begin to pass the blame, you have a serious decision to make. Should you continue trading or give it up? Are you tough enough to take the pounding the market gives us all from time to time? Unfortunately, it is most severe during this learning stage. Occasionally, we all get to the point when we have taken enough punishment or are under so much stress that we just yell "Uncle!" Time to take a break. Just walk away and rest until you really want to come back and trade. But passing blame on others will never be the formula for success; therefore, realize now that this learning process is tough on your attitude, but it is worth the effort.

Though I believe we all need a break now and then, I have been accused of being a workaholic. In a sense I guess I am when it comes to trading, but a workaholic is not a bad thing if properly defined. To me, a workaholic is more a state of mind than a state of time. Taking the time required to rest and recharge your batteries is important, but it makes more sense to "press" harder when you have the groove and rhythm of the market than to walk away from it. There will be times that you are in almost perfect harmony with the market, and you should stay with your system during these times. If that means the pattern lasts for an extended period of time, stay with it and do nothing to dismiss it. If that is the definition of a workaholic, I can live with that.

I think about attitude in terms of support and resistance levels in one's mind. Arrogance, cockiness, and close-mindedness live at the resistance levels. When strong trading patterns occur to the point where I begin to develop some of these negative qualities, I remind myself to be humble by remembering this critical rule, **The market is always right,** and it has a unique way of punishing these qualities. Maintaining a support level in your mind means remembering what brings success. Like the trends of markets and stocks, a trader is best served by avoiding the breakouts and breakdowns in attitude. Manic-depressive swings based on performance can bring only failure. Traders who learn to control emotions will fare much better.

In conclusion, many people are in search of some magic to help them find easy money. While this view seems a bit cynical, it is true for the masses. Few possess the motivation required to be a true professional trader. As their experience grows, I believe traders continually adjust the ratio of cognitive intelligence and emotional intelligence toward the latter, whether the balance of power to be successful in trading is 80 percent emotional intelligence and 20 percent cognitive/mechanical intelligence, or 90/10, or some other ratio. The likelihood is that it is probably different for everyone. What is the same for all traders is that adopting rules of thought and a proper perception of the market is, and will remain, the best approach to trading stocks. The next chapter will introduce you to some of these professionals. Your mindset and attitude are the greatest tools and allies you have, so don't ignore their value.

12

INTERVIEWS AND INSIGHTS FROM THE "ONE PERCENTERS"

What is most fascinating about traders is that, while they all have differing opinions on strategy and market engagement, they share many common opinions on the rules for the mind and on trading psychology. Out of the many interviews I have conducted, I have decided to share the views and insights of the particular five traders presented in this chapter not only because of their profitable and consistent results but also because of their mindset and activity that lead to the result.

Unlike false seers who sell their services promising great success for all that subscribe, these gentlemen put their capital at risk each and every day, walking the talk, and making their own decisions. No chat rooms, subscription services, or false prophets are in their lives, just hard work born of their passion to trade. None of them have been paid to volunteer their insights, nor do any of them have an ax to grind. They simply share a common attribute that many successful traders possess, a willingness to pass along what they have learned from many great traders before them. While it is my belief that great traders are few, those who have conquered the art of trading are often too successful to feel the need to write and share knowledge, unless there is some other motivation to do so. In the case of these five professionals, all shared a somewhat humble philosophy of life that I found particularly attractive. As I have stated throughout this book, many of the attributes required to trade successfully are the same virtues we hope to possess in other facets of our lives: humility, grace, passion, patience, generosity, and discipline. All are rare qualities singularly, and it is even rarer for a person to possess them all. I have come away with this simple belief: Those who lack any of these qualities usually lack most if not all of them, and those who possess any of these qualities usually possess most if not all of them. This is comparable to the extreme polar ends that we often see in the market: those who make great money versus those who lose big, with very little population in between. Because of these virtues, these men were willing to share what knowledge they have acquired so far on their journey, all the while acknowledging it is just that, only a journey and not a destination.

DARIN CORT

I could not help but like this young speculator. At first glance he seemed conservative and reserved, even quiet. It didn't take long, however, to realize this 31-year-old professional possesses a rare combination of aggressiveness and intelligence. His aggressiveness came through in many ways, including his passion for sports and his highly competitive nature. I made the mistake of telling him I liked to wrestle for fun (after a few social beers) only to find myself the victim of very quick hands that obviously have greater application than just rapid-fire trade execution on the keyboard!

Q: Darin, how and when did you get started trading? And how did you do?

A: I started trading three years ago in early 1997 with $50,000 in capital. My good friend was already trading and finding success, and I was very unfulfilled with my career in banking. Within the first six months I had lost $26,000 of my stake and promised myself that if I drew down my account by 50 percent I would quit, and that is what I did. I returned to my banking background with substantial reservation. Part of me refused to admit I had failed, and the other part of me knew I wasn't chasing my passion. Neither realization was very palatable.

Q: How did you make it back?

A: I recapitalized myself and returned with $35,000 to trade. Being properly capitalized is important, and I knew I was undercapitalized, but the lessons I had learned during my first run at trading taught me to forget about the money and trust my instincts and training. I knew the odds were against me with this amount of capital, but my short time away allowed me to clear my head and reach a level of focus I did not have before. I felt this would be my edge. This translated to having conviction when I had an idea, instead of being overly literal in terms of losses, measuring every loss strictly by price. I learned that making trading decisions goes far beyond just prices relative to my cost basis and has more to do with where stocks are strong and weak based on volume and activity. This proved to be a breakthrough for me.

Q: **If you were to teach your best friends or a close relatives to trade, what advice would you give them?**

A: I would have them sit next to me while I traded and made sure they had ideas and insights to offer me as they learned. Once new apprentices have thoughts and opinions about the market, they begin to activate the neural networks within their own mind. They show they are becoming independent thinkers, relying on themselves and not others. They begin to know themselves as a trader, which I consider to be the greatest advantage. Once their level of confidence is evident, I would have them engage the market. I make this statement with the caveat that they must have the mechanical skills to trade first. I would then have them spend 20 to 30 minutes reviewing their trades every day and keeping a journal of what had transpired. They need to know why they make decisions. If I make a trade for the right reasons, I don't evaluate the decision based on my P&L. I base the decision on my discipline to work the trade within the parameters I set. I know the odds will work toward my favor in the long run if I do. If I have been disciplined to follow my plan and the net result is a loss, I don't punish myself for that; in fact, I journal this and remind myself I still did the right thing. I would make sure a new trader I was teaching did the same things from day 1. When an abandonment of the discipline exists, even if the trade is profitable, I am equally critical of myself for not being disciplined so I do not confuse this activity with skill when, in fact, it is luck. These are some of the lessons I would teach.

Q: It sounds as though you know exactly what you would teach, but what about setting financial goals?

A: I do have unwritten financial goals, but I am more interested in setting activity goals that lead to the desired result. Most of these goals are centered on discipline. I expect to make $100,000 per month at this stage, but my goals are more associated with maintaining my disciple of looking for low-risk–high-probability trades. For example, I will not risk a dollar to make a dollar. I want setups where I risk 25 cents to make a dollar, for example. If I can consistently do that and remain patient for these opportunities, I realize my financial objectives anyway, so my financial goals take care of themselves.

Q: Do you have a bias of the market in terms of the long side versus the short side?

A: I trade both sides. I have no real bias, although I do go long about 60 percent of the time and short the remaining 40 percent. I guess from my actual experience, I am more weighted to the long side, but that is really a function of the market and my ability to measure its direction more than it is a result of any mental bias I have.

Q: Do you have a strategy that you employ more than others? A favorite strategy, so to speak?

A: Yes I do. I like to step in front of the market. For example, I will buy stock a level above a support level when I see indications of a turning point. I will also short a stock a level below a resistance level. I feel this ensures that I am in the trade early on when most others are waiting for an impending move to show itself. That way I get into more trades and earlier when other people seem to be missing them. I find that the tendency to chase a trend is more likely once a move or turning point is in play, and this is the most difficult scenario to make money at. It also flies in the face of my discipline, looking for lower-risk–higher-opportunity trades. When the market provides these opportunities and more importantly when I recognize them, I trade aggressively. To me that is what trading is about, knowing when to press and knowing when to stand aside.

CHRIS JOHNSTON

Chris started his trading career in Canada on the Ontario Stock Exchange. The skills necessary to trade on the floor are very much the same as the skills needed in the electronic environment. This training has served Chris very well, and he now trades full time electronically. Chris has a very competitive spirit that shines through his otherwise very likable and direct manner. You know almost immediately that Chris is profitable. He is quick to answer questions and make decisions and does not have to think about things very long. This is not to say he is not thinking things through but rather, that he is very decisive and direct—qualities that serve traders well. On average, Chris trades 100,000 shares a day and averages over 2 million shares per month.

Q: Do you do research, and if so, how much time do you spend on average each day?

A: I am definitely a believer in research. A lot of day traders want to trade in a vacuum with no news or outside noise to jade their thinking, but I differ in that sense. I want to study the market every day, which I do religiously one to two hours before the open each day. I like to review charts and technical patterns because it helps form a broader bias for the stocks I plan on trading each day. I will not trade a session without knowing exactly what I am trading for that day; that way I am not wasting time surfing the market looking for ideas. I know where I am trading in terms of sectors and stocks before the opening bell. If my stocks are flat or stale for the day, so be it. I do not believe in forcing something to happen.

Q: How active are you on the short side of the market?

A: Shorting is my strategy as a whole. The research I do is to look for overbought situations that rise rapidly on overreactions. I short 70 to 80 percent of the time.

Q: Why is shorting so attractive to you?

A: I believe the natural flow of the market is definitely bullish, but so many stocks run ahead of the herd, so to speak, that they stand out. I like to sell into those stocks when the levels and trends show they get tired. Also, you make more money when they come in.

Q: What strategy or technique do you employ when shorting?

A: I hate the answer I am going to give you, but most of trading is psychological—the psychology for yourself and the markets' psychology. I believe in the end it is touch and feel. This is difficult to teach. I can tell when pressure is building in a stock; for example, when prints are active at a price level, yet still not able to penetrate that level, I find that many issues will come in a bit and then get strong again, sucking in a lot of dumb money to the long side. I stopped falling for that years ago. I remember where those thick spots are in the stock following a weak up-trend, and therefore like to short into the top end of that minor trend. I think the odds are much more with me than against, and I think the trader who can see a broader perspective of the market on tape over the course of time forms a better feel than the super microtrader.

Q: What about risk. Isn't shorting a riskier play especially while shorting into a strength move?

A: I think shorting for the short-term trader is less risky if you have discipline and will cover when prices drive through those thick spots. If I am short, and the stock makes a higher high within the trend I am studying, I buy and cover. It is that simple to me. But when I am right and the stock falls, it's a beautiful thing! The profit opportunities are greater when a house of cards falls. If I can control my losses, the profitable trades will take care of themselves. I also believe panic and fear are easier to spot in the market than greed. Lots of people will stare at a move and never get in because the perception is that it is already over, but most people will bail out once they get their fill of a bad trade. I like to be there when that happens.

Q: What is the sole reason for your success?

A: No secrets in this game! I work really hard. I treat trading like a business because it is a business to me. I get seven to eight hours sleep every night before trading, I don't drink on "school nights," and I am dedicated to trading. Also, I love to win, but not because I am thinking about the money. I don't think too much about the money anymore. I consistently make it, so it has to be something else for me. I guess you could say I work for the medals as well as the money. I am proud to say I am a trader. I like what I do and work hard to keep my job. It is my passion, period.

RICHARD LACKEY

When I think of the word *discipline,* the first thing that pops into my mind is trading, the second is martial arts. Discipline and martial arts always seem to go together, and, in Richard's case, that is definitely true. Richard earned two black belts, one at age 13 and the other at age 18. His early training serves him well as a highly successful and disciplined trader. Today, Richard makes his living sharing his time between trading and mentoring new traders as an instructor. His success at both translates in this interview into some very insightful advice from which every trader can benefit.

Q: Richard, of all the people you have trained, what do you find to be the single common denominator of the successful traders?

A: The best traders I find are those that treat this truly as a business. Like an entrepreneur who opens a new business, most don't expect to be profitable right away. People who engage trading with the same philosophy seem to possess many of the right qualities that trading requires. Those wanting to become professional traders should begin the endeavor as they would if they were intelligently approaching starting any new business. Learn everything possible from people that are already successful and follow the rules and reasoning that they share. Most importantly, have a plan. Have a plan for learning the art and science of trading. Follow a plan that allows you to start small and build your trading size and volume at a rate consistent with your improvement in both proficiency and consistency.

Q: What is the biggest reason traders fail?

A: Proficiency and consistency: We have little problem making good trades. It is making good trades more often than poor trades or, perhaps more importantly, limiting the losses of the poor trades consistently that is the discipline of great traders. It is a psychological breakthrough when a trader realizes that effective trading has nothing to do with being aggressive versus conservative; it has to do with combining an understanding of calculated risk, a feel for the momentum of a market or a stock, and a measure of instinct drawn from experience. In my experience there are two polar ends: One is instinct and one is discipline. I have known traders with great instinct that blow themselves up because they have a few bad days. Even with great insights and instincts, there is no way to be correct all the time, and the only sure-fire way to maintain a steadily increasing income is to maintain some standard of discipline.

Q: How do traders acquire this quality of discipline that seems so elusive?

A: I give new traders exact numbers by which they can measure their progression (or regression, as is occasionally the case) from managing a single trade to managing a month of trading. People perform better when there is structure to their trading. I recommend a military-like approach through which everyone starts by using the same rules and guidelines until they reach a certain competency level. When they have pushed their way through our required levels of proficiency and consistency, they are able to develop a more personal, more unique trading style of their own while maintaining a consistent profitability. On the other hand, there are people who are incredibly disciplined and follow all the rules but have very little feel for the market or for momentum. The good news is these people rarely lose much of their capital. The bad news is they must work just as hard to develop instinct as the instinctual trader must work to develop discipline. The best

traders seem to be in the middle. Finally, traders are successful by being micromanagers of the market and even of a security. If there is any concern at all, they exit their position
immediately. If they change their mind or find reason to get
back in a security, they can do so just as quickly. There is no
reason to take inordinate risk with instant access to the markets and falling commission rates.

**Q: When you recruit new traders, which I know is a big part of
your job, what do you look for?**

A: I look for what you talk about a lot. Passion. The drive to be
successful is not quite the same as the love for the sport. In
pro sports today we have a lot of great athletes who are driven
by the money. Mind you, there are a lot of great things you
can do with money, but the greatest traders, like the greatest
athletes, have a passion for the game. I love to trade. I love to
match myself, my abilities, and my instincts with the masses.
My work is one of my favorite hobbies. I do other things just
because I enjoy doing other things, but I really love to trade.

Q: What is your core strategy?

A: I love volatility. Almost without exception the best traders
make the most money day in and day out in volatile markets.
It is much easier to assess the direction of a tiger than a snail.
It is much easier to steer a bicycle that is moving than one
that is standing still. Stocks that are moving, whether up or
down, are simpler to trade than those going sideways.

**Q: Words of wisdom in a few words or less, and don't make me
count!**

A: Keep it simple. The best traders use simple measures to make
decisions. Start with only a few stocks and very simple charts
(two to three minimum of candlestick of stock, and ND/SP
futures). Trade these until you are consistently profitable
before you try new things. When starting out, spend more
time learning how to exit trades turning against you than
learning how to find more trades to enter. Goal number 1
should be preservation of capital. You can't earn a return on
something you don't have. I use the example that if you start

with 100K and lose 70K or 70 percent, you are in an uphill battle in that coming from a losing trend, you now have to change the direction of the trend, which is difficult in and of itself, but you also must earn significantly more than a 70 percent return to get back to even. In fact, with only 30K you must earn more than 330 percent to get back to where you started. Ben Franklin's urging that a penny saved is a penny earned really doesn't do justice to the real cash flow crunch that can be created by the inability to produce such a dramatic change in your rate of return.

JOHN WALTERS NICK, JR. (JACK)

Jack was a specialist and member on the New York Stock Exchange (NYSE) for 17 years. As a specialist, Jack has made markets for many listed stocks and has transacted millions of trades. The lessons that Jack has learned over these years of trading on the world's most vibrant exchange are not only invaluable but also transferable if the words you are about to read are internalized and trusted.

Q: Jack, let's cut to the chase. What are the single most important words of advice you can give to a trader, new or experienced?

A: You are not going to believe this. . . . Specialize! After years on the floor as a specialist, this is my great word of wisdom! I'm serious. I truly believe that when individuals learn to focus on just a few stocks, as I have over my trading career, they know those stocks so well that the only real reason they lose money in those stocks while trading them is because they abandon discipline and ignore the actions that they know to be correct. I am talking about knowing when to cut a loss but not doing it. When you specialize in a few stocks, you gain strong insight about where key price levels are, where these levels get thick with volume, and where they grow strong or weak. This gives you a tremendous advantage and to ignore these signals is simply an abandonment of discipline. In my opinion, specializing gives you the single greatest advantage, period.

Q: But Jack, didn't you have a huge advantage on the floor as a specialist, if not even an unfair advantage?

A: At one time I did, but not as much today. This is why I am now an electronic trader rather than a floor specialist. Yes, there are great advantages to seeing order flow, but the obligations to provide liquidity and buy and sell stock as last resort when supply and demand imbalances occur put a great burden on the specialist. Additionally, the capital needed to provide liquidity as a specialist in a given issue, not to mention the increasingly stringent rules we as specialists needed to follow to protect the public, all contributed to my decision to trade off the exchange through electronic technology. Therefore, what I took away from the floor in terms of advantages is my belief that specialization in a few securities is the single greatest advantage a trader can have, and because of technology, everyone can now have it.

Q: Do you still concentrate on listed stocks?

A: I still have a bias for listed stocks because they are what I know best. I also believe that there is less room for manipulation of listed stocks in comparison to NASDAQ issues, due to the multiple market-maker system of NASDAQ. But, I also like to trade NASDAQ stocks because of the transparent access to the market now available.

Q: Jack, how can a day trader benefit from what a former exchange specialist like yourself has to teach?

A: I apply my trading knowledge from the floor to the electronic market by focusing on this simple-yet-undeniable fact.

"Buyers stay together when stocks are strong, while sellers stay together when they are weak."

What this means is that when stocks are strong, the buying crowd, which has the capital to move a market, will continue buying strong stocks at the onset of a move, knowing that by the time the public reacts to the buying, the stock will have already moved significantly upward relative to its level prior to the buying and money flow into the stock. Professionals know that amateur buying will continue to move the stock higher, but only very temporarily. Therefore, professionals who wish to exit the stock with a profit will do so during the buying stage. This provides the professional liquidity needed to exit the stock. Put simply, the public is buying what the professionals have to sell. The opposite is true when stocks are weak. Professional sellers will sell stocks aggressively and push prices lower. Professionals know that what may appear to be a low price at any given moment will be perceived as a high price once the stock continues to sell off. Think of it this way: When today's lows become tomorrow's highs, you will be glad you traded with the professional sellers by exiting sooner rather than later. Hence, professional buyers and sellers stay together, while amateurs rarely run with any herd. They are aimlessly roaming the Serengeti, not even knowing that they are market prey.

Q: How does this view of the market translate into electronic trading?

A: I look for signals that indicate when professional buyers and sellers are entering or exiting the market. These signals come in the form of increased daily volume, sector leaders, the advance decline line, the bond market, the oil market, and other market indicators. Many believe that a specialist is completely micro-oriented in that all we pay attention to is the stock we make markets in, but this is a complete myth. The market indicators I mentioned are critical tools we use to anticipate market trend. While we do enjoy the benefit of seeing order flow, we are limited to trading in issues that may or may not be market leaders in terms of activity. Electronic trading allows me to trade whatever I want, whenever I want. As a specialist I am committed to trading only the stocks I specialize in. As an electronic trader, I monitor sector rotation and sector strength, as I did when I was a specialist, but I can shift my trading attention to the stocks with the most opportunity. I did not have that opportunity as a specialist. While I believe that specializing on just a few issues is important for the electronic trader, having the ability to shift to different sectors and stocks as money flow shifts is a great advantage. Therefore, my view of the overall market as a specialist, while important to monitor, didn't always translate into opportunity in the stock I made markets in. Electronic trading has opened the entire market to me; therefore, paying attention to broad market indicators is even more valuable to me.

Q: Where do you see the specialist system in the future?

A: In my opinion, the human intervention the specialist provides will always be needed. When severe supply and demand imbalances occur, chaos sets in. The specialist is there to provide order and liquidity, and I believe there will be a need for this intervention as long as market volatility exists. So I do not see the specialist system going away, but I do see it changing.

Q: In what way?

A: I believe the playing field will be leveled by allowing the public to participate at an even deeper level than we see today, such as having the ability to monitor the specialist book. Today, the specialist book is not open to the public; therefore, transparency to the market is still very limited in this respect. Even the regional stock exchanges, such as the Boston, Cincinnati, Philadelphia, Pacific, do not have access to the specialist book on the New York. While they are members of systems, such as the Intermarket Trading System (ITS), that allow them to trade with the NYSE, they are limited in seeing the depth of the market in terms of buyers and sellers. I feel that in the very near future the public will have this ability, which, in turn, will only add efficiency to the listed market.

Q: What advice would you give to electronic traders in terms of where to focus and how to develop their skills?

A: I would remind them that on the floor, we do not have the luxury of taking the time to do in-depth analysis. Once the opening bells sounds, we operate on supply and demand imbalances, sector strength, money flow, and attention to indicie leaders, as I mentioned before. Therefore, we have been conditioned through the very nature of the NYSE to react to these signals and not to try and predict the future too far in advance. I am convinced that nobody can do that. So this is where the focus must remain. Follow the sector leaders and the stocks that lead their respective sectors. Know where the bonds are trading, oil, technology, retail, and so on, and let the market show you the way. I think most amateurs make trades and then hope for a bounce when they go against them, instead of cutting the loss and turning the other way. Because of the new order-handling rules set by the SEC in 1997, all customer orders must be filled or displayed; therefore, the ability to get out of a losing trade in a liquid stock quickly makes the argument clear why holding on to a loser is not because of technology limitations or because of the rules. It has the most to do with people's psychology of losses and the fact that they have little practice developing this needed skill. Most new traders today come from a mutual fund background at best. That investment vehicle teaches nothing about cutting losses; in fact, that job is left to someone else, the fund manager. Therefore, this is where I feel people need to focus and develop once engaged in a trade. In fact, when teaching new traders, I force them to trade out of stocks early just to get into the habit of taking losses and reacting fast. Being "whipsawed" is not a concern to me when I am teaching people to trade. I want them to become emotionless and indifferent to profit and loss, and instead focus on market direction. You rarely lose money when you are on the right side of the market.

Q: Isn't that obvious?

A: No, believe it or not, it isn't. When a stock is strong with the market or indicie it trades in, it is easy to short into a rally and buy it back on a light pullback and make money. The problem is, a trader who is shorting into an up trend may make money on any number of trades on these light volume and shallow pullbacks, but any money made on these trades in this example will be given back with greater losses when a stocks "rips" $5 or $6 into a short position. The trend in this example is strong, and the trader is 100 percent on the wrong side by being short. Because these "rips" occur so fast on light volume, a trader can be several points under water in moments. If you look at a chart, strong stocks on rally days have few pullbacks, and the pullbacks are shallow. It is better to buy the dips to open the trade than to buy the dips and close it. This is an example where a trader can make money fighting the trend, but he or she elevates the risk dramatically. This is what is meant by being on the wrong side of the market. Buying weakness and selling strength on strong days is far more profitable than selling strength and buying weakness to cover shorts, as a rule. The exception to this is to over sell when liquidating longs to get short, and overbuying when covering shorts to get long. This is a more advanced strategy that is very effective once experienced.

Jack's insights are invaluable. In fact, the real value of them can only be appreciated fully once you have gained some experience. Oftentimes, to truly appreciate the lessons of professionals, you must first experience the pain of your mistakes as an amateur. This helps explain why there is no better teacher than making actual trades. The premise of engaging the market while learning and cutting losses fast allows for experience and survival while the lessons are given one trade at a time. It is later that the insights of professionals will have their greatest meaning. The deepest level of learning occurs when you can look back on your own mistakes and learn from them while a professional is helping you understand why you made the mistake in the first place. That's called insight, and I could not help but think about many situations in which I had done the exact same thing Jack was describing in the last example. We all continue to learn from each other, even if the lesson is a lesson we have learned before. This is perhaps why high-level traders love to associate with each other. They are constantly feeding each other with new insights or reminders of things they already knew but were glad to have been reminded of.

The trader who possesses the psychological makeup to stay interested and to continually learn and execute new methodologies and mechanical techniques is the trader who wins. The final interview is with a friend of both mine and Jack's who possesses all the attributes I have described.

The final interview with Bill Lupien continues to build on some of the mechanical knowledge you need to trade listed stocks and also focuses on personal psychology.

BILL LUPIEN

Bill has spent 17 years as a specialist on the Pacific Stock Exchange, 5 years as chairman and CEO of Instinet, and 5 years as chairman of his own market-making firm. Since 1994, Bill has also been chairman of OptiMark Technologies, one of the newest technologies that I spoke about in the book. As impressive as Bill's background is, what is even more impressive is watching the man trade. I have had the pleasure to trade side by side with Bill many times, and I can tell you the experience has enhanced my trading considerably. You can never know too much or have been in the market too long to learn something; Bill has taught me plenty.

The wealth of knowledge a trader has is like a well of knowledge that can be tapped in an instant to formulate new ideas and strategies based on situations that may not have been encountered before. The ability to use one's intellectual resources on a moment's notice to decipher trading opportunities is the essence of floor trading and day trading. The greater the resources in the well, the more opportunity one can discover. What impresses me the most about Bill is his ability to see things that most would not; he can do so because his well of knowledge and experience is deep and full.

Q: You have many years' experience on the floor. Could you explain how you use that depth of information and knowledge to trade electronically today?

A: I think the opportunity is simply incredible that the average person today can trade on a level playing field with professionals. I will even say that the average person has an advantage over the market maker and specialist since there are no restrictions on the individual trader. The only barrier to piercing this veil is that individual traders do not see themselves, in general, as professionals, whereas, floor traders do. Floor traders have an imposed perception to act and acquire the skills of a professional. Most people see themselves as carpenters, accountants, attorneys, teachers, businesspeople, and so on, with an interest in trading, as opposed to traders who makes their living trading stocks. Greek mythology tells a story of Pygmalion, a Greek god who expressed so much love toward an inanimate statue that represented his perfect mate that the statue actually came alive to fulfill the god's greatest wish. The expression of love was so strong that the statue became real, somewhat of a self-fulfilling prophecy. The metaphor can be used today to explain the high level of expectation traders must have of themselves. It is called appropriately, the "Pygmalion effect." The metaphor is based on the premise that the expression one has toward something must be so strong that it creates a reality in the eyes of the participant. I believe most individuals are missing this level of expectation due to peripheral demands that tug on their attention such as their careers. This deep expression for success is usually present for floor traders because trading is their career, and most of their thinking regarding excelling in their respective field is aimed toward the result of successful trading. This desire runs consciously and subconsciously through the minds of traders and is an intangible element that creates a very tangible edge. So before answering the question, I believe this level of expectation of oneself must exist to compete with professionals who knowingly or unknowingly have it.

Q: **That is a strong insight, Bill, and it could have been formed only through many years of training and developing traders, which I know you have done, both on the floor of the Pacific Stock Exchange and as the chairman of Instinet. Now assuming an individual has that level of expectation, the passion, what insight could you offer to the electronic trader of today based on your experience?**

A: There are so many subtle indications that exist in the market that the public is not generally aware of. While they are not complicated, they are also seldom disclosed to the public.

Here is one example. The NASDAQ market is fragmented, as you know. This means that when this market opens, trade executions occur all over the board between the multiple market makers and ECNs. This means there really isn't a consolidated opening for a stock on the NASDAQ market. This begins to explain why so much chaos is often present with NASDAQ issues, especially on the open. With listed stocks, this is not the case.

My years on the floor can be directly applied to an electronic environment in many ways. Here is one example. Because one specialist is controlling any given stock on the listed exchange and regionals across the country, the opening price of a listed stock is a consolidated open. This means when a listed stock opens, it opens fairly and indiscriminately. Therefore, if a listed stock is indicating an opening range in terms of price before the actual opening, electronic traders can place strategic limit orders through electronic systems like SuperDot for the New York, or Scorex for the Pacific, without being subject to the inequities often associated with the fragmented NASDAQ negotiated market by comparison to a fairer auction market for listed securities. So if the indication for HWP is bid 35 to 37 offered, few traders realize that before the open, traders can enter a limit order that can protect them through the nature of limit-order protection while still leaving the upside should the stock open higher then their limit price. Therefore, if a sell limit order is entered to sell 2000 HWP at 36, and the specialist opens HWP at 37, the electronic trader will be filled at 37 due to the consolidated opening. The downside protection exists if the stock opens at 35 because the trade will not be executed since the opening price is below where the seller is willing to trade, but the upside is not limited if the stock opens higher at 37. This is one of many examples of how an understanding of the listed market can benefit the electronic trader. Because this type of information is not commonly known, most day traders today focus only on NASDAQ issues, and I believe this is a mistake. Just as traders must trade the long and short side of the market, electronic traders must understand how to trade both listed and OTC markets.

Q: Bill, that is very good information. What other thoughts could you add that could be applied to electronic trading?

A: I believe there still exists a form of arbitrage in the equity market beyond the obvious futures market in terms of market timing. I don't mean arbitrage in the sense of money flow from one market to another or execution inefficiency from one exchange to another. What I am referring to is more related to an indication. Although what I am about to share is not a true arbitrage, the indication works from the same premise. Here is what I mean. Because the NASDAQ market opens at 9:30 a.m. EST (not considering premarket trading), we get to see where sectors are strong and weak prior to many listed stocks' opening. This creates a great indication of where a listed stock will open. If, for example, the Internet index is getting hit in the NASDAQ market, although there are not many listed stocks in the Internet sector, there are stocks represented on the listed exchange directly and indirectly related to this market segment that are likely to follow the trend set by the NASDAQ market. This can be a great indication of how you will trade the open for listed stocks once they open.

Q: Bill, how much of what influences a trader is psychological?

A: I think almost all of it once the mechanics are learned and learned properly. The problem is, most people do not truly understand the mechanics of the market well enough. Most are in too much of a hurry to begin, which is a psychological issue itself, by not taking the time to learn to trade properly. I have trained many people to trade over the years, and I have come to the conclusion that most people can learn the mechanics if they dedicate themselves, but because most don't or won't, their introduction to trading is often a poor experience, which can forever jade their psychological perspective, leaving them short on both sides in terms of market mechanics and psychological perspective. I don't know how anyone could survive those odds.

Q: Final question: How did you and how would you train people so that they don't fall victim to that fate?

A: For the most part, they have to decide if they are willing to dedicate themselves; otherwise two people waste their time.

If people really want to learn, I would have them take at least three months to study the market, if not longer. If they can pass the truth test during this period, then I would have them by my side learning by doing and watching. It doesn't take long to tell if the psychological elements are present after that. I have interviewed many traders in the market, and through that experience, I have come to realize that this rule is critical: **If you have the opportunity to get inside the head of a true professional for even a few hours, do it!**

The consensus among traders is that most of trading is weighted on the psychological aspects of trading. Who knows what the literal numbers are. In fact, I am sure it varies by individual, yet as stated numerous times throughout the book, most people are in search for that magic software system that will yield windfall profits. By this time, and at the risk of being redundant, I hope that you subscribe to this fact so that you can focus on the discipline and psychology of speculation in the market. The question you may ask is, "Why is it the most neglected subject regarding the market?" The answer is twofold. First, countless books on technical analysis, fundamentals, and market theory have and will continue to be written, teaching mechanical techniques, which is much easier because they are definable. Second, quantifiable, measurable techniques and formulas are what most novice traders want. Unfortunately, those who look for certainties in the market have far to search and little to find. Psychology is the one part of trading you must teach yourself. The *Harvard Business Review* conducted a study regarding leadership qualities for businesspeople. The study showed the balance of power between cognitive intelligence and emotional intelligence. Emotional intelligence won out by almost 5 to 1 in terms of importance. If you choose to believe these studies and opinions, you can then begin to build yourself into the trader you want to be. But it is important to recognize that cognitive intelligence without emotional intelligence is prone to be overanalytical, while emotional intelligence without cognitive intelligence is prone to be vulnerable to swings in the market and gambling. Therefore, the synergy that is generated by utilizing both sides of the mind (right and left brain) creates the right formula.

How do you gain this cognitive and emotional edge? Read, study, take risk, and engage the market. Write down what you learn, and talk to other passionate people who love the market. While they are not the majority, they are still abundant.

COMMITMENT

At this point you are probably asking, "How long does it take to learn to trade?" Again, without being too literal, it is my experience that it takes a minimum of 1000 trades to become a proficient day trader. Certainly, results vary per individual, but this number represents a good estimate. Remember, time is not the barometer; experience is. Obtaining that experience in a shorter period of time accelerates the learning process. The style you choose will determine how active and how quickly you can scale the learning curve.

Are you prepared to take the time, expend the energy, and absorb the losses that will surely occur? From watching and working with traders, I know very few become successful in their first quarter of trading, if you define success monetarily. If you view the learning experience itself as a degree of success (as most good traders do) regardless of the financial implication (within reason), this attribute of good attitude is a good leading indicator of overall trading success. If these sound like the words of an optimist, they are, but I don't know many successful pessimistic traders. Once again, like life itself, optimists tend to find much more gratification and success than those who possess the alternative personality trait; hence this is another self-evaluation tool you can use to determine if active trading is for you.

AFTERWORD

While most of the rules covered throughout the book are less likely to change, rules do in fact change; therefore, it is important not to become mesmerized by changes in the market, good or bad. That is part of the evolution of the market. As our economy takes on new paradigms and processes orders through new media such as wireless communications, it may leave behind many traders who will fight the change. Many are still in search of value, or they are looking for their faithful technical indicators to work as they did five years ago. But we are truly in a new economy that goes beyond just the technology revolution. It scales into the very culture of the market and the people who trade it. Those of you who weather the change well will not only fare better financially in the short term but will fare better in the long term as you train yourselves to embrace change and move with it rather than fight it.

The final rule I leave you with is one that, if you follow it, will continually feed positive energy through your mind. It relates to one of the biggest obstacles to success in life. The rule is **Live within your means**. Many people will live far beyond their means in the belief that things have always worked out and will continue to. This is unfair pressure to put on yourself if you are to be of healthy mind while trading. Financial pressure is precisely a reason that you should not trade. The emotions associated with such pressure when living beyond your means jades objectivity and, in the end, cheats you. When money motivation is the only reason to trade, danger is not usually far behind. This rule can apply to life in general as well. Those that have too much motivation for money are more prone to cheat themselves and even others to get the results they desire. Trading is one discipline that is far too unforgiving for "scared money" or greed.

I have always subscribed to the theory that living within one's means leads to an enjoyable lifestyle. The good news is, as success grows, you can still have all the great material things you desire (assuming you are normal). You can live in an expensive home and drive a nice car, and so on, relative to your financial condition. It is when impatience and ego set in that people acquire a lifestyle they cannot afford. I like the way a friend of mine Jason puts it; he describes this self-imposed pressure as "the treadmill of life," which constantly requires a faster and faster pace.

The best traders I know find joy beyond their material things. They are wholesome, down-to-earth people who have a balanced perspective on life. They are quite different from "Gordon Gecko" (who was portrayed as the greed-driven trader in the movie *Wall Street*), whose image was purely a media invention. If you think about it, trading successfully requires the same personal regimes that every other occupation requires. Traders will be at their best when their stress is at its lowest levels. Many traders will not trade when they are upset, sick, tired, or fatigued because they have learned the hard way what result ensues. Simply put, they know themselves.

Resting at night during those quiet moments should be a time to reflect and appreciate what you have, even if you don't have as much as your neighbor. The fact is, you never will have more because the next, wealthier neighbor is never far away. If your paradigm is to constantly want more, you ride the treadmill of pressure forever, and that mindset will not only hurt your trading, but your quality of life as well. In fact, you aren't free at all, regardless of your net worth. You will be forever fighting demons during these quiet times that disguise themselves under the guise of competition. True competitors compete because they love the game; individuals who live outside their means do it because they have to. Again, to use the invisible-hand theory, those with the right motivations get the results they deserve, and those with poor motivations get what they deserve as well. The stock market has an uncanny ability to expose human motivation, for good or ill.

Day traders want to be free. True freedom comes with a healthy mindset born from living within your means. Even if you can afford everything you own, you will never have true freedom if you can never own enough.

Active trading is like taking two steps forward, one step back when you are successful. When you are not successful, it is the inverse or worse. The common element in either case is that setbacks will occur. Those that deal with setbacks the best seem to have the financial and emotional means to engage the market. While this is disheartening to many, it is the reality. Better to accumulate the proper capital for tomorrow and forgo trading today. A poor start at trading, whether undercapitalized, or a poor outlook such as greed, leads to the same result in almost all cases, and the risk goes beyond just losing money—it also threatens your attitude. Money is much easier to replace. Once your attitude is destroyed, it is doubtful that you will ever retrieve it, so give yourself the proper start. Be patient, and begin only when you have the time and resources to give it 100 percent. In the meantime if you are not ready financially, start educating yourself by reading all that you can. When the time is right, you will be glad you made the effort.

I hope that you gained some ideas from this book. That is the goal of any trading book, to deliver a few ideas that you can incorporate into your trading style. I have at present read many books on the market. I have not regretted reading any of them. Some were certainly better than others, but all were worth my time. I hope you see it the same way. We priced the book with that belief in mind, so that you can get several books on the market for the same price that some charge for one. My belief, as I said throughout the book, is that you must form your own melting pot of trading ideas. Don't expect any one book or course to give you even most of what you need. Only experience, time, and dedication to the market can provide that.

Thank you for your valuable time in reading my work. To write a book requires the use of a two-edged sword. On one edge, I am forced to think more about how I trade to become more conscious of it in order to write. On the other edge, some critics have argued that those that truly find success in the market are too busy to write and are too rich to feel the need! However, the challenges notwithstanding, I have enjoyed the opportunity to share my ideas with others who also have passion for the market, for it has contributed to my own trading growth and development; for that, I thank you, the reader.

Remember, true success is found through balance: a great family, health, and an appreciation for taking the time for both defines balance. In short, have fun! I am a big believer in fun. Many market participants approach the market with such intensity that it isn't fun. Trading should never become an unhealthy obsession. If you stay balanced, you are much more likely to reap the rewards trading has to offer, which goes beyond just financial rewards.

TAX LAWS SPECIFIC TO TRADERS AND SECURITIES

Congress has passed a series of tax laws very specific for stock traders, or as they term it, "traders in securities." This appendix is not designed to provide comprehensive coverage of tax laws applicable to stock traders; rather, it is intended to make readers aware of alternatives in tax reporting for their stock trades. These laws are very beneficial for the trader, and we highly recommend that the trader either become familiar with these laws or seek professional advice from someone who is.

The applicable Internal Revenue Code (IRC) benefits for active traders are found under IRC Section 475, "Mark to Market Accounting" (MMA). Additional information can be found in Revenue Procedure 99-17 and Revenue Ruling 97-39. Mark to market accounting was significantly discussed and defined in the 1997 through 1999 tax revisions.

To gain an understanding of the benefits of MMA, it is beneficial to review the basic categories of investors and traders and the tax law applicable to each. Individuals who are active in the stock market typically fall into three categories:

- Investor
- Trader in securities without a qualifying MMA election
- Trader in securities with a qualifying MMA election

INVESTOR

Most people treat trading activity on their tax returns as investors. An investor reports all trading activity on Form 1040, Schedule D. Trades are treated as either long or short term depending on the holding period. Trading losses can be deducted against trading gains, plus up to $3000 per year. Excess trading losses that are currently not deductible may be carried forward to future years to offset future gains. Investors may deduct only "realized losses" (subject to the wash sale rules); they may not deduct "unrealized losses." Unrealized losses are losses on open positions held at year-end.

The *wash sale rules* state that a taxpayer may not deduct a loss on any security sold if that security is repurchased within 30 days. This obviously creates problems for the active day trader, and it is an accounting nightmare as well.

Deduction of investment-related expenses is limited and is reported on Schedule A. A deduction for margin interest expense is limited to investment income. Investment income is limited to dividends and interest and does not include capital gains. Nondeductible margin interest may be carried forward to future years.

Other investment-related expenses are also deductible on Schedule A as a miscellaneous itemized deduction and are limited to the extent that they cumulatively exceed 2 percent of a taxpayer's adjusted gross income. Nondeductible expenses may not be carried forward.

These restrictive tax rules can cost the individual who reports his or her trading activity as an investor would a tremendous amount of tax dollars.

TRADER IN SECURITIES

Internal Revenue Code 475 created a new broader classification of active stock trader, termed a "trader in securities" (TIS). A TIS is in turn classified into two subgroups, a TIS who elects MMA and a TIS who does not elect MMA. If a TIS elects MMA, that individual must continue under that method of accounting for as long as he or she is actively engaged in the business of trading in securities.

TIS WHO DOES NOT ELECT MMA

A trader in securities who does not elect MMA reports all trading activity on Form 1040, Schedule D. All trading activities are treated as capital gains and losses and are subject to the restrictive rules applicable to investors discussed above. The major difference is that the definition of "trading expenses" is expanded, and they are fully deductible on Schedule C. A TIS may qualify for this qualification even with long- and short-term holdings.

TIS WHO DOES ELECT MMA

A trader in securities who elects MMA reports all active trading activity on Schedule C as ordinary income or loss. In other words, gain or loss from active trading activity becomes ordinary income in nature and loses its capital transaction classification. Losses are not limited per the investor rules discussed above. In addition, losses may be deducted on open positions held at the end of the year. Expenses are also deducted on Schedule C and are not limited in any way.

Should the active trader report a profit during the tax year, the gains are not subject to self-employment tax.

A qualifying TIS may maintain long-term investment accounts and report those holdings on Schedule D as long as they are clearly held in separate accounts and are not mixed with the trader's active trading account. Therefore, the active TIS with a proper MMA election can still take advantage of the beneficial long-term capital gain rates while also taking advantage of the relaxed rules for his or her active trading accounts.

All TISs with MMA may currently deduct trading losses against other income such as a spouse's salary or other earned income. If after offsetting other income, the qualifying TIS with MMA has a net operating loss (NOL), that NOL may be carried back 2 years and then forward 20 years, thereby enabling the qualifying individual to receive refunds of taxes paid in other years.

MMA essentially means that the active trader in securities is engaged in a trade or business and reports gains and losses on both open as well as closed positions. Open positions at end of year are marked to current market value as if the position had been sold and a corresponding gain or loss is recognized on the transaction. The following tax year the "tax basis" in the security becomes its market value at the end of the previous tax year.

As one can see, this methodology of reporting gains and losses from trading activities is of great benefit to those qualifying individuals. Any individual who otherwise qualifies should therefore make an election with the Internal Revenue Service to be treated as a "trader in securities" with a valid "mark to market" election.

A P P E N D I X

TYPES OF ORDERS

There are two basic classes of orders you can use in your trading: *conditional* and *unconditional.* Conditional orders put time, price, or quantity stipulations on your orders. Unconditional orders have no restrictions. Using the right order at the right time can often mean the difference in profit or loss. Also keep in mind that many of these orders are not acceptable to various electronic trading systems.

all-or-none order—Your order is to be filled completely or not at all.

cancel former order (CFO)—Your current order is to be canceled and replaced by the new order. You would use this type of order to change one element of the order such as the price or quantity.

day order—Your order is good only for the "day" or trading session in which it has been entered.

discretionary order—You are giving trading authority to someone else, often your broker. This could be *full discretion,* in which the broker makes all the trading decisions. Or it could be *limited,* in which you decide on the security, whether to buy or sell, and the quantity. The broker has discretion on time (when to execute the trade) or at what price to execute.

fill-or-kill (FOK) order—Your order must be filled completely and immediately or it is canceled.

good-'till order—You set the time or date the order is to be canceled.

good-'till-canceled (GTC) order—Your order is to remain in the market until the order is filled.

limit order—You set a limit on the price you will accept. Your order must be filled at that price or better.

market order—Your order is to be filled immediately, no matter the price.

market-if-touched (MIT) order—When the security reaches the price you have specified, your order becomes a market order and is immediately filled.

market-on-open order—Your order should be filled during the opening period of a trading session.

market-on-close order—Your order should be filled during the closing period of a trading session.

stop order—You place a "stop" price. When that price is hit, your order becomes a market order.

stop limit order—You place a "stop" price. When that price is hit, your order becomes a limit order.

WEB RESOURCES

The World Wide Web is populated with some of the finest web sites pertaining to electronic trading—online and EDAT. At the same time, it is a fertile hunting ground for unscrupulous stock manipulators. "Know Who Is Behind Each Web Site You Consult!" Trading and investing are businesses in which it pays to be paranoid. Just as you have been taught to look for confirmation in the leading indexes, seek more than one opinion before following advice, particularly freely offered advice, found on the Internet.

Always take your time. Check and double check. Do not jump into a trade on a tip. Search reputable web sites for confirmation and more details. You will never be out of good trades. No trade is so special you cannot pass it up.

With that said, take some time and become familiar with the web sites listed below. Naturally, we would first like to invite you to our web sites, *www.maketwise.com* for EDAT traders, online traders, and for information on our stock trading schools.

GENERAL WEBZINES AND FINANCIAL NEWS SITES

ABC News	www.abcnews.com
Barrons	www.barrons.com
Bloomberg	www.bloomberg.com
Business Week	www.businessweek.com
CNBC	www.cnbc.com
CNNfn	www.cnnfn.com
Dow Jones	www.dowjones.com
Economist	www.economist.com
Financial Newsletter Network	www.financialnewsletter.com
Financial Times	www.ft.com

Fortune	www.fortune.com
Fox Market Wire	www.foxmarketwire.com
Holt Stock Report	www.holtrepoet.com
Inc.Online	www.inc.com
Investors Ally	www.InvestorsAlly.com
Kiplinger Online	www.kiplinger.com
Market Technicians Association (MTA)	www.mta.org
Money.com	www.pathfinder.com/money
Motley Fool	www.fool.com
News Alert	www.newsalert.com
Red Chip Review	www.redchip.com
Red Herring Online	www.herring.com
Reuters	www.reuters.com
Silicon Investor	www.siliconinvestor.com
Small Cap Investor	www.smallcapinvestor.com
SmartMoney Interactive	www.smartmoney.com
Stock City	www.stockinfo.standardpoor.com
Stock Detective	www.stockdetective.com
StockScreener	www.stockscreener.com
StockSite.Com	www.stocksite.com
StockTalk	www.stock-talk.com
StockZ.Com	www.stockz.com
StreetNet	www.streetnet.com
TheStreet.Com	www.thestreet.com
Thomson Investors Network	www.thomsoninvest.net
USA Today Money	www.usatoday.com/money
Wall Street Journal	www.interactive.wsj.com
Worth	www.worth.com
Yahoo! Finance	www.yahoo.com/finance
Zacks Investment Research	www.zacks.com

SPECIALTY SITES

Insider Buying and Splits

Company Sleuth	www.companysleuth.com
EDGAR Online	www.edgar-online.com

Insidertrader   www.insidertrader.com
Insider Watch   www.cda.com/investnet
Stock Rumors   www.stockrumors.com

Up and Down Grades

Briefing.com   www.briefing.com
JagNotes   www.jagnotes.com
Theflyonthewallcom   www.theflyonthewall.com

Stock Exchanges

American Stock Exchange   www.amex.com
Chicago Board of Options   www.cboe.com
Chicago Board of Trade   www.cbot.com
Chicago Mercantile Exchange   www.cme.com
Chicago Stock Exchange   www.chicagostockex.com
NASDAQ Exchange   www.nasdaq-amex.com
New York Stock Exchange   www.nyse.com
New York Mercantile Exchange www.nymex.com
Philadelphia Stock Exchange   www.phlx.com
Pacific Stock Exchange   www.pacificex.com

Government

National Association of
   Securities Dealers   www.nasdr.com
Securities and Exchange
   Commission   www.sec.com

Data Feeds

Data Broadcasting Corp.   www.dbc.com
Data Transmission Network   www.dtn.com
Omega Research, Inc.   www.historybank.com
PCQuote   www.pcquote.com

Tax Accounting

Mann & Company   www.daytradertax.com

Education

Market Wise Securities, Inc.   www.marketwise.com
Dr. Yardeni's Economic   www.yardeni.com/
  Network   econews.html
FinanceWise   www.financewise.com
GreenJungle   www.greenjungle.com
Teachdaq   www.teachdaq.com
Market Technicians Association www.mta.org

BOOKS OF NOTE

Cohen, Bernice. *The Edge of Chaos.* Wiley, 1997.
Farrell, Christopher A. *Day Trading Online: Start Trading for a Living Today.* Wiley, 1999.
Jurik, Mark (editor). *Computerized Trading: Maximizing Day Trading and Overnight Profits.* Prentice-Hall, 1999.
Lefevre, Edwin. *Reminiscences of a Stock Operator.* Reprint, 1994.
McCafferty, Thomas A. *All About Options: The Easy Way to Get Started.* McGraw-Hill, 1998.
Nassar, David S. *How to Get Started in Electronic Day Trading.* McGraw-Hill, 1998.
Schwager, Jack D. *Market Wizards: Interviews with Top Traders.* Simon & Schuster, 1989.
Schwager, Jack D. *The New Market Wizards: Conversations with America's Top Traders.* HarperBusiness, 1992.
Seligman, Martin E. P. *Learned Optimism: How to Change Your Mind and Your Life.* Simon and Schuster, 1998.
Wolfe, Tom. *The Bonfire of the Vanities.* Bantam, 1988.

INDEX

ABOUT THE AUTHOR

David S. Nassar is chairman and CEO of Market Wise Securities, Inc., one of the nation's first electronic trading brokerage firms. Market Wise Securities is recognized as a leader in the training and development of highly active retail and proprietary traders. An active trader and a pioneer in the electronic trading industry, Mr. Nassar is the author of the *New York Times, Business Week,* and *Wall Street Journal* bestseller *How to Get Started in Electronic Day Trading.* David is a powerful and highly sought after public speaker on the markets and has spoken and appeared at venues such as MIT, CNBC, CNN, Fox News, and the *NBC Nightly News with Tom Brokaw.* Public speaking engagements and company contact information can be obtained at *inquires@marketwise.com* or visit *www. marketwise.com.*